Intelligent Drawings

THE McGRAW-HILL DESIGNING WITH SYSTEMS SERIES
Eric Teicholz *Consulting Editor*

Daryanani *Building Systems Design with Programmable Calculators (1980)*

Stitt *Systems Drafting: Creative Reprographics for Architects and Engineers (1980)*

Stitt *Systems Graphics: Breakthroughs in Drawing Production and Project Management for Architects, Designers, and Engineers (1984)*

Stitt *Designing Buildings that Work: The Architect's Problem Prevention Sourcebook (1985)*

Teicholz *CAD CAM Handbook (1985)*

Gerlach *Transition to CADD for Architects and Engineers (1987)*

Radford and Stevens *CADD Made Easy (1987)*

Teicholz and Orr *Computer-Integrated Manufacturing Handbook (1987)*

Terrence G. Schilling, AIA

Patricia M. Schilling

Intelligent Drawings

Managing CAD and Information Systems in the Design Office

McGraw-Hill Book Company

New York St. Louis San Francisco Auckland Bogotá
Hamburg Johannesburg London Madrid Mexico
Milan Montreal New Delhi Panama
Paris São Paulo Singapore
Sydney Tokyo Toronto

Library of Congress Cataloging-in-Publication Data

Schilling, Terrence G.
Intelligent drawings.

(The McGraw-Hill designing with systems series)
Bibliography: p.
Includes index.
1. Engineering design—Data processing. 2. Computer-aided design. I. Schilling, Patricia M. II. Title.
III. Series.
TA174.S35 1987 620'.00425'00285 86-27414
ISBN 0-07-055317-3

1234567890 DOC/DOC 893210987

ISBN 0-07-055317-3

The editors for this book were Nadine M. Post and Rita T. Margolies, the designer was Naomi Auerbach, and the production supervisor was Thomas G. Kowalczyk. It was set in Primer by T. C. Systems.

Printed and bound by R. R. Donnelley & Sons Company.

To our fathers,

Samuel J. Fitzpatrick
Dr. Melvin J. Schilling

Contents

Preface

Our background is architecture. In writing, therefore, we address architects, planners, designers, and drafters who do not wish to become computer programmers or system managers but do want to take advantage of the data processing tools now available. As a result, we have minimized any discussion of hardware or programming languages. Instead, we focus on methodologies for design, planning, and production drafting which can be automated with data processing tools.

The procedures described in the book rest on an analysis of how decisions are actually made and recorded during the design process. Consequently, certain design procedures are discussed at length, though we avoid discussion of the theoretical underpinnings of the design process itself. In our view, software for planning, design, and drafting must reflect methodologies currently used within the profession. Too often, this software reflects the view of programmers; such software mimics rather than serves the needs of architects. Unless software development is derived from an understanding of both existing design procedures and the objectives of the design process, it is of no value.

Increasing the Content of Design Documents

The economic justification for computers is based on the increased productivity and the improved document quality they make available. However, developing the skills within a design office for using computer-aided design (CAD) and related systems at high levels of effectiveness is a formidable undertaking. Many offices are having difficulty achieving cost effectiveness when using computers. Often, this reflects shortcomings in the administration of project work rather than the real limitations of the equipment or software.

Existing design methodologies, both hand drafting and overlay, are widely understood, mature tools which have proven to be successful. In many ways, they are very efficient. Replacing our existing methodology with one based on computers, a technology which has a brief history and is just becoming understood within the profession, requires significant redirection of time and resources for retraining and reorganization. In order to realize the higher efficiency promised by computers, new procedures for creating design documents must be defined along with new ways of administering project work.

Although speed is an important benefit to the architect and the client, using CAD to compete with hand drafting for the sake of speed alone is not a primary objective. We believe the benefits of using intelligent drawings are derived primarily from increasing the content of design documents that can be read and processed by computer systems. Recording information in a processable form not only speeds production, it also enables information to be transferred with ease and accuracy from one document to another. Consequently, new design services become available as a by-product of basic design and drafting.

The concept of who reads and uses design documents expands as their computer-processable content increases. The users of intelligent drawings include those who interpret them visually during the planning, design, bidding, and construction phases. However, users also include the machines that assemble the documents to start with and the individuals that manage, maintain, service, and supply the building or facility when it is occupied.

In the not-too-distant future, the readers and users of intelligent drawings will include the inspectors and machines that check and approve projects as well as the people and machines that build them.

The expansion of the audience for architectural documents, which intelligent drawings makes possible, is what we find exciting. Often the intent of a building design (recorded in the original design program before drawings are initiated) is lost after construction in the expediencies of facility administration. With intelligent drawings, initial programming concepts are carried forward through construction into documents which assist the ongoing management of the final project.

When setting out to write this book, two concepts intrigued us. The first was the possibility of showing how the intent of a design can be carried beyond construction into the day-to-day life of a building project. After increasing the efficiency of drawing production, this seemed to be an obvious extension of CAD. It is rewarding to see so much current software development and market interest concerned with facilities planning and management. The second, more fundamental, concept was the application of data processing to planning and architectural document production, which we had struggled with from the early 1970s onward. Like a new set of graphic standards, the fundamental procedures for the use of data processing, yet undocumented, were emerging. If spelled out, others in our profession could take advantage of these techniques and procedures.

A General Purpose Users' Guide

Photographs of computer equipment, such as digitizer tablets, plotters, CRT terminals, and tape drives, are included in most books on the topic of computers in architectural design. Configurations of hardware, including relationships between computer components such as a central processor arranged with peripheral workstations, plotters, and printers, are frequently portrayed in marketing literature and books on the subject. Writing in 1986, we assume readers are familiar with what computers look like and are generally aware of how they are configured. Architects can recognize the physical components of a CAD system. Consequently, we have excluded illustrations of computer hardware from this book.

Rather than pictures of equipment, we have included indirect illustrations of the capabilities of CAD along with examples of output. With the exception of Fig. 11-1, a copy of the historic floor plan of Independence Hall, all of the figures in the book were created on CAD systems and plotted for reproduction.

Many books on computers in architecture have been written that describe the functions of internal operating software of a graphics computer, the writing of programs for creating architectural drawings, or idealized computer functions. Writers on such deservedly important topics reflect their background, usually in the field of programming, education, or software development. However, readers looking for algorithms will not find them here, although several examples of procedures that use custom software are illustrated along with an outline specification for the software required.

In contrast to programming, our emphasis is on the practical use of data processing equipment, including CAD systems, word processors, and business or personal computers, within architectural design practice. Rather than discussing how the software and hardware actually work, we have focused on:

1. Procedures for assembling and managing architectural documents using data processing equipment, including both graphic and written information.
2. Procedures for organizing information used in the design and planning process that take the greatest advantage of computer software and hardware.

While establishing and operating a CAD and data processing service bureau (Design Logic, Inc.), the lessons we learned about using computers were acquired dearly. Successful methods emerged slowly after a great deal of experimentation, trial and error, and input from many individuals, both staff and customers. Out of this experience developed an overriding concern for how architects and planners can successfully use existing computer systems as well as expand their grasp of advanced data processing applications. Successful equipment and software is available, although there is still a need for continued development. So rather than focusing on software or hardware developments, we felt that it would be more challenging to develop and redefine office procedures so that automation can be used to full advantage within the unique requirements of the design process.

It is our intention to provide the reader with a general purpose users' guide, not a buyers' guide. With the exception of Table 3-1, where general characteristics of CAD systems are compared, we avoid references to specific manufacturers or vendors.

Given the dynamic state of system development, a meaningful comparative analysis of systems is found only in publications which have a short-term focus (6 months to 1 year), such as magazines or marketing surveys. We have, however, included broad guidelines for selecting a system in Chapter 3. Rather than a comparative analysis, these guidelines recommend the development of an office automation plan. Such a plan can be developed by each individual design firm. With it, systems can be selected which satisfy the particular requirements for automation of individual offices based on near- and long-term objectives.

Procedures described in the following chapters make use of CAD and related system functions that are generally available today. However, functions that offer greater efficiency than high-speed drafting alone, and which are only available with certain system configurations, are also outlined. A few of these, such as the automatic transfer of furniture symbols onto drawings with the aid of an architectural space program, or automatic generation of room data sheets including both written tables and symbols, have only been demonstrated with custom-designed software. Other software utilities, such as lettering and dimensioning directly on the projected views of a three-dimensional model, are included as recommendations for future software development. Software functions that are known to be currently unavailable are so indicated.

The Viewpoint of a Systems Analyst

A *systems analyst* is defined as "a person who defines a problem, determines exactly what is required in the solution, and defines the broad outlines of the machine solution." [P. Jordain and M. Breslau, 1969]

The systems analyst is typically responsible for user liaison, systems specification, systems design, and project control. Notice that the emphasis of this role is on defining the problem so that it can be solved with data processing tools. The distinction between a computer programmer and a systems analyst is similar to the distinction between a drafter and a designer. The analyst, like the designer, is oriented to the needs of the user and directs programming, much as the designer directs drafting. Whereas the drafter usually performs the bulk of production activity, the designer, similar to the analyst, is charged with defining and satisfying the requirements of the user in an efficient and aesthetic manner. On most small design project teams, the roles of designer and drafter are combined; similarly the roles of analyst and programmer are often combined. Yet in each case, there are two distinct roles with two different areas of emphasis. A programmer who lacks the ability to analyze problems and provide satisfactory solutions is like a drafter with no sense of design—their efforts are misplaced and the results are lackluster. When developing software applications for future office practice, the systems analyst is a key consultant.

The viewpoint of the systems analyst underlies our overall approach; however, statements are made from the point of view of the designer. When using data processing equipment, the designer wants to take advantage of the speed and convenience provided by the equipment, but his or her primary concern is integrity of the design. This implies control of the design process, regardless of the medium used, and faithful reproduction of design concepts. When using CAD, the designer must understand how the development of design documents is affected by data processing. The designer's needs will not be satisfied by trying to reach this understanding through discussions of the computer programming process alone. The limitations of existing CAD software often result from an overemphasis on computer programming at the expense of systems analysis, rather than from a complete lack of exposure to the architectural profession (after all, CAD system developers usually employ architects). The emphasis in this book is on how methods used in the design process are translated into automated procedures. From this perspective, the designer and the systems analyst have a common objective.

An Evolving Topic

Writing in the mid-1980s on the use of computers in any field is admittedly like trying to spot a moving target in dense brush. You must lead the target, yet it is difficult to distinguish it from the background and foreground. One can easily miss. However, at this time, an important phase in the commercial development of CAD is ending. CAD has been in use within design offices for just over a decade. Although much experimentation and development lies ahead, the capabilities of CAD systems, including functions for design, drafting, three-dimensional modeling, and text or word processing, are established. Their general operating characteristics have become distinct.

If we compare one system with another we find each CAD vendor provides quite different software features. Over time, however, most systems tend to offer the same core of basic functions—those that have obvious utility regardless of the hardware environment or the history of the particular software involved. As a result of striving for uniqueness, one system may have an advantage over others in certain applications. However, competition drives system developers toward common features. For example, currently not all systems directly connect objects on drawings to a data base of nongraphic attributes. Nevertheless, the usefulness of such a mechanism is widely understood. Most system developers are either pursuing or expanding this capability for future versions of their software.

In many important ways, the automation achieved with existing systems only scratches the surface of possible increased productivity. For example, as a rendering tool, the capabilities of three-dimensional modeling systems are just beginning to be seen outside of software development laboratories. Most commercially available three-dimensional model-based design systems create somewhat cartoonlike views of architectural projects. Eventually, these modeling tools will combine video images of the actual site with automatic shading and shadows, multiple light sources, along with surface characteristics, including reflectiveness, transparency, and textures. Separate colors will be mapped to each major element in a composition such as the foreground, background, sky, and building. With these tools in the right hands, the architectural renderings they produce promise to be spectacular.

Terrence G. Schilling
Patricia Schilling

Acknowledgments

It is impossible to acknowledge adequately Fred Stitt, of Guidelines, who provided, from inception of this book and at every stage to completion, unflagging guidance, support, and encouragement. We owe special thanks to Connie Myers, of Whistler-Patri, Architects, who combines skills as an editor with knowledge of computer systems and their operations, for her thorough editing of this book, which she carried out with professionalism and generosity.

Those who reviewed our manuscript deserve acknowledgment: Michael Schley, AIA, of Facility Systems Group, who reviewed the entire manuscript and contributed key improvements; Michael Holland, who provided insight based on his considerable experience as both a CAD user and a software developer; and Paul Divan, III, who identified needed corrections.

Thanks are also due to the staff of Design Logic, Inc., particularly: Joe Ouye (currently with Facility Technics) for his pioneering work in architectural programming which provides the source material for much of the architectural planning procedures we describe; Tom Lau, systems analyst (currently with Cadam), for software enhancements that enabled the procedures described; and those innovative people who contributed to the development of standards, which are also published in this book.

Without the support provided by CalComp, the organization and people, particularly Marty Stein and Ken Johnson, this book would not have been written. Much of the experimentation that led to the development of ideas contained in this book were made possible by the many capabilities of the CalComp interactive graphic system. Finally, with few exceptions, we created the figures contained in this book on the CalComp System 25.

Illustrations and examples of output were also made available by Ken Sanders, Santa Ana, CA; Skidmore, Owings, and Merrill, Houston, TX: Union Mutual Life Insurance Co., Portland, ME; Whistler-Patri, Architects, San Francisco, CA; and The Pyros Partnership, Costa Mesa, CA.

Introduction

Intelligent drawings make the connection between traditional drawing content and design information that can be manipulated by computers. Obviously, we do not mean to imply that drawings are cognizant and actually capable of perception or thought. The title of this book simply expresses the capability of certain computer-aided design (CAD) systems to perform automated functions on drawings. These functions are normally not available or are associated with separate non-CAD systems and procedures, e.g., global revisions or querying of drawings for nongraphic information. The essential concept implied by the phrase "intelligent drawings" is that both graphic and written information can be organized for efficient computer access and reuse. This implies the use of architectural drawings as more than graphic instructions for putting together a building.

Intelligent drawings are readable not only by visual inspection. They can be interpreted by multiple software applications as well. Drawings and text files, when combined correctly in a data processing medium, generate architectural drawings while building an information resource for the architect. The reusable contents of intelligent drawings can be transferred from project to project as well as from one project phase to the next, from preliminary space planning, through design, to facilities management. When transferred, design information can be restructured with data processing procedures. Consequently, additional design services, such as drawings of tenant boundaries, can be produced from information already stored with working drawings.

The graphic objects on architectural drawings, even if assembled with CAD, are visually familiar to designers. However, designers are generally unfamiliar with the characteristics of objects in a CAD medium, with the relationships between such objects, and with their connection to files and records that store nongraphic design information. Drawing characteristics that are not visible, such as levels and nongraphic attributes, are at work along with the visual record of the design. Even recognizable graphic objects take on specific and carefully assembled relationships to each other, such as groups and symbols. These relationships are essential to revising drawings and creating reports, though invisible to the casual observer. Intelligent drawings need to be correctly recorded in the first place. Otherwise the accuracy and efficiency that an automated combination of text files and drawings makes possible will not be achieved.

Book Organization

This book is organized into four sections. Section 1 discusses the impact of CAD on design office management: The roles of production manager, system manager, CAD operator, and data processing assistant are described, and lists of their functions and responsibilities are included. Detailed explanations of mechanisms for creating and revising CAD drawings, including groups, symbols, and drawing layers, are described in Section 2. Section 3 illustrates the structure and use of nongraphic files with cases from design practice, such as door schedules. Transferring written information both to and from architectural drawings is also covered. Section 4 reviews computer-based three-dimensional modeling. Throughout, lists of detailed guidelines for putting CAD systems to practical use are provided including:

1. General recommendations for operating speed and efficiency.
2. Recommendations for creating and using drawing layers, groups, and symbols.
3. Conventions for naming symbols, files, and records.

Most important, this book emphasizes the organization of information used in design practice, both drawn and written information, so that it can be used, reused, and managed as a resource on project after project.

Design Information

Data processing of design project information differs from data processing for other applications. For instance, an automated billing system for a department store will contain a large volume of data, but all of it can be represented in a short list of accounting categories. Another example, accounting data, is predominantly numbers and titles: Numbers are combined with rules defining how they are assembled into reports such as income statements, balance sheets, and invoices. Procedures used with this type of information are highly repetitive. The system may include thousands of accounts receivable, yet each one is entered, processed, and output much like all the others.

An architectural design project also includes a large volume of data. In contrast to accounting, however, it is distributed into a diverse array of data types, including numeric, written, and graphic. The variety both of functions performed and of documents created is much broader than that required for accounting data. Documents include contracts, correspondence, planning reports, occupant surveys, both architectural and consultant drawings, notes, schedules, details, specifications, cost estimates, shop drawings, and change orders. The data included with these documents is also characterized by a high rate of change. Design information is manipulated frequently yet the number of items manipulated during each procedure is relatively small compared to accounting.

The unique character of design information requires that data processing procedures be incremental, or staged. Equally important, procedures must allow for convenient review of the work performed. With traditional design methods, the continuous pace of drawing production makes it possible to review work on a day-to-day basis. With data processing, drawing progress moves forward swiftly. Drawings and reports are generated automatically and presented all at once. In other words, work is done in batches. As a result, procedures for review of work must be given special emphasis.

The recommendations included in this book organize design information for both efficient assembly of documents and convenient review. Information must be stored in files that are set up for reporting and can be summarized easily. In this way, error checking is convenient, drawing information is accurate, and the designer's control of the process is maximized.

The unique character of design information is used to organize and plan the flow of project work on data processing equipment. In a completely automated office, the designer interacts frequently with the system in a variety of transactions. Since manipulations are frequent and the volume of information is small, thorough planning of procedures is essential to prevent the loss of design information and to optimize its reuse. At any one time, the contents of documents are distributed among a variety of systems and files. Given the increased pace of work and the complexity of a data processing environment, an overview of progress, achieved easily with a traditional set of progress prints, is not as easily achieved without a thorough understanding of the procedures involved. Storage of information in the correct form for convenient retrieval is the real key to project control. In addition, understanding the process of interaction with the system is vital to the efficient use of data processing on a design project. An orderly and predictable interaction with the system, based on a clear understanding of when and in what form information must be submitted, provides for true efficiency and high productivity.

Section 1

Office Organization

Section 1 focuses on the impact of CAD on the human resources of a firm. The general problems of staffing and system selection when integrating CAD into an existing practice are addressed. The roles and specific responsibilities described apply to any size CAD system—single-station personal computer (PC) or larger multistation systems. The outline of an office automation plan is presented along with a comparison of broadly defined system characteristics.

Chapter 1

New Roles within Design Offices

Architect: "How do you put the drawings into the system?"

CAD Operator: "You don't put the drawings in. You get drawings out of the system."

When computer systems are used in a design office, issues arise which challenge the management of the office and the roles of professionals on the design team. It is a mistake to think that computer-aided design (CAD) affects drafting only. For successful integration of data processing into a professional design office, new responsibilities must be defined. The entire office, not just the drafting staff, must realize that work will be performed in fundamentally different ways. As a result, roles will be modified and new roles will emerge; every job description will have to be reevaluated. Cost justifications that describe a 3-to-1 increase in productivity are generally correct. However, when these justifications are prepared, the adjustments required for the entire management of a design office must be taken into consideration. To make the lease payments on computer equipment, an office with a CAD system must:

1. Maximize its design skills.
2. Market its services more effectively.
3. Secure more design contracts.
4. Perform the work faster.

In the time currently spent on one set of drawings, an office with CAD equipment is able to perform three times as much work. This means that in the same period of time, there will be three times as many drawings to check, three times as many instructions to give, and three times as much work to coordinate with consultants, the client, and reviewing agencies. This higher productivity requires greater coordination between members of the design team and modifies the responsibilities and roles of design professionals involved.

Responsibilities described in this chapter are defined in terms of functions for specific roles, such as operator or system manager. Such functions reveal the demands a CAD system places on the design firm. Our objective is to detail system-related functions rather than recommend a specific organization for delegating responsibilities or specific designations for individual roles. Responsibilities must be distributed among staff and roles defined to take advantage of both the human and the equipment resources of individual offices. For instance, we assume here that the design team's key interface with CAD resources is the project architect. This role could as easily be performed by the project principal, the designer, the job captain, the chief engineer, or others.

The number of individuals required to perform various functions is determined by the amount of computer equipment involved and the volume of design work carried out by the firm. Specialized roles can emerge as the officewide computer system becomes more complex and the volume of work expands. A moderate-size system, perhaps one or two work stations or several PC-based CAD stations, does not need a full-time system manager or production manager. Nonetheless, someone, perhaps the CAD operator and the project architect, will still carry out the responsibilities of these roles. In this case, the functions described in this section will be more broadly dispersed throughout the staff.

Depending on the size of the system, separate roles can be blended into each other and performed by a single individual. The system manager and the production manager have overlapping responsibilities, for instance. The first focuses on the hardware and software and making sure that the system runs smoothly, whereas the second is concerned with the output from the system and the interface between the project architect and operators. Both, however, work with the system and the production staff. Also, there is no reason that a system manager or production manager cannot contribute time to creating documents as operators.

The System Manager

Unlike flat drawing files, CAD systems do not take care of themselves. Like the railroad engineer with an oil can, the system manager keeps the system running. He or she is in charge of the entire computer environment, i.e., whatever affects the operation of the system. Rather than being concerned with the design project per se, i.e., its documents and progress, the system manager is concerned with the hardware and software that comprise the system.

The responsibilities of the system manager include:

1. Maintain the operating integrity of the system.
2. Supervise periodic maintenance of the system and, when necessary, request field service from system vendors.
3. Maintain a log of system problems and communicate them to operators and outside vendors.
4. Install and test upgrades and improvements to the hardware and software; notify outside vendors of weaknesses or defects in their software or equipment.
5. Coordinate the archiving of drawings from disk to tape or other mediums and monitor the tape and disk library.
6. Take overall responsibility for documentation of files and software on the system; see that outdated or unused files are deleted or archived.
7. Monitor and troubleshoot production operations; assist operators in analyzing drawings and using system resources.
8. Train operators in the proper use of equipment and specific software procedures.
9. Consult with the design staff on specialized software needed for upcoming project work.
10. Provide, where necessary, new documentation and condense, expand, or reinterpret existing written material from vendors.
11. Supervise the accounting of work performed on the system.
12. Specify and create, where possible, programs which enhance production.
13. Keep abreast of technical developments and advise design staff on the desirability of such developments.

The problems faced by the system manager are distinct from problems found in the course of professional design practice. To an architect, many system parameters will not be visible at all. The architect may not appreciate their complexity. For example, how and when are drawings and files backed up? When should drawings be moved into archive storage? Will all the project drawings fit on the main disk? Drawing management issues such as these are only one concern of the system manager.

As the office explores new data processing capabilities and as new products become available, the system configuration will frequently change. Storage is a key aspect of system configuration. How much storage is required? What type of storage is necessary: hard disk, tape, or floppy disk? Will there be enough computer memory available for additional software applications? Items that appear intangible or incomprehensible to an architect, such as hardware for a "fast floating point" or "double precision," can have a significant impact on the overall speed and performance of a CAD system. These, and a long list of other issues, affect the configuration of the system.

The day-to-day control of system configuration is in the hands of the system manager. He or she must plan any system changes in cooperation with everyone who interacts with the system. Changes must be performed with the utmost care to prevent loss of work. Of course, changes must be timed not to interfere with ongoing project work. During these changes, and when the inevitable problems arise, the system manager represents the office with the computer vendor. This is often a delicate relationship concerned with major resources of the design office.

The complete environment for the equipment, room temperature, air quality, ionization, electrical power, lighting, and so on, must be carefully managed. Periodic maintenance is required to avoid system breakdowns. Timely response when problems do arise is essential. The system manager must maintain good communication with service groups. Allowing a service contract to become delinquent, for instance, can result in drawings that are locked up for days while the system is down and the contract is renegotiated.

The system manager must also be able to distinguish between a system problem and an operator problem. Eliminating such problems requires a certain amount of discipline because CAD system procedures are more physically sensitive than manual drawing procedures. Operators must be guided carefully. People have conflicting ideas about the use of computers—those with destructive habits, for instance, should not be allowed to use the system. Since banging on the keys will eventually cause the keyboard to fail, a light touch is recommended. It is up to the system manager to impose discipline and protect the equipment.

An office usually does not have the resources to train someone in data processing skills. Since the system manager is often a new staff position within a design office, he or she must already have these skills. Even if no one else in the office does, the system manager should know the difference between a bit and a byte. It may be necessary to recruit such an individual from outside the design profession; system managers may come from a computer science or data processing background. In this case, they should not be expected to fully understand the requirements of the design profession. Some appreciation, however, is essential. Wages in data processing fields tend to be higher than in design professions, so income expectations will be greater.

The system manager should enjoy dealing with issues that center around a computer system. The management of a computer is an intellectual challenge requiring considerable technical and analytical skills. System managers should love the equipment and take pride in its smooth operation. However, since the system manager has a strategic role between the system and the design staff, do not overlook the need for skills in human relations when considering an individual for this position.

The Production Manager

Perhaps a new role in the small- or medium-size office, the production manager has existed for some time in design offices of 100 employees or more.

The position extends some of the control normally exerted by the project architect while reviewing work with drafting staff. In a computer environment, the production manager is an intermediary between the project architect and those that operate the CAD system. In contrast with the system manager, the focus of the production manager is on drawing standards, the content of documents, and the progress of work.

The responsibilities of the production manager involved with CAD include:

1. Develop and maintain standards and guidelines for the content and organization of project documents.
2. Develop, implement, and enforce procedures for control of document quality.
3. Effect procedures for setting up standard macros, pen tables, drawing layer lists, symbol libraries or files, and nongraphic files.
4. Endeavor to maximize use of the firm's resources, specifically, system hardware and software as well as personnel, to achieve project goals.
5. Review project scope, prior to start of project work, and help derive schedule and budget; develop a strategy with the design team and operators to derive estimates of time and projected completion dates.
6. Review standards and apply them to the project prior to start of project work; direct revisions and additions to standards as required by the project.
7. Monitor and provide direction and support to operators to deliver documents on schedule, within budget, and up to office standards; interpret drawing content where necessary.
8. Coordinate and monitor all project schedules for efficient personnel assignment and balanced work load.
9. Troubleshoot project problems, including complaints from the design team.
10. Review all check plots, final plotted drawings, and reports.
11. Work with system manager to identify and resolve system problems.
12. Review each project's status frequently. Review and update accounting reports and budgets, and take appropriate corrective action as required.
13. Approve major changes and estimate extra work.
14. Hire CAD operators that are technically efficient in system operations.
15. Train operators by developing and conducting a phased training program that includes basic, intermediate, and advanced training sessions.

The production manager has responsibility for creating drawings that are architecturally correct. In the past, drawing requirements were passed on through a verbal process, along with the use of published graphic standards, directly from project architect to drafters, who often worked as trainees or apprentices. Now, however, the project architect will not necessarily have the time to see that CAD operators understand every aspect of architectural drawings. Nonetheless, someone must ensure that drawings meet the standards required for professional documents. Drawings and reports must be complete, clear, well coordinated, and dimensionally accurate. It is up to the production manager to see that documents are produced correctly in this new computer medium. Operators must be trained in the application and use of drawing standards and techniques.

Drawing standards must be created, in some cases for the first time, and published for all employees. Any existing drawing standards must be revised, expanded, and applied to the characteristics of the particular CAD system in use. Each system has unique capabilities and parameters for such things as dimensioning, lettering, grouping structure, symbols, drawing layers, and drawing resolution.

Although they do not produce revenue directly, drawing standards are essential to the efficient use of CAD. Unfortunately, work performed on standards often seems to be of a lower priority than project work. However, this work should not be considered a thankless task. Work progresses so quickly on a CAD system that, without standards, problems can become embedded in the drawing, difficult to analyze, and expensive to correct. Regardless of revenues, standards must be developed and recorded. Systems tend to reinforce the use of standards. Once operators are trained in their use, carefully developed and recorded standards will be used automatically by everyone on the project with little or no opportunity for arbitrary variation.

The production manager should become the single point of control for distribution of work to CAD operators. This individual checks the drawings as they are returned as plots from the computer and turns them over to the project architect and finally the client.

The form of the production manager's job is not significantly altered. For example, the production manager does not always need to master the high-speed input techniques used by operators. However, to supervise computerized drafting procedures, the production manager must understand both the software and hardware and must be familiar enough with their operation to enforce efficient procedures.

The production manager in a CAD environment has to deal with some new pressures. Rather than managing drafters working with paper, pens, and pencils on drafting boards, the production manager is now in charge of operators, working three times as fast with computer terminals, and pen or electrostatic plotters. Adjusting to this new environment will require reorientation along with some retraining. Managing it successfully requires inventiveness, perseverance, and substantial powers of persuasion.

The project architect will need considerable assistance working with the client on one hand and a computer system on the other. It is difficult for one person, either the project architect or the operator, to fully understand the requirements for both computer systems and architectural documents. In this new medium, the importance of a production manager dedicated to the quality and progress of drawings as well as to the maintenance of standards will become apparent.

CAD Operators Are Not Drafters

The job of a CAD operator is not the same as that of a drafter. A drafter is an apprentice to the project architect. A variety of professional skills other than drafting are learned by drafters working with a project architect. CAD operators, in contrast, must learn new techniques for work with data processing equipment. Techniques for recording design information in a data processing medium are complex, and learning them requires a considerable amount of time. While focused on learning these techniques, the operator may not have the opportunity for tutoring in either the basic aspects or the subtleties of professional practice from the project architect. The project architect, on the other hand, may never be required to learn CAD input techniques. Rather than converting sketches into drawings with hand drafting skills, the CAD operator translates sketches into electronic documents on a computer. Realistically, the operator's attention is focused on the CAD system rather than the drawings.

The responsibilities of the CAD operator include:

1. Plan, set up, construct, and edit drawings and related documents on the CAD terminal.
2. Organize graphic objects on the drawing in an efficient manner.
3. Provide comprehensive knowledge of the CAD terminal.
4. Provide a knowledge of production drawing standards and understand how to interpret drawings.
5. Control the quality and completeness of drawings, checking and correcting them as necessary.
6. Produce check plots, final plotted drawings, and extractions or reports as necessary.
7. Communicate with the design team about the overall status of the drawings and clarify any ambiguous or missing information.
8. Coordinate progress of work with the design team and observe estimated time to completion.
9. Participate in meetings for project strategy planning, including initial orientation and periodic project status reviews.

In a computer environment, receiving instructions and reporting on the status of drawings take on new importance. Since drawings progress at such a rapid pace, instructions to the operator must be complete and precise. The project architect will not have an opportunity to look over the operator's shoulder and correct the work as it is being drawn. It is not as convenient for operators, who may even work on a different shift, to stop and clear up uncertainties in the drawings as they are discovered. As a result, the redlined drawings from the project architect must be thorough, well-organized, and timely.

The project architect is familiar with drafting techniques and drawing organization using traditional drafting mediums. However, CAD imposes new requirements for drawing completeness and organization. The content of a computer drawing is organized into primitive objects, groups, layers, symbols, pen numbers, direct files, and records. The organization of the drawing, and the responsibility for these new requirements, will be controlled by the operator, not the project architect. This is a new distinction. As a result, some of the control of the document is removed from the project architect.

In spite of the high degree of technical skill involved, there is no reason to think that operating a CAD system is a career unto itself. Similar to drafters, operators should eventually move into new roles within a design team and become designers or project architects. After all, operators have the advantage of contributing to more project drawings in a shorter time than is possible with traditional drafting mediums. With a background in computer operations as well as in design project work, current CAD operators should eventually become a new and more versatile breed of design professional.

The CAD operator, a new professional technician, has a pivotal role on the design team. Because operators translate the instructions of the design team into documents on the system, much of the success of the production effort rests with them. Performing CAD operations at three or more times the speed of ordinary drafting requires concentration, dexterity, and a high degree of mental coordination. Operators can produce project drawings rapidly in a complex machine environment. Not all drafters have the inclination to work at this pace nor the capabilities required. At a higher rate of productivity, and with an increased responsibility for drawing organization, CAD operators must have more skills than drafters.

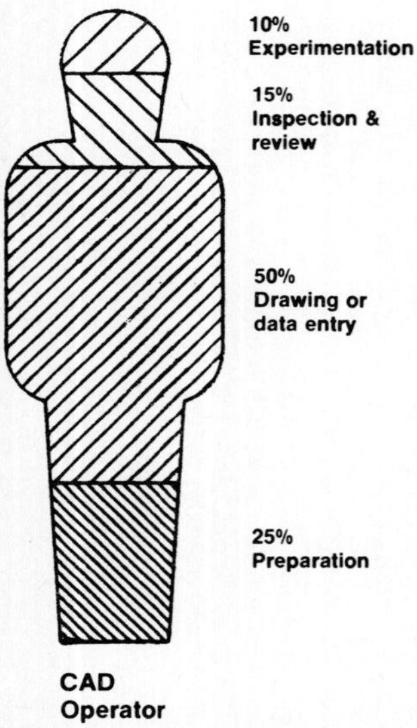

Figure 1-1 Recommended allocation of time on major activities for a typical CAD operator.

Allocating an Operator's Time

It is unrealistic to assume that operators will work uninterrupted on a CAD system for a full 8-hour day. Although drawings can be created three or more times faster than with traditional drafting, checking the results takes just as long. Also, planning the organization of a CAD drawing takes more time. Proportionally more time must be allocated for this task. Ideally, operators should spend a maximum of 50 to 60 percent of their time entering and editing project drawings directly on the system (Fig. 1-1). The balance of time is spent in preparing future work, inspecting and checking completed work, and communicating with others on the design team. Of course, the actual amount of nonsystem time varies depending on the type and phase of the project, the stability of the system, the skill of the operator, and the quality of instructions.

Some amount of operator time should include experimentation with new computer techniques. Expanding one's skills with computers is a process that goes on well past initial training, for several years in fact. Experimentation is required to discover new input techniques as well as new relationships among the objects on drawings and reports that might yield higher levels of efficiency. Shortcuts and simplified procedures often result. Such experimentation should be encouraged and rewarded.

Data Entry Assistant

A new position that appears with the introduction of computers is that of data entry assistant. In a design office, many tasks are essentially data entry. Such tasks can be laid out and reviewed by professional staff and performed effectively by someone with only a casual understanding of design project work. The individual need not have an architectural or even a drafting background. Following is an outline of tasks that can be performed by a data entry assistant.

1. Entering furniture and equipment inventory information.
2. Entering construction cost items.
3. Entering survey results.
4. Entering files of architectural drawing notes or keynotes.
5. Entering files for architectural space programs or construction specifications.
6. Transcribing meeting notes and other information into a design decision file.
7. Running reports or extractions from project drawings.
8. Expanding symbol libraries or files.
9. Operating the plotter.

Notice that these tasks are project-related—in contrast with the administrative responsibilities of a secretary. A data entry assistant is an entry-level position. For tasks such as those mentioned, hiring an assistant will be more cost-effective than using others on the design team.

The Project Architect

The increased pace of work impacts both the form and the content of the project architect's job. The need for project planning and control is more acute with CAD than with traditional drafting. During the accelerated design and production drawing phases, the client's monthly cost is increased. Clients will be alert to this and need to be reassured that the entire team can successfully manage this rapid pace. Such reassurance must come from the project architect. He or she is going to have to make decisions three times as fast.

It follows that the client is also going to have more design work to review in a shorter time. As we all know, delayed decisions from the client often retard progress and, in some cases, create additional expense for the design team. As the key interface, the project architect must prepare the client for the pace ahead with a detailed schedule of review and approval intervals tied to drawing production. One of the strategic aspects of the design and construction process is the project architect's task of leading the client through review to approval. On projects over a certain size, perhaps $10 to 20 million of construction value, the client is encouraged to provide a project manager dedicated to monitoring the progress of design work and anticipating upcoming approvals.

To stay on top of a job, the project architect will not be able to divide his or her attention among several different projects. During the construction document phase in particular, the project architect must concentrate solely on the project being developed on the system. In particular, the architect will not have time to personally perform some of the drafting. The complexity of the new project team and the cost of operating the computer makes getting out of step with the progress of the drawings expensive. If instructions and responses to questions are delayed, problems can be multiplied very quickly throughout the drawings. Many of these problems do not even arise with traditional drafting. Rather than wait while the project architect and designer work out a detail, operators tend to keep right on entering new line work.

The degree of change possible with CAD systems amplifies an existing problem for the project architect. With traditional drafting mediums, changes to the design, if unrestrained, needlessly consume time and resources. With CAD systems, the amount of change that can be carried out is much greater. It is hoped that this greater capacity for change facilitates the perfection of design. Unfortunately, without a system for controlling changes, such as a sequence of predefined iterations for drawing input, overall productivity is undermined. Design offices with CAD systems have discovered that as much as 75 percent of operator time on project documents is spent making changes. This level of change, clearly intolerable with manual drafting, offsets the increased productivity of CAD, and the final result is as expensive as manual drafting. Although there is no absolute rule for the right amount of change, judgment is required. The project architect must exert additional control over modifications to the drawings, or expectations about productivity and speed will be unsatisfied.

The use of CAD systems expands the reporting responsibilities of the project architect. When drawings are created at an accelerated pace, proportionally more time is required for communicating with operators, consultants, reviewing agencies, and the client. In fact, new reporting documents are needed. At this pace, the prints on the project architect's desk are out of date very quickly. The original drawings will now be stored on the system. With current plotters, it is not as convenient to run off a complete set of check prints, unlike prints of a flat file of drawings. However, the increasing availability of high quality electrostatic and laser printers makes this a transitional phase. A greater quantity and variety of intermediate documents are required, such as partial drawings, "quick" plots, extractions from drawings, and reports. Fortunately, most systems, when set up correctly, have convenient utilities and peripheral devices for creating these reports and quick plots. CAD is still a new tool in the design office, and it is the rare project architect or office principal that has the time or inclination to learn the complex operations of a CAD system. Several years' experience as a drafter allows a project architect, skilled in the medium, to easily pick up the tools of drafting and to occasionally participate directly in the creation of construction documents. Becoming highly proficient at CAD drafting requires an apprenticeship as an operator of at least 1 or 2 years, similar to that of a drafter. A simple error can disrupt the integrity of a complex drawing for use by other operators or design disciplines. Consequently, unless project architects are willing to undertake additional training, it is impractical to expect them to occasionally contribute to the actual production of contract documents on a CAD system.

The separation between the project architect and the drawings implied by this evaluation is expected to be a transitional phase. After all, some of today's CAD operators will soon become project architects. Also, future software enhancements should better incorporate CAD standards and procedures so that more people can interact with CAD systems.

The project architect's basic responsibilities for direction, control, and overall progress are unchanged with the introduction of CAD. However, these responsibilities are brought into sharper focus. Management of this increased pace will rest largely on the project architect, who will have to work faster. Problems tend to reach the surface sooner in a computer environment, and, as always, the project architect will be expected to anticipate these problems. Consequently, communication assumes greater importance. An emphasis on good communication will certainly benefit the quality of a project.

The increased pace of work creates a new mental environment also. Adjusting to it is a serious challenge for the project architect.

The Designer

The role of the designer in the new computer environment is a provocative subject. At this stage of computer use in architecture, how CAD will transform the designer's role is unclear.

Some offices are experimenting with a scenario where designers work with personal computers while drafters work as operators on larger CAD systems dedicated to producing construction documents. With this scenario, designers work with drafting, sketching, three-dimensional modeling, or perspective software applications. Similar to traditional drafting procedures, they develop preliminary drawings and sketches. These are passed onto the drafting staff or transferred directly to the production CAD system. If, for example, design sketches are not drawn to scale, and working drawings are created from scratch, it is not necessary to transfer them directly from the designer's system to the production CAD system. If, however, transferring the design drawings and preliminary nongraphic information directly from personal computers to larger systems is desirable, compatibility between systems is essential for an efficient operation.

With computers, the designer has access to more information. Information also becomes available more quickly. Computer systems make the following items easier to produce and generally more available to the designer:

1. More two-dimensional drawings, including automatic generation of drawings for stairs, bathrooms, elevator cores, etc.
2. Extractions from drawings, including material and equipment quantities, boundaries, and areas.
3. Views or drawings from three-dimensional or solid models, including shading and color.
4. Architectural programming documents, such as facilities-planning layouts, space projections, occupancy loads, standard furniture and room configurations.
5. Design testing, such as analysis of compliance with building codes; circulation projections or models; shading analysis; projections of solar gain and heat loss; analysis of lines of sight and visibility.
6. Interference checking.
7. Access to centralized data banks for construction materials and environmental information, such as weather, earthquake faults, traffic, and populations.
8. Quantity takeoffs and construction cost estimates.
9. Design decision tracking.

CAD systems are currently perceived, within the design profession at least, as effective at producing construction documents. Software applications for design tasks are either not as well-developed, well-understood, or well-marketed. Certainly, as project documents are created at an accelerated pace, the designer will have more decisions to make in a shorter time. However, the question of how designers are impacted by computers is really one of where a firm sees the limit of design work. Are design tasks separate from the creation of the drawings? More fundamentally, does design include analysis? The answers to these questions may lie in whether designers come to actually create drawings and reports directly on CAD systems.

Not to Be Overlooked, the Financial Manager

Two final roles, the financial manager and the director of marketing, are worth highlighting. Without an emphasis on these positions, the investment in new equipment and training either will not get under way or will soon erode. Financial managers will face new demands.

The billing cycle must keep pace with increased productivity. Equipment lease payments and maintenance expense for computer systems require that fees for design services be paid in a businesslike manner, generally in fewer than 60 days. To make the most effective use of capital resources, billing, job cost, and reporting systems must be in place and operate smoothly. Fortunately, the success of computers is well-founded in software applications for accounting. Also, regardless of industry, an automated accounting system is a logical first step in a phased development program for computer use.

Design offices have traditionally had to invest only a modest amount of capital per employee for equipment. The funding and maintenance of capital equipment is a new problem. The lease payments for CAD systems are carried on the books as a fixed cost. In other words, the cost will not vary with regard to workload. As a result, equipment-leasing companies require offices to project their income streams several years ahead. This accounting calculation brings several issues to the surface, such as the net worth of the office, the ownership of the office vis-à-vis the equipment, and the investment of the principals. Although these are straightforward business issues, they are often hard to resolve.

A New Emphasis on Marketing

Whether the role of marketing director is a full-time position or is shared by the office principals, more design work will have to be generated. For the first time, modern marketing techniques may be required, including: specialization, positioning the firm in the marketplace, development of new services, and forecasting by market segment. Usually new marketing techniques such as these have to be acquired in training outside of the design office.

Advanced software applications make available new marketing opportunities for design firms, including applications for facility planning, space projections, and construction-cost estimating. With these applications, new skills are acquired that can be developed into additional design services.

Even with the increased productivity that CAD systems provide, three times as many design projects are not likely to be available. However, more services can be performed on the same project, if they are marketed so that clients understand they are receiving additional value. For example, boundaries, which are valuable to facilities management, can be extracted from construction documents and sold separately on specially edited drawings. Design office management must search for similar opportunities in which data, originally captured during the documentation process, is reused and sold as part of a separate design service. Integrating new services into traditional marketing techniques, however, will take special emphasis.

Chapter

2

A New Project Team

"Of course, any potential increase in efficiency from changing methods must be balanced against the training and adaptation costs of switching users over to the new methods. A typical strategy is to first computerize the current methods, then switch to better, more efficient methods once the users have become familiar with the computer." *[FOLE82]*

The integration of CAD modifies the allocation of human resources within a design team, altering not only the roles of professionals but also the composition of the design team. The team expands and new positions emerge (Figs. 2-1 and 2-2).

At the head of the team, the office principal will have less time to devote to any one project. Since marketing is given new emphasis, the principal must be concerned with more projects during the same period. Also, CAD compresses the time for project completion.

Project architects, however, must devote their undivided attention to the project at hand. The complexity of the team, the increased pace, and the new focus of the office principal make the role of the project architect all the more important.

The system manager and the production manager play key roles in the new project team. Smooth operation of a CAD system requires the attention of a system manager, who gives special attention to drawing standards and the organization of project documents. More resources are devoted to planning and controlling project documents—the production manager's job. To a

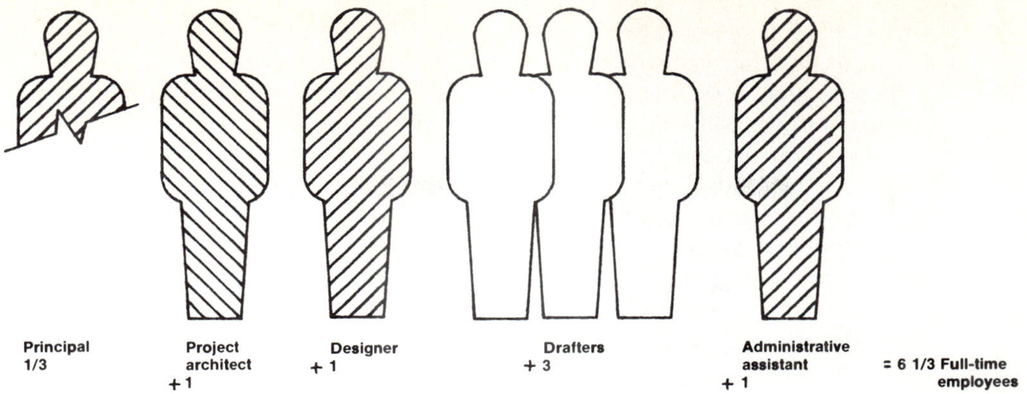

Figure 2-1 Organization of an architectural project team using traditional drafting methods, showing distribution of time on a typical project.

greater or lesser degree, the system manager and production manager are involved with every project in the office. If these functions are performed by different individuals, part of their time is allocated to each project.

A single operator can perform the work of at least three drafters. However, this does not necessarily mean that personnel should be eliminated. In fact, new opportunities for growth and mobility within the firm are created. Rather than providing the same amount of work for fewer people, CAD systems enable the same number of people to deliver more design service. The cost justification for computers is the increased productivity and the improved quality of work they make available. Taking advantage of this by converting computer capabilities into improved design services requires adjustment and reorientation.

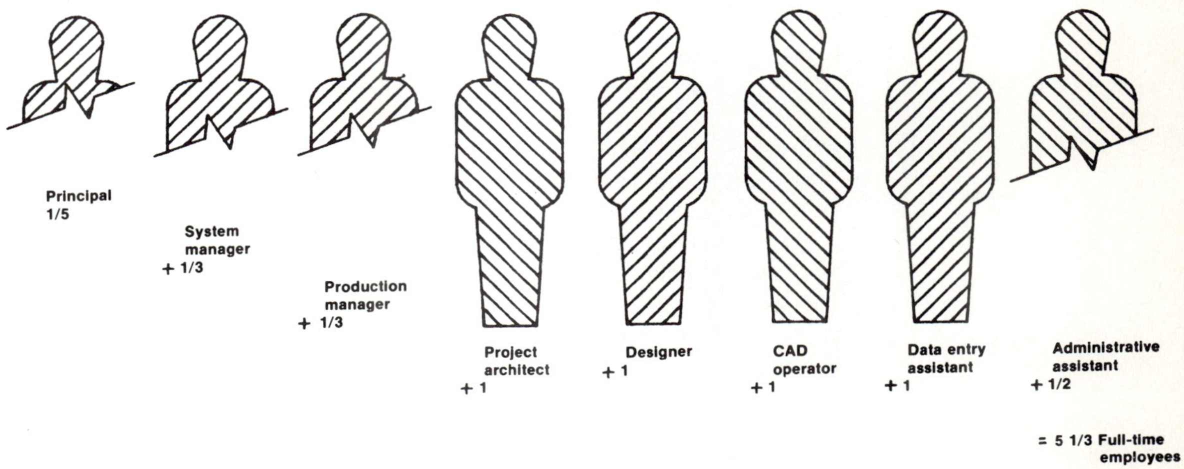

Figure 2-2 Suggested organization of architectural project team working with CAD, showing assignment of time on a typical project.

The focus of new roles performed with the use of computers does not necessarily mean that individuals are more narrowly specialized. On the contrary, computers tend to decentralize, not only the flow of information, but the distribution of tasks as well. Some degree of specialization, such as for system management, is essential. However, several design firms apply a studio approach to project work with computers. The objective is for the core of the design team to participate in every task in the design process, from design to documentation. Applying this method to computers, most members of the design team become proficient with several computer applications including word processing, computer-aided drafting, and reporting on the drawings. Thus different roles in a computer environment are spread across the design team.

Since CAD systems produce drawings quickly, time devoted to project activities is reallocated. Although the amount of time spent on production drawings is reduced dramatically, all the time saved is not spent on design activities. This is a common justification when an office is considering the purchase of CAD equipment, but the complexity of a computer environment tempers this expectation (Fig. 2-3).

Some additional time will be available for expanded and more thorough design studies. As we know, CAD systems simplify the problem of generating and rendering design alternatives. Nonetheless, a considerable amount of time is required for activities that are not directly related to project work. Simply managing the system requires additional overhead resources as well as time.

To completely master the use of computers requires a learning period of several years. The amount of time currently allocated for education and training should be doubled. Also, to generate more work for an automated design team, additional time must be spent on marketing activities.

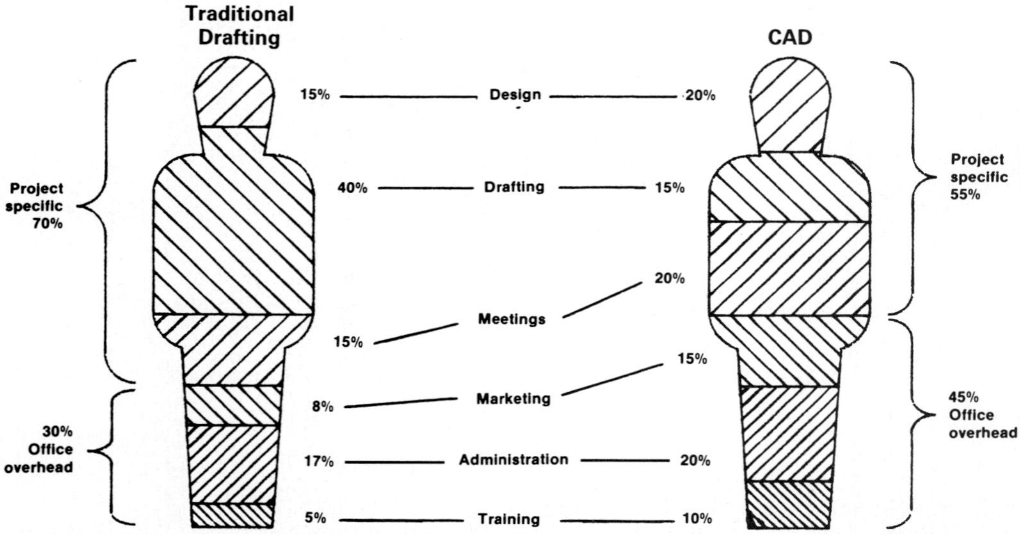

Figure 2-3 For a typical architect, comparing allocations of time to major activities for traditional drafting methods versus CAD.

Finally, since work progresses at an increased rate, proportionally more time is required for the administration of a project. More time is spent in communication and meetings. Activities such as giving instructions to operators, setting up project standards, and reviewing the progress of drawings and reports require greater emphasis. Reports and schedules as well as drawings tend to proliferate with the use of CAD systems. In fact, this is one of their benefits. But this information must be communicated to the client.

In summary, a project which makes use of CAD has a larger percentage of time devoted to activities other than specifically creating drawings. Some of this additional time, such as that spent in meetings and review, is project-related. Activities such as marketing and system management, however, must be absorbed as ordinary administrative expenses.

Emphasis on Training

Do not expect a significant improvement over established and well-understood production techniques such as hand drafting without changes in the form and content of professional service jobs. In the words of a design office principal experienced with the integration of CAD into professional practice, "Be prepared to restructure the entire management of the office."

In any field, the essential element in the successful use of data processing equipment is training. Training takes place both at start-up and when computers are used in office procedures other than drafting. Training is the largest single expense accompanying the use of computers, larger even than the cost of equipment. It is also the most difficult cost item to quantify. Even more important than the equipment, training (or retraining in the case of professionals in practice) is the key to increased productivity.

As staff moves onto new positions, it is important to effectively train incoming staff so that carefully developed office procedures are not lost. A training manual that quickly brings entry-level operators to productive skill levels is essential. Rather than rely on the material supplied by the CAD vendor, which is not specialized for a particular firm, the design office must develop its own training manual. Over time, a series of exercises, from remedial to advanced, should be developed to reflect the type of design work performed. In this way, both office standards and CAD procedures are transmitted in the same training experience. Documenting system procedures for this purpose is one of the functions of the production manager.

New capabilities represent an investment in modernization, for both the individual design office and the design profession as a whole. Once staff members have been retrained to work at higher levels of productivity with data processing equipment, they are more valuable and more difficult to replace. In spite of fears that computerization will eliminate jobs, there is a shortage of qualified people with both professional and computer skills. Competition among employers for people with these skills exists and will probably continue into the foreseeable future. At the outset of training, an employment agreement should be considered for the well-being of all parties.

Despite sales hyperbole and testimonials by professionals already working with CAD, assume that it requires one full year of retraining and extra effort to master production drafting on a CAD system. This does not mean productive work cannot be carried out on the system during this period. With most CAD systems, initial training enables operators to generate drawings within a matter of weeks. Assume, however, that it will take a year before a complete project can be carried out on budget and on time without having to train or learn at each major step in the process.

On the positive side, firms that have mastered the use of CAD find they can tell clients, "We can produce work as fast as you can review the drawings." Relief from this bottleneck is well worth the extra investment in time and energy.

Chapter 3

An Office Automation Plan

"The better the computer tool, the sooner it becomes obsolete."
MICHAEL HOLLAND, SOFTWARE DEVELOPER

A CAD system should not be seen as an isolated piece of data processing equipment in the architectural office. It must be considered part of an office's strategic plan for delivering design services that combine human resources and automated tools. Computer use must reflect an office policy for integrating data processing with design services. Each office should have a written strategy for the acquisition and use of computer software and equipment. Such a plan integrates the CAD system with the goals and objectives of the firm.

An office automation plan should discuss the current and near future methods of implementing automated accounting, word processing, communications, data base organization, and CAD. It must outline specific goals for each of these application areas, such as tripling drafting productivity. The plan must be open-ended to accommodate the inevitable changes which technological advance dictates. Key areas of an office automation plan are capital requirements, equipment ownership, and staffing. The plan will not cover all eventualities, but it will bring the firm's thinking about computers into the open. It should address the reorganization of the office which will result from office automation.

Although system integration is important, all software applications need not be performed on the same system. Office systems are considered integrated if the desirable links between separate files and software applications have been established.

Some questions raised by an office automation plan are: What is the firm's policy on purchasing application software? Does the firm have the resources to develop its own software? What is the current and proposed use of each application? Who will be trained on systems? Will systems be integrated through a network or through central processing? Which systems will handle which applications (for instance, can the accounting be done as a background process once a month on the CAD system computer)? What are the "blue-sky" goals of the firm? A terminal on every project manager's desk with access to multiple applications? A terminal for each project designer? A terminal dedicated to each project?

System Selection

Because the selection process must reflect the resources and requirements of an individual office, we cannot recommend specific system criteria. The following are general recommendations intended for planning or establishing a procedure for selecting hardware and software:

1. The selection should be part of an integrated office automation plan rather than a series of isolated purchases.
2. Involve at least two people in the selection. As with employee selection and review, two views supplement each other with profit.
3. Computer systems are complex, so expand your understanding of the possibilities available by reviewing as many publications and books on the topic as possible.
4. From your reading, pick out the three or four most qualified alternatives. Request thorough, individual demonstrations from each of these vendors.
5. Establish a list of criteria—requirements which the system must meet—that reflect the emphasis of your particular design practice. Weight these criteria as to which has the most importance for the selection you are currently considering.
6. Visit sites where the system is already installed.
7. Based on typical drawings from your design practice, develop a benchmark test for objective comparison of different system performance.
8. Wherever possible, use published checklists and benchmark procedures.
9. Evaluate the company as well as the software and hardware. The long-range relationship with the company, and its methods and attitudes, will affect your company for years to come.

10. Evaluate each vendor using the criteria established. A blind evaluation by each member of the selection team can be useful.
11. Make a decision and implement it.

Realize your decision will be based on the best available information at any one time. Good business decisions must often be made with incomplete information. Change is inevitable, but fear of change should not inhibit anyone from becoming involved with technology.

Comparative System Characteristics

CAD systems and application software are characterized by design intentions developed for the system or application when it was first created. Understanding the underlying design program for a system, similar to appreciating the design program for a building, enables an office to develop CAD and data-handling procedures that optimize the capabilities of a particular system.

Table 3-1 lists characteristics of CAD systems and graphic software applications which reflect the design of a system and influence its use, providing examples of currently available systems that typify each characteristic. The list does not necessarily reflect industrywide terminology; rather the terms are those used in the following chapters in discussions of the organization of drawings on CAD systems. The systems and applications are not always opposites or mutually exclusive, but designations are paired to accentuate contrasting characteristics.

For reference, we also cite examples of currently available CAD systems which, to the best of our knowledge, typify each characteristic. Those listed are intended as examples only, and the list is not based on a complete survey of all systems available. This list is not intended as an evaluation of the comparative capabilities of different systems, nor is it intended to be used for justifying a particular selection. The authors offer no judgment here as to the relative merit or shortcomings of systems named.

TABLE 3-1 Characteristics of CAD Systems and Graphics Software Applications

Characteristic	Description	Examples
Session-based	Update or replace drawings at session end.	1,2,3,4,6,10
Live	Work directly on graphic file.	5,7,8,9
Addressed attributes	Supports attributes or properties that are referenced by pointer. Direct files.	1,2,3,4,5,7
Keyed attributes	Attributes referenced by key words. Indirect files.	1,3,4,6,7,8,9
Local symbol	Unique copies of data defining graphic objects inserted into graphic file.	(most)
Systemwide symbol	Pointers to central reference copy inserted into graphic file.	2,4

TABLE 3-1 Characteristics of CAD Systems and Graphics Software Applications (Continued)

Characteristic	Description	Examples
Data base–oriented	All files, including graphics, handled by a data base management system, providing data independence.	1,5,6
Optimized	Format of graphic file designed to optimize performance of graphics software.	(most)
Deep-grouped	Groups with an unlimited recursive hierarchy.	1,2,3
Shallow tree	Groups with only set number of levels.	4,5,6,7,8,9,10
Object-based	Appearance or other attributes assignable to any object.	(most)
Layer-oriented	Appearance or other attributes assignable to nonobjects such as drawing layer.	1,7,8
Menu-oriented	Commands entered from tablet or screen menus.	(most)
Command-oriented	Commands entered with the use of a command syntax.	1,4,6,7,8
Drawing-oriented	Drawings are independent files complete unto themselves and serve as the master or source file.	1,2,3,6,7,8,9,10
Project-oriented	Drawings accessed through a master project grouping.	4,5,6,7,9
Model	Single source description of a design.	4,5,6,8
Two-dimensional	Coordinates are recorded or displayed only as X and Y values.	1,2,3,7,8,9,10
Three-dimensional or solid	Coordinates are recorded and displayed as X, Y, and Z values.	3,4,5,6,7,8,9
Extendable	User-extendable at source code level.	1,2,3,4,7,8
Proprietary	Turn-key software only, no provision for user extensions.	5,6,9,10
Stand-alone	Drawing file stored in workstation-dedicated processor.	1,2,3,4,9
Multiple access	Shared access to drawing files.	5,6,7,8,10
Distributed	Networked, communicating, or linked with other systems or using distributed processing.	3,4,5,6,7,8,9,10
Isolated	Not designed for, or not installed in an environment conducive to, frequent exchange of data with other systems.	1,2
Speed in millions of instructions per second (MIPS)		
1 MIPS (approx.)	Micro, supports single workstation.	1,4,5,6,7,9,10
Multiple MIPS	Mini or supermicro, supports two or more workstations and/or processes.	2,3,4,5,6,7,8
10s of MIPS	Mainframe, supports multiple workstations and processes at multiple sites.	2,4

TABLE 3-1 Characteristics of CAD Systems and Graphics Software Applications (Continued)

Characteristic	Description	Examples
Virtual files	Partial drawing is resident in central processing memory with paged access to entire drawing.	2,5,6,7,8
Real files	Drawing remains resident in central processing memory.	1,3,4,9,10
Portable	Software written to run on multiple computer operating systems.	1,4,5,8,10
Machine-dependent	Software written to run on only a specific hardware environment.	2,3,6,7,9
Raster graphics	Screen image composed with grid of individual pixels from sweeping beam.	(most)
Vector graphics	Screen image composed with vectors, drawn from point to point. Longer redraw interval.	8
Windowed	Multiple-window drawing views, or multitasking software operations.	2,4,7,9
Single image	One view of a drawing, or single function operation.	1,3,5,6,8,10

[1] AUTO CAD v2.17, Auto Desk, 2320 Marin Ship Way, Sausalito, CA 94965.
[2] Design Bldg & Mngr System, and 3D Interactive Package, CADAM INC, 1935 N. Buena Vista St., Burbank, CA 91504.
[3] System 25, CALCOMP, 2411 W. La Palma Ave., Anaheim, CA 92803.
[4] AEC Software, ComputerVision, 100 Crosby Drive, Bedford, MA 01730.
[5] RUCAPS, GMWC North America, 1417 4th Ave., Seattle, WA, 98101.
[6] HOK Draw, HOK/CSC, 100 N. Broadway, St. Louis, MO 63102.
[7] IGDS/DRMS, APDP Integraph Corp., One Madison Industrial Park, Huntsville, AL 35807.
[8] McAuto, McDonald Douglas Automation, St. Louis, MO.
[9] Point-Line, Point-Line Co., 2280 Powel St., Suite 300, San Francisco, CA 94133.
[10] VersaCad, T&W Systems Inc., 7372 Prince Dr., Huntington Beach, CA 92647.

Section 2

Drawing Organization

Section 2 describes the basic elements, such as drawing layers, groups, and symbols, which organize the graphic information on two-dimensional drawings created on a CAD system. With some variation in both naming conventions and degrees of freedom, these elements are common to all currently available systems, both PC-based and larger. Chapters 4 through 10 include guidelines and lists of recommendations for creating, organizing, and working with these elements to efficiently manage graphic information on CAD systems.

Chapter

4

Elements of Drawing Structure

Architect: "What do you do when a drawing occupies nearly all of the space available for it in computer memory?"

System Manager: "Pack the drawing."

Drawings created on a CAD system exhibit striking differences from those that are created in a manual drafting environment. Features of drawings which do not exist in a manual drafting environment emerge for the first time. The origin of a line, for instance, does not exist with traditional drafting, yet it is basic to graphic operations on CAD systems. Other drawing parameters, which are familiar and well understood, are translated into a new terminology. Line weights are analogous to both pen numbers and intensities. Drawing layers are like the different sheets used in overlay drafting. Often the differences are profound. In many cases, a CAD system confronts the designer or operator with concepts that have no analogies and either seem absurd, such as packing a drawing, or present barriers to operation which are difficult to overcome.

This chapter focuses on the new characteristics of drawings on CAD systems. The operational aspects of any particular system, such as the procedure for drawing a straight line or a circle or for storing a drawing, are not considered. We assume that an understanding of such operations is acquired more easily from training or from documentation that is specific to a system and its application software. Certain aspects of computer-generated drawings apply, in one form or another, to most systems, however. These are discussed here, as well as the new terms, which define the organization of a drawing on a CAD system. In general, the aspects of drawings discussed in this chapter make up a core of graphic standards for CAD drawings.

We selected the terms defined in this chapter because of their pivotal relationship, from the perspective of an operator, to the control of objects on a CAD drawing. An understanding of their nature and use is essential to efficient use of CAD systems for architectural drawings. Certain topics, such as groups and symbols, are described in some depth in later chapters. This chapter defines much of the vocabulary used throughout the book.

The final section in this chapter includes a list of recommendations. These rules of thumb summarize conditions that must be considered when creating drawings on a CAD system.

A Few New Terms

In a CAD environment, every part of a drawing, such as a point, line, arc, or lettering, is a discrete element. Terms for these are distinct from those which define a design element made up of such objects. To some extent, this has always been the case in traditional drafting. Standard line weights and lettering sizes are defined in the office graphic standards. However, on CAD systems, drawings are more complex. They have more parts which must be defined with a new terminology. Sometimes, the terminology reflects terms used in traditional drafting. Often, it does not.

Using CAD, every object on a drawing can be manipulated by the operator. Objects can also be manipulated as a class. Since they can be manipulated, objects not only are named, but they also have characteristics specific to their class. These characteristics define what operations can be performed on objects as well as the relationships between them. Making distinctions between the objects on a drawing and identifying the characteristics and operations associated with them are an important part of the dialogue that surrounds the use of CAD.

Creating architectural drawings with CAD systems requires a new basic drawing unit that is neither as traditional as a line nor as specific to computers as the bit or pixel. The *graphic object* serves this purpose. A graphic object is any element within the drawing, such as a point, line, arc, string of letters or numbers, which can be defined with geometry. Groups and symbols which are made up of these elements can also be treated as graphic objects for specific operations.

Notice that on certain CAD systems, the term "object" has a particular meaning distinct from that defined here. (See the entry under "Shallow tree" in Table 3-1.) On such systems, an "object" is analogous to a drawing layer as described and used in this book.

Groups and symbols are combinations of simpler graphic objects that are treated as a single object. Simple graphic objects, which are not made up of any other elements, are referred to as *primitive graphic objects*, or simply primitive objects. In this book, the term *object* refers to either a primitive graphic object or a group or symbol acting like a graphic object.

The concept of a graphic object defines a general category. The category includes the entire spectrum of objects on a drawing that can be created, recognized, modified, and acted on by the system. In fact, the only material excluded from the category is written information that is stored in text files which are themselves connected to graphic objects. Since they can be connected to graphic objects, text files and their contents are sometimes referred to as *nongraphic objects*.

Every graphic object has an *origin*. The origin can be defined as a reference point that defines the geometric location or pivot of a graphic object for the purpose of finding, moving, rotating, or mirroring the object by the system.

The *geometric location* refers to the *X* and *Y* cartesian coordinates of the origin within the boundaries of a drawing. Frequently, the origin is the first, or starting, point of a line. Some systems prompt the operator to designate the position of the origin when first creating an object. An origin does not have to coincide with a line in the object, however. It can fall outside or within the line work (see Fig. 7-8). System utilities make it possible to relocate an origin after an object is drawn. In a sense, the origin is a handle for an object. Since it is a reference point, an operator can pick up and move an object by its origin. The origin of a group, for instance, is the origin of the first member of the group. As described in Chap. 7, objects can be located in relation to a separate line in the drawing by having the system place the origin on the line.

The origin must not be confused with the location of an object within a project in the architectural sense. The location of an object within a room or a department, for instance, can be determined automatically with the use of boundary objects and location fields. Origin only defines the *X* and *Y* coordinates of a reference point. By itself, the origin cannot convey its position relative to an architectural boundary. Although the origin is used to find location on a drawing, it does not cite a designated room location specific to the project.

Designers are very familiar with *line weights*. In the manual drafting environment, line weights have been developed to allow precise differentiation between elements on a drawing. Variations in line weight provide a graphic vocabulary that heightens the visual distinctions between structural elements, built-in items, drawing borders, and drafting guidelines.

On most CAD systems, line weights are illustrated on the screen in one manner and reproduced with a plotter in another. On a plotted drawing, which is the output from CAD procedures, line weights define graphic distinctions just as they do in hand drafting. For the purposes of plotting, when objects are created on drawings their line weights are designated with *pen numbers*, sometimes referred to as *pen weights*. (On systems where pen numbers are not used, the line style carries the line weight.) Plotters, either pen or electrostatic, interpret the object pen numbers to define the thickness of a line. This is achieved on pen plotters either by using pens with tips of different thicknesses, or by instructing the plotter to redraw with the same pen, two times or more, each time with a slight offset, along the same line. When different pens are substituted, pen numbers can be used to define the color of a line as well.

The pen number is assigned to a graphic object when it is first created on the system. In fact, pen number is one of the data fields that defines an object within the system. Functions are available that enable an operator to change the pen number for an object at any time.

When displayed on the cathode-ray tube (CRT), line weights in all but a few CAD systems have the same thickness. To distinguish between them, the brightness, or the *color* of the line, must vary. Consequently, all graphic objects are also designated with a color number or *intensity*. This number indicates either the brightness or color of an object as it is displayed. On black-and-white screens, intensity is usually limited to two or three levels of brightness. On a color screen, the possible distinctions are much greater. As with pen numbers, color is a data field that is part of the definition of an object within the system. Line color can also be edited at any time to a new value.

Pen number and color, although related, are not one and the same. Lines of different thickness, when plotted, can have the same intensity when viewed on the CRT screen and vice versa. The distinctions between colors are finer than those which can be reproduced economically on a plotted drawing, which is usually restricted to black and white. However, intensity, or color, can be used to enhance operations on a CAD system. First, with different colors, a particular design element, such as the load-bearing walls, can be readily distinguished from others, such as the light-weight partitions. So, colors make new distinctions, entire classes of elements, easier to identify within the drawing. Since distinctions can be readily made, the use of color can simplify the visual identification of objects and improve the overall speed of interactions within the system. As a result, different intensities, and particularly the use of color, provide a new level of organization to an architectural drawing. Obviously there are limits to the number of colors and other display characteristics that can be distinguished by the eye (Table 4-1).

Objects can also be drawn with distinct *line styles*. Line style refers to the graphic characteristics of a line, for instance, a solid line, dashed line, or centerline. The software supplied with a system usually includes several standard line styles. A software utility is also available for creating special line styles. The versatility and response speed of different line styles depend on the characteristics of the particular CAD system. For instance, to conserve memory, line styles are not always shown on the CRT screen as they will

TABLE 4-1 Graphic Characteristics Easily Distinguished Without Error[a]

Coding method	Maximum number of codes for nearly error-free recognition
Color	6
Geometric shapes	10
Line width	2
Line type	5
Intensity	2

[a] Reprinted with permission of J. D. Foley and A. Van Dam.

appear when actually plotted. Instead, a simplified version is shown. Some systems do not use pen numbers, and the line style defines the thickness of the line along with its graphics characteristics. In these cases, the relative line thicknesses are shown on the CRT screen, since they are invariable.

Special Flags

A graphic object can also be designated with a *special flag*, sometimes referred to as a "kind" number. A *flag* is a short field, possibly an integer, which is part of the block of attributes, or control record, for the object. The field is similar to that for color, pen number, or drawing layer, since all these characteristics are stored in the object's control record. Unlike the pen number, layer, and color, which have prescribed functions, a special flag usually does not. The special flag is a wild card.

Because it is a simple number included in the control record for the object, rather then a separate record with several fields, the system can read a special flag swiftly. Consequently, the system can search very quickly through the entire graphic display file for objects with a specific number in a flag. These flags can be found more quickly than can information searched for through nongraphic records associated with the objects. Special flags have the advantage of speed and simplicity.

Special flags are assigned to objects in one of two ways. First, with an interactive procedure, objects, such as symbols, are selected by an operator. Then, using an editing function much like that for changing color or drawing layer, the flag is assigned and given a specific number.

Second, special flags can be automatically assigned by the software when an object is first created. Here, the function of a special flag is defined by the software vendor. In this case, the flag number has a prescribed function. For example, by automatically assigning a special flag to wall lines, they are distinguished from other lines when inserting a symbol or performing an area takeoff.

If the software recognizes a specific value for a flag that value cannot be used as a special flag for other purposes. For example, by assigning a specific value to a flag on door symbols, the system is triggered to draw door jambs automatically when a door is located on a wall. If not otherwise prescribed, flag values can be assigned by the operator for project-specific purposes such as takeoffs of furniture and equipment.

Rather then affecting the final plotted output directly, as pen numbers do, special flags are applied to assist operations during the creation of a drawing. A special flag provides a reference that cuts across other parameters of the drawing, such as drawing layer and color. This is its most important characteristic. Since it is a cross index, it can be assigned to all objects of a certain category. Combined with fast system recognition, this characteristic can be used to advantage on many drawing management problems. Separate phases of work, for example, can be designated with a special flag. Items that are not provided by but are installed by the contractor, can be identified by a special flag. Thus they can be identified conveniently regardless of drawing layer.

In another example, all items of furniture, including desks, tables, and chairs, can be assigned the same special flag number. The system will thus identify every item of furniture and display it very quickly. Once found, other operations can be performed on the objects, including counting the furniture and creating a furniture inventory report or updating the nongraphic files that are attached to the furniture. Special flags are a powerful project management tool.

Drawing Parameters

In traditional drafting, the fundamental dimensional parameters of a drawing are the drawing size, such as 30 by 42 in, the unit of measure for the drawing, such as feet and inches or meters, and the scale of the drawing—such as $\frac{1}{8}$ in = 1 ft. On CAD systems, these parameters are assigned either when the drawing is first initialized or when it is plotted. Although essentially the same, drawing parameters on CAD systems are more dynamic.

For example, drawing size is no longer entirely fixed. On certain CAD systems, when a drawing is first initialized its size is not even designated. Instead, size is determined by the drawing scale. However, on these systems drawing scale is defined as part of the procedure for plotting the drawing. To correctly size lettering and sheet borders, the operator must know the drawing scale, but the system has no record of drawing scale, and therefore size, except for plotting.

On other systems, the size and scale of the drawing are designated when the drawing is initialized. However, a drawing that is initialized at one size can be plotted at many different sizes. As a result, drawing scale is also varied. Plotters have the capability to rescale the drawing when it is plotted. A drawing created at one size can be plotted at half its original size. The resulting plotted drawing will have a scale double that of the initialized drawing.

This rescaling capability affords several advantages. The same drawing can be used for full size plans as well as enlarged plans of designated areas, such as bathrooms, stairs, and elevator cores. When a project begins, initialize the drawings at double their final size. For example, if the final plotted drawings will be 40 by 30 in, initialize them at 80 by 60 in. Create the full-scale plans with a working scale of $\frac{1}{4}$ in = 1 ft. When complete, $\frac{1}{8}$-in scale drawing can be produced by plotting the CAD drawings at half size. As work progresses on the full size plans, areas within them can be plotted at full size. Thus, nearly complete plans of $\frac{1}{4}$-in scale for stairs and baths are created with one additional operation. In addition, if changes are made to the $\frac{1}{4}$-in–scale drawing, they are reflected in the $\frac{1}{8}$-in–scale plan at the time of plotting.

Since the full size plans are plotted at half size, the plotted drawings have greater clarity and the line quality is improved. Objects on plotted drawings are composed with straight lines regardless of whether the object includes arcs and curves. At half size, curves and line intersections appear sharper with this technique.

Regardless of the size of the plotted drawing, however, some things remain fixed. The area represented on the drawing in real-world dimensions remains unchanged. Similar to traditional drafting, the scaled length of the longest line on the drawing is determined by the size of the drawing combined with the scale of the drawing. As a result, the largest possible dimension on the drawing is fixed when the drawing is initialized.

On many CAD systems, the unit of measure, such as feet or meters, is also fixed. This cannot always be modified after drawing initialization, although some CAD systems provide this flexibility.

On most systems, however, the working scale of a drawing can be changed at any time. This is similar to traditional drafting, where switching between scales of $\frac{1}{8}$ and $\frac{1}{4}$ in per foot is as simple as rotating the wooden scale in the drafter's hand. A software utility enables the operator to change the current working scale of the drawing. Realize however that a drawing-oriented system usually has no means of associating scale with each line or object on the drawing. As with traditional drawings, changing scale is used for drawing operations that are restricted to only part of drawing, such as combining enlarged plans of utility rooms on the same drawing with the complete floor plan. Consequently, if line work that was originally created at one scale is dimensioned while another scale is in use, values will reflect the current rather than the original scale. At any point in time, the entire drawing is perceived at only one scale, designated by the operator. This flexibility pertains to drawing-oriented systems. On a model-based system, the dimensions of an object are constant and independent of the drawing.

Along with the traditional parameters, a new parameter is associated with CAD drawings. *Drawing resolution* defines the smallest segment of a line, or the smallest distance between two points, that can be represented on the drawing. Drawing resolution also determines the length of the longest line that can be represented. Aspects of drawing resolution become noticeable with systems that record coordinate values in a field of only 2 bytes. On systems that record coordinates in relatively larger fields, for example, floating point fields with 4 bytes or more, the upper and lower bounds of resolution are less likely to be a limitation. Notice that if coordinates are stored in short integer fields, system performance is generally faster.

Drawing resolution is determined by a ratio that includes three variables. The combination of the scale and the size of the drawing is divided by the precision of the hardware and software in the system. Since it is a ratio, drawing resolution is usually designated with a decimal to several degrees of accuracy. The drawing resolution is assigned when a drawing is first initialized.

Since it is a ratio between the precision of the system and the combined scale and size of a drawing, resolution determines the geometric accuracy of the drawing. Keep in mind that there is no point in having more accuracy than the smallest dimension that can be measured at the construction site. For architectural projects, this is typically $\frac{1}{8}$ in. This measure sets a practical limit to the resolution, and therefore the accuracy, of drawings on a CAD system.

For CAD systems using raster graphics (see Table 3-1), resolution is the size, in scaled units of measure, of a single pixel on the CRT screen when the system is zoomed completely in on the drawing. The screen can be visualized as a very fine grid of dots. Drawing resolution determines the real world size of the distance between two dots. For example, with a resolution of $\frac{1}{8}$ in, when the system is fully zoomed in a single pixel represents a line $\frac{1}{8}$ in long. In turn, this line is translated into a specific length, depending on the scale of the drawing, when measured in the field.

Panning across and zooming in and out of a drawing may blur the relationships between drawing size, scale, and resolution. However, with the exception of drawing resolution, drawing parameters are essentially unchanged. These once familiar parameters are managed on CAD systems with functions that are more dynamic and allow greater flexibility.

Graphic Display Files

Objects displayed on a CAD drawing are defined and stored in graphic display files that are internal, that is not immediately accessible to the operator. The configuration of these files depends on the design of the hardware and software. As a result, display file configurations vary from one system to another. Graphic files for two-dimensional work are organized with one of two approaches: by drawing or by project. In the first case, one or more files is required for each drawing. With the other approach, the project as a whole, including several drawings, may be defined in a single file. Again, the entire project may also be stored in a set of interrelated files. A drawing and the configuration of graphic display files do not always relate one-to-one.

Fortunately, the record for each graphic object is defined in the same manner regardless of how display files are organized. Typically, a graphic object is defined with information stored in two separate records or blocks—display and geometry blocks. A *block* can be thought of as a list of data.

Display blocks store the display attributes of an object. Display attributes identify the object and include some of the characteristics of the object's appearance. This block is used to control interactions with the object at the CRT screen, digitizer tablet, and plotter. A typical display block includes data which defines the following: color, pen number, drawing layer, any special flags, object type (such as line, curve, or lettering), the extents of the object (the maximum and minimum X and Y cartesian coordinates); the object origin; a pointer to a direct nongraphic file; flags for mirroring, rotation, or scaling, any group membership flag; the number of group members; and usually a pointer to a geometry block.

Notice that the display block does not include any information about the shape of the object. This is stored in the second block, referred to as a *geometry block*. For a primitive or basic graphic object, such as a point, line, or arc, the geometry block specifies the following: coordinates of line-segment endpoints; the number of line segments; where applicable, the number of times a segment is repeated; for arcs, a description of how the arc was constructed. For a group, the geometry block stores a list of the group members.

The two blocks, geometry and display, are sometimes stored in two separate but parallel files. On other systems, the two blocks are stored together in the same file for efficiency.

Planning, Control, and Efficiency Recommendations

To improve operating efficiency and economy in the process of creating architectural drawings, consider the outline of general operating recommendations provided below. This outline focuses on planning drawings and managing them while on a CAD system. These recommendations use terms that can be applied to most CAD systems:

1. Organize the drawing task before starting at the workstation. When possible, decisions should be made ahead of time. Disorganized work habits will decrease the efficiency of high-speed drafting.
2. Plan the organization of a drawing carefully. Usually, a period equal to 25 to 40 percent of time spent operating the system should be allocated for planning and coordinating the structure of documents. Good preliminary planning will speed up initial input and later editing. Also, review the current progress on a drawing before logging onto the system, not after.
3. Use a sequence of stages or iterations to build up a drawing in a logical and systematic manner. This allows everyone on the project to understand what stage of development has been reached with the drawings. It also simplifies coordination between CAD drawings and the hand-drafting and overlay documents that are used in the same project.
4. Conclude each stage or iteration with a plot of the status of the drawing. Use plots generated between iterations for checking and planning only, not for distribution. Distribute plots to the design team from completed iterations only. This reduces the time-consuming and confusing proliferation of plotted output.
5. Single out repetitive parts of a design. Develop a strategy for reusing these parts—with a rational grouping structure, for instance.
6. Use a drawingwide orientation and minimize changes between functions during the initial stages of building up a drawing. For example, insert all openings into walls in one continuous operation. Note: Ignore this recommendation when using vector-oriented systems which require significant time to redisplay the graphic screen.
7. When making revisions to the drawing, use a specific drawing area orientation; complete tasks within one area at a time, using as many functions as necessary. Delays while panning and zooming with a nearly complete drawing are thus avoided.
8. Avoid proliferating objects that will have to be deleted. Objects that have been deleted still occupy drawing memory; to recover this drawing mem-

ory on some systems, the drawing may have to be packed.[1] Packing a drawing is time-consuming, especially if the drawing is fairly dense with line work.

9. Use the most efficient operation available for copying objects. For multiple objects, use an operation that eliminates the need to pick each object and drag it into place. For instance, when possible, enter the quantity and dimension for spacing between repeated objects at the keyboard.
10. Familiarize yourself with every command in the system. Find out the fastest and most reliable way to perform each operation.
11. Think ahead. Get inside the drawing, and always be aware of the next three functions that are going to be performed.
12. Prepare a complete list of appropriate symbols prior to starting drawing.
13. Wherever possible, simplify the graphics of a drawing. In particular, avoid elaborate line styles. In general, elaborate line styles occupy more memory than simple ones and therefore slow the system's response to certain commands.
14. Save a backup copy of the drawing frequently. Do not wait until the end of a drawing session. Make a backup copy at the following points: after a drawing is first initialized, after a drawing has been packed, and whenever you expect to have to backtrack from a trial operation.
15. Always be aware of the current pen number and drawing layer you are working on (or the object on systems on which layer is defined by names of sets of objects). Frequently check these against the office standards.
16. Use a combination of reference and active layers to minimize the possibility of inadvertently selecting the wrong object (see Chap. 5). Where available, set your editing capability to exclude objects you do not wish to access.
17. Use macros to speed up frequently used procedures when possible.[2] Be aware of unique aspects of a project that lend themselves to work with macros. Be familiar with writing macros and carefully build a library of them for use on all projects. Procedures with macros are essentially faster than operating basic system utilities with human interactions.
18. Pack the drawing at the end of each iteration, unless the system does so automatically. Packing removes obsolete records from the file for the drawing and makes more space available in computer storage. When nearly complete drawings are being revised, pack whenever necessary. Be aware that packing a drawing may affect the speed of operation at other workstations.

---

[1] *Packing* a drawing is a computer procedure which reduces the amount of storage required to hold the entire file for the drawing. Records of objects which have been deleted from the drawing are removed, and thus the file for the entire drawing is shortened. Rather than adjust the entire file each time an object is deleted, the file is adjusted in a separate operation.

[2] A *macro* is a series of commands which is recorded and named by the operator and can later be replayed and executed with a single operator input.

19. Assemble typical graphic information about a project into a reference package, preferably on 8.5- by 11-in notebook sheets. Typical graphic information would include: project standard layers and pen numbers; a copy of all named symbols to be used; typical partition and wall delineation and thickness; typical door sizes and locations in relation to corners or columns; other repetitive items, such as baths, stairs, and utility rooms.
20. Create checkplots, with complete pen numbers, of architectural background drawings before they are copied or distributed. An effective tool for checking and analyzing the assignment of pen numbers before distribution is a test plot substituting a different colored pen for each pen number.
21. Establish a drafting manual that includes operating guidelines for work on the system. Have the production manager coordinate the manual. However, assign written topics to individual staff members according to their areas of expertise or interest.
22. Instruct designers and project architects about the need for clear and orderly presentation of sketches, red-lined drawings, and other source material or instructions to system operators. Encourage designers and architects to review plotted drawings thoroughly at each stage of completion, revising the current plot only. Thus, errors can be avoided which may be difficult to correct when the drawings are 90 percent complete.
23. Debrief a project after the documents are completed. If the project had to be run again, how could drawings and reports have been created more economically or efficiently?

The appropriateness of these recommendations depends on both the system in use and the nature of a specific design project. Additional recommendations are contained in later chapters about symbols, groups, names for objects, and key fields.

Stages for Drawing Input

Work that is done randomly or piecemeal with a CAD system is not cost-effective. The continuous drafting procedure used with manual working drawings is also discouraged. These methods can be improved on with a simple procedure that arranges an order for adding elements to a drawing. The assembly of an architectural drawing can be broken down into logical stages, or iterations.

An *iteration* is a single input and output cycle. Floor plans are completed in four or five iterations. During each iteration, certain drawing elements are entered for the first time. The sequence begins with those design elements, such as building grid lines, that determine the location of elements added in later iterations. Each iteration builds on the previous one.

Begin an iteration with instructions from the design team. These take the form of sketches, notes, and what are referred to as "red-lined" drawings:

copies of drawings from the previous iteration marked with red pencil showing additions and revisions to the drawing. As the operator translates this information onto the system, he or she marks off the red-lined instructions with a yellow pencil as completed. Once all such instructions are entered, the iteration is complete.

During the current iteration, make revisions to or edit previous iterations as requested. Postponing revisions to a following iteration is discouraged. Unless revisions are translated onto the actual CAD document, they are lost. If a plotted drawing is modified using traditional drafting techniques, for example, the revisions are not captured as data. Consequently, they won't appear on following iterations of the drawing.

Notice that a system of iterations works hand-in-hand with a well-organized system of drawing layers. Enter line work on walls and columns on different drawing layers from built-in fixtures, for instance. Enter built-in fixtures not only on a separate layer but also during a later iteration. Using drawing layers and iterations together allows complex project drawings to be assembled in an orderly and predictable manner. Table 4-2 outlines a sequence of iterations for architectural floor plans, key plans, roof plan, reflected ceiling plans, and elevations. The sequence in Table 4-2 coordinates with the sequence of drawing layers listed in Table 5-1.

TABLE 4-2 Drawing Stages[a]

Architectural Floor Plans
First iteration
▪ North arrow, graphic scale, title, date
▪ Partitions, doors, and swings
▪ Room names and numbers
▪ Plumbing fixtures
▪ Structural grid dimensions
▪ Casework outline where known
Second iteration
▪ Partition types, glazed partitions
▪ Exterior walls
▪ Casework
▪ Equipment
▪ Ceiling heights, soffits
▪ Floor drains
▪ Floor depressions, slopes, curbs
▪ Toilet partitions
▪ Date
Third iteration
▪ Door types
▪ Room finishes
▪ Corner guards
▪ Window and louver mark or group numbers
▪ Miscellaneous specialties
▪ Sheet notes
▪ Casework mark or group members
▪ Date
Fourth iteration
▪ Hardware mark or group members
▪ Dimensioning

- Detail references
- Date

Architectural Key Plan
First iteration ■ North arrow, graphic scale, title, date ■ Partitions ■ Room names ■ Grid dimensions ■ Partition types (fire separations) Second iteration ■ Corrections and/or update ■ Date
Roof Plan
First iteration ■ North arrow, graphic scale, title, date ■ Column grid and dimensions ■ Roof drains, slopes ■ Roof openings Second iteration ■ Walks ■ Roof penetrations ■ Canopies ■ Skylights ■ Access hatches ■ Detail references ■ Sheet notes ■ Date
Reflected Ceiling Plan
First iteration ■ North arrow, graphic scale, title, date ■ Background Second iteration ■ Ceiling tile layout ■ Specially lighted areas ■ Soffits ■ Light fixtures, diffusers Third iteration ■ Sprinkler heads ■ Exit lights ■ Detail references ■ Sheet notes
Exterior or Interior Elevations
First iteration ■ Graphic scale, title, date ■ Profiles, column grid ■ Windows, doors, louvers ■ Floor level lines ■ Key plan with references Second iteration ■ Materials ■ Detail references ■ Sheet notes

[a] Table reprinted courtesy of Design Logic Inc., San Francisco, CA.

Chapter

5

Drawing Layers

CAD Operator: "The system won't let me pick that line. I can't copy it; I can't even move it. What's wrong with the system?"

System Manager: "Is the drawing layer active?"

The separation of drawings into many layers or levels characterizes the organization of a drawing on a CAD system (see Fig. 5-1). Those acquainted with overlay drafting techniques are already familiar with the usefulness of organizing a drawing in this way. With overlay drafting, separate transparent films or drawing layers contain different drawing elements: walls on one, dimensioning on another, and lettering on still another. A complete drawing is produced by creating blue line prints from a combination of layers.

Drawing layers on a CAD system are analogous to the sheets of transparent film used for overlay drafting, only they are considerably more flexible. Creating different components of a CAD drawing on separate layers uses the same principle as overlay drafting. Drawing layers may seem complex, but they are a useful organizing tool.

Since the layers are separate, work can proceed at different rates on each layer. Different operators, or consultants, can work on a drawing layer without monopolizing the whole drawing. More important, elements of one drawing can be plotted with elements from other related drawings without having to be redrawn. A typical illustration of layering is the generation of an architectural background drawing. The same configuration of walls, columns, doors, and windows, which makes up the architectural background, is used by each consulting discipline. By creating these elements on a single drawing

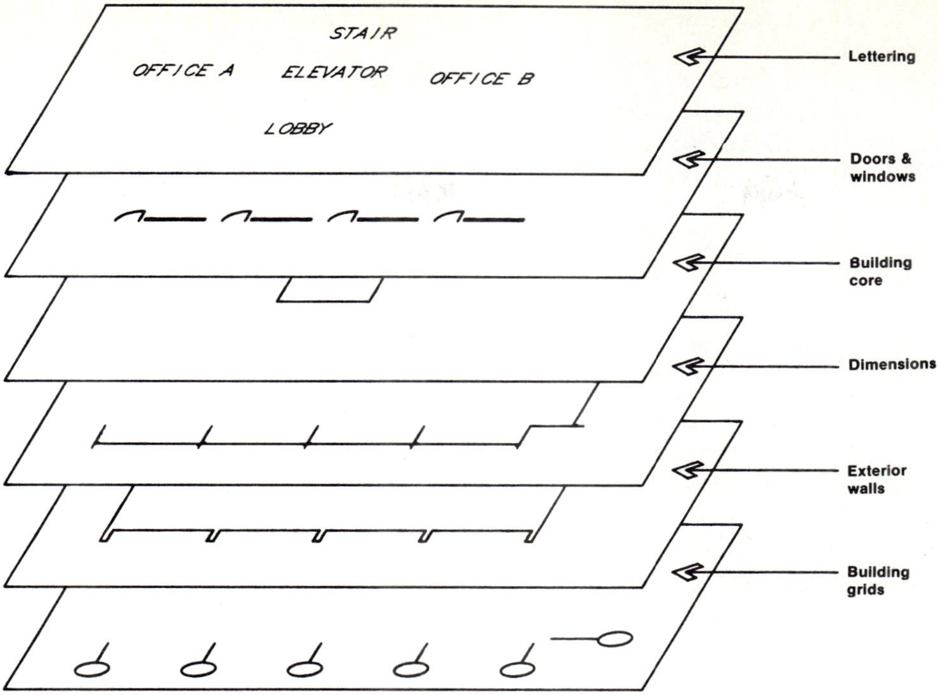

Figure 5-1 Representation of a drawing subdivided into layers.

layer or set of layers and assigning notes and dimensioning to other layers, each consultant can work with a copy of the graphic information for the background without having to reproduce the line work involved.

On CAD systems, drawing layers are created by using one of several computer processing methods. One method defines each drawing layer as a separate file within the computer memory, and the amount of memory required for operations on a specific layer is less than would be required if all the layers in the drawing were called up at once. This method can be developed in the design of the CAD system so that separate layers can be conveniently passed from one drawing to another. However, the speed of operation when calling up or switching between drawing layers is comparatively slow.

A second method for creating drawing layers divides the drawing by assigning a number (or name) that corresponds to a specific drawing layer to each graphic object on the drawing. All the objects on the drawing are stored in a single file within the computer memory regardless of layer. This system design, referred to as "drawing-oriented," emphasizes storing objects in a single drawing, and the response when switching between drawing layers is very prompt. However, exchanging the same layer between different drawings is impossible without making a copy of the layer.

One CAD system does not use the term "layers" at all, but achieves the same effect using a combination of "phases" and object names. Obviously, terminology can differ between computer systems that produce the same results.

These methods produce essentially the same result for most graphic operations. Both have advantages as well as disadvantages. Both methods enable the CAD system to operate on a subset of the objects stored on a drawing, which is important to the efficiency of operations. If the drawing is segmented it can be redisplayed more quickly. The time required for certain operations, such as panning across the drawing, can be minimized by the careful selection of drawing layers.

Degrees of Freedom with Drawing Layers

Although the concept of drawing layers is similar to that of overlay drafting, the degree of freedom available with layers on a CAD system is significantly greater. Procedures for the use of layers are thus more complex as well as more dynamic. With overlay drafting, the sheet that represents a layer can be physically picked up and handled. This simplifies the problem of understanding what is on a particular layer. It also provides a practical limit to the number of layers that can be assembled into a single drawing while retaining a sharp image of all information. A CAD drawing, however, has no such limitation.

Although the methods of separating drawings into layers differ radically, the principles for the use of drawing layers as a whole apply to all of them.

For the method that stores layers in different files, the number of layers in a single drawing is unlimited. New layers are added as they are needed. The number of layers is determined by what the system will permit on a single layer. A separate layer may be required for lines which have a different line style, for instance. Drawing elements that are shown dotted, such as overhanging items, cannot be included on a layer with elements that are shown with a solid line. Lines that are drawn with different line weights, that is, different pen numbers, or different colors, also require separate layers. Each layer can include only one color, pen number, or line style.

Appearance characteristics, such as color and pen number, are applied to the drawing layer as a whole when this method is used. The system does not have to store these characteristics with each graphic object and would be considered layer-oriented as opposed to object-based (see Table 3-1). Although efficient for conserving memory, this method does not enable the system to search for and highlight all the line work for a design element that is drawn on several different layers. This is a drawback when trying to analyze the characteristics of design elements, such as stairs, that are drawn with more than one pen weight and line style.

The drawing-oriented method makes available a specific and limited number of layers with each drawing. A certain number of layers, 256, for instance, is set aside for the drawing when it is first initialized on the system. Whether or not the layers are actually used, the drawing has the specified number of layers. Here, each drawing layer can be associated with a specific design element, such as exterior walls or stairs. There is no limit to the number of different line styles, colors, or pen numbers that can be used on a single layer. They can be combined as needed. Pen number, color, and line style can also be changed independently of each other and of the drawing layer for the graphic object. This enables the architect to modify the appearance characteristics of an object while working with a stable system of drawing layers. Most importantly, by activating the required drawing layers, the system will find and highlight all the line work associated with a design element, enabling the operator to find, analyze, and modify design elements.

Depending on the particular CAD system in use, each drawing layer is designated with either a name or a number—this applies to systems that include an unlimited number of layers as well as those that work with a specific number. Remembering a drawing layer or recognizing what is drawn on the layer is easier if the layer is named. However, commands for displaying, changing, or plotting drawing layers are quicker and easier to enter if the layers are designated with two or three digits rather than names.

Reference and Active Drawing Layers

Separate drawing layers, even entire subsets of layers, can be turned on and off at will with simple commands. At any time, a selection of layers can be seen, displayed on the screen, or plotted. The selected layers, those that are currently active, work together like one sheet of transparent drawing film in overlay drafting. However, since layers can be easily activated on a CAD system, changing between separate layers is more convenient than with overlay drafting.

Selected layers can be seen even though they are not available for drawing operations. Such a layer is known as a *reference* drawing layer. Reference layers can be seen along with other drawing layers that are active for graphic operations such as adding and modifying line work. With a combination of layers, some of which are active while others are referenced, work can proceed on the active layers without affecting objects that are visible on the referenced layers. Within the limitations of the CAD system, drawing layers can be designated as either active or reference at any time. Again, this process is similar to overlay drafting, where work proceeds on one layer with several other layers stacked below it as references. Obviously, this mechanism aids coordination between the architectural background drawing on the one hand and reflected ceiling plans, furniture plans, and consultant drawings on the other. It also provides a degree of security for drawings such as the architectural background. If the architectural background is available as a reference layer only, it cannot be modified by members of the design team other than the architect.

Different CAD manufacturers have developed the capabilities that are available with reference layers to various degrees of sophistication. On a few systems, the reference mechanism is not available at all. Some systems have a reference layer which is not editable but is "hitable." This means objects can be accessed by the operator to relate new objects to them. Thus an object which cannot be edited can be used to place another object.

On some CAD systems, layers can be designated as reference and viewed as long as they are included as part of the drawing that is currently activated on the system. Usually, it is also possible to transfer part of one drawing, such as the layer for the architectural background, to another drawing. This is done by making a copy of the layer. However, without copying, a reference layer from one drawing can not be displayed while a separate drawing is activated.

On other CAD systems, especially those which organize files by project, one or more entire drawings, including all layers, can be brought in and viewed as a reference while a separate drawing is available for active work. This technique enables work to proceed on many different drawings at the same time while each member of the design team uses the same drawing as a reference. Usually, this capability requires an investment in additional computer hardware. It is currently available only on large CAD systems.

Principles for Organizing Drawing Layers

The coordination of graphic design information, some of which is shared or reused on different drawings, is the primary reason for working with a system of drawing layers. This requirement provides the basic organizing principle for drawing layers. Two common examples illustrate how the principle is applied: On most projects, the architectural floor plan is coordinated with a reflected ceiling plan, with plans for each of the consulting disciplines, such as the structural, mechanical, and electrical engineers, and with facility and furniture plans. A set of drawings for a large building project may have as many as 10 or more consultant drawings for each architectural floor plan. Providing each consultant with the same architectural background drawing ensures coordination among these drawings. In another example, work performed during different phases of a construction project, such as a staged addition, are shown in outline on the same plan along with the current phase. When the initial phase is complete, additional phases are shown in greater detail. Since each phase will have project elements in common with other phases, different phases can be shown on different layers of the same drawing. In both cases, the objective is the same as that of overlay drafting: the coordination between, and reuse of graphic design information from, one project drawing and another. Any system of drawing layers should be organized to achieve this fundamental objective.

Secondary principles to keep in mind when analyzing a system of layers for a CAD drawing involve the characteristics of the CAD system in use. Operations can be performed on a drawing layer as a whole, and certain drawing changes can therefore be managed very efficiently and quickly with drawing layers. First of all, finding an object is easier if it is on a known layer. Every occurrence of an object, such as all the dimensions, is found by displaying the layer for the dimensions and no other layers. Once found, the system can be instructed to modify every object on the layer. For example, the pen number or color for all the lettering can be modified with this technique without having to select each item.

office graphic standards (Table 5-1). Make sure anyone working on a project is using drawing layers organized according to the office standard. In this way, all CAD operators are able to find things on the drawing in a predictable manner, and standard procedures are used throughout office projects.

TABLE 5-1 Recommended Sequence of Drawing Layers for CAD System with 256 Layers

Levels	Contents
1–69	Architectural plans
1–19	Drawing definition and text information
20–39	Architectural background
40–54	Built-in plan items
55–59	Material indications
60–64	Demolition
65–69	Site work
70–74	unassigned
75–99	Reflected ceiling plan
100–119	Structural drawings
120–139	Mechanical or HVAC drawings
140–159	Plumbing drawings
160–179	Electrical drawings
180–189	Signal drawings
190–199	Unassigned
200–206	Master groups
207–219	Unassigned
220–245	Furniture and equipment plans
246–256	Unassigned

Level	Pen	Drawing element	Comments
		Drawing Definition and Text Information	
1	0	Sheet border and title block	For screen reference only.
2	1	Sheet title, number, etc.	
3	1	Work point	
4	2	North arrow, match lines	
5	1	Architectural dimensions and	Not shown on background.
	1	dimension text	
6	1	Column or grid dimensions and	Shown on background.
	1	Dimension text	
7	0	Reference points, construction lines, other invisible objects	
8			
9			
10	1	Elevation, section, detail number or letter	
	1	and symbol	
11	1	Room name or number and	Shown on background.
	1	symbol	
12	1	Room finish	Not shown on background.
13	1	Ceiling height,	Not shown on background.
14	1	Door number and	
	1	symbol	
15	1	Door hardware number	
16	1	Window number and	
	1	symbol	
17	1	Equipment/furniture number and	See also levels 221, 225,
	1	symbol	228, 233, 243, 245.
18	1	Casework number and	Automatically assigned.
	1	symbol	
19	1	General architectural notes	
200		Master groups, architectural objects	

TABLE 5-1 Recommended Sequence of Drawing Layers for CAD System with 256 Layers (Continued)

Level	Pen	Drawing element	Comments
		Architectural Background	
20	1	Column lines and annotation	
21	2	Structural columns	
22	3	Structural walls	
23	1	Other structural elements	
24			
25	3	Exterior walls (nonstruct.)	
26	2	Exterior window sills	
27	3	Exterior window centerlines	
28	1	Exterior overhead items	
29			
30	3	Partitions and furring	
31	2	Low partitions	
32	3	Glazed interior partitions	
33			
34	2	Floor openings and shafts	
35	2	Conveying systems	
36	2	Stair treads, arrows	Shown on background.
37	1	Stair handrails, up and down	Not shown on background.
38	1	Interior overhead items	
39			
237	0	Top-level APP composite wall	Automatically assigned.
238	0	Layout line APP walls	Automatically assigned.
239	0	Top-level group APP basic walls	Automatically assigned.
		Built-in Plan Items	
40	3	Doors and swing (swing = pen 1)	See also levels 14 and 15.
75	3	Door ceiling lines	
200	0	Door group and placement circle	
41	3	Door and window elevations and sections	
42			
43	2	Plumbing fixtures and equipment	See also Plumbing drawings.
44			
45	2	Casework, lockers, etc.	
46	2	Equipment and special construction	
47	2	N.I.C. equipment	
48	2	Miscellaneous plan items	
49			
50	2	Toilet partitions, etc.	
51	2	Toilet accessories	
52	0	Room boundaries	
53	0	Department boundaries	
54	0	Floor boundaries	
147	7	Fire hose cabinets	See also Plumbing drawings.
169	7	Electrical panel boards	
185	7	Telephone and signal boards	See also Electrical drawings.
		Material Indications	
55	1	Floor finish patterns	
56	1	Exterior material indications	
57	1	Partition type indications	Symbol or line style.
58			
59			

		Demolition	
60	3	Existing to remain	
61	2	To be demolished	
62			
63			
64	1	Demolition notes	
		Site Work	
65	0	Property lines and civil engineering data	
66	1	Built-in site work	
67	1	Topography	
68	1	Landscaping	
69			
		Reflected Ceiling Plan	
75	3	Door ceiling lines	See Insert symbol.
76	7	Interior overhead items	Trace over level 39.
77	7	Upper casework	Trace over level 46.
78	6	Ceiling-tile pattern	
79	6	Access doors	
80			
81	8	Light fixtures, ceiling mounted	See also Electrical drawings.
82			
83	8	Registers, grilles, diffusers	See also Mechanical drawings.
84	8	Hoods, flues, etc.	See also Mechanical drawings.
85			
86	7	Exit signs	See also Electrical drawings.
87	7	Speakers	See also Signal drawings.
88			
89			
90	6	Equipment-mounting tracks	
91			
92	7	Fire sprinklers	See also Plumbing drawings.
93	8	Smoke detectors	See also Signal drawings.
94			
95			
1	0	Sheet border and title block	For screen reference only.
96	1	Sheet title, number	
97	6	Dimensions and	
	6	dimension text	
98	6	Detail number of text and	
	6	symbol	
99	6	General notes	
201		Groups	
		Structural Drawings	
20	1	Column lines and annotation	
21	2	Structural columns	
22	3	Structural walls	
23	1	Other structural elements	
100	8	Framing members	
101			
102			
103			
104			
105	8	Foundation elements	
106			
107			
108			
109			

TABLE 5-1 Recommended Sequence of Drawing Layers for CAD System with 256 Layers (Continued)

Level	Pen	Drawing element	Comments
		Structural Drawings	
110	6	Schedules	
111			
112			
113			
114			
115			
1	0	Sheet border and title block	For screen reference only.
116	6	Sheet number, title	
117	6	Dimensions (structural) and	
	6	dimension text	
118	6	Detail number or text and	
	6	symbol	
119	6	Structural notes	
202		Groups	
		Mechanical or HVAC Drawings	
83	8	Registers, grilles, diffusers	
120	8	Supply-air system	Ducts, registers, etc.
121			
122	8	Return-air system	Ducts, registers, etc.
123			
124	8	Exhaust-air system	Ducts, registers, etc.
125			
126	8	Cold-air system	Ducts, registers, etc.
127			
128	8	Hot-air system	Ducts, registers, etc.
129			
130	8	Mixing boxes	
131			
132	8	Coils	
133			
134			
135			
1	0	Sheet border and title block	For screen reference only.
136	6	Sheet number, title	
137	6	Dimensions and	
	6	dimensions text	
138	6	Detail number or text and	
	6	symbol	
139	6	General notes	
203		Groups	
		Plumbing Drawings	
43	2	Plumbing fixtures and equipment	
140	8	Domestic water	
141	8	Sanitary piping	
142	8	Gas piping	See also Mechanical drawings.
143	8	Storm sewage system	
144			
145			
146	8	Sprinkler-system piping	See also Reflected ceiling plan.
147	7	Fire-hose piping	Includes fire-hose cabinets.
92	7	Fire sprinklers	See also Reflected ceiling plan.
148			

149			
150	7	Isometric drawings	
151			
152			
153			
154			
155			
1	0	Sheet border and title block	For screen reference only.
156	6	Sheet title, number	
157	6	Dimensions and	
	6	dimensions text	
158	6	Detail notes or text and	
	6	symbol	
159	6	General notes	
204		Groups	
		Electrical Drawings	
81	8	Light fixtures ceiling mounted	See also Reflected ceiling plan.
160	7	Light fixtures, other	
161	8	Light circuit and switches	
162	7	Life safety lighting	See also Reflected ceiling plan.
163			
164			
165			
1	0	Sheet border and title block	For screen reference only.
166	6	Sheet title, number	
167	6	Dimensions and	
	6	dimensions text	
168	6	Detail notes or text and	
	6	symbol	
169	6	General notes	
170	8	Main service and distribution	
171			
172	8	Power circuits	
173	7	Electrical outlets, wall/floor	
174	7	Electrical outlets, ceiling	
175	8	Electrical panel boards	
1	0	Sheet border and title block	For screen reference only.
176	6	Sheet title, number	
177	6	Dimensions and	
	6	dimensions text	
178	6	Detail notes or text and	
	6	symbol	
179	6	General notes	
205		Groups	
		Signal Drawings	
180	7	Signal speakers and outlets	
181	8	Signal circuit	
182			
183	7	Fire alarms	
184	7	Telephones	
185	7	Telephone and signal boards	
1	0	Sheet border and title block	For screen reference only.
186	6	Sheet number and title	
187	6	Dimensions and	
	6	dimension text	
188	6	Detail notes or text and	
	6	symbol	
189	6	General notes	
206		Groups	

TABLE 5-1 Recommended Sequence of Drawing Layers for CAD System with 256 Layers (Continued)

Level	Pen	Drawing element	Comments
		Furniture and Equipment Plan	
210	0	Boundaries	
211	0	Boundaries	
220	2	Furniture panel[1]	
221	1	Furniture panel lettering[1]	See also level 17.
222	2	Power lines and outlets[1]	
223	0	Panel connectors[1]	
224	2	Desks, tables[1]	
225	1	Desk and table lettering[1]	See also level 17.
226	2	Miscellaneous furniture items[1]	
227	2	Furniture, lighting[1]	
228	1	Lights, lettering[1]	See also level 17.
229			
230			
231			
232	2	Chairs and sofas[1]	
233	1	Chairs lettering[1]	See also level 17.
234			
235			
236			
237			
238			
239			
240	2	Equipment	See also level 46.
241	2	Plants and planters	
242	1	Dimensions	
243	1	Workstation number	See also level 17.
244	1	Furniture notes	
245	1	Equipment lettering	See also level 17.
52	0	Room boundaries	
53	0	Department boundaries	
54	0	Floor boundaries	

[1] Used by Haworth furniture symbol library.
Table reprinted courtesy of CalComp, Anaheim, CA.

Drawing Layers, Some Closing Thoughts

It is not possible, on a CAD system, to pick up the corner of the sheet in one's fingers. As a result, drawing layers can be somewhat confusing to work with. Merely looking at the drawing on the screen will not reveal the difference between reference and active layers, and they can easily be confused in the rapid pace of operations. Although layers are easily explained, it takes time to master their use. Fortunately, layers can be accessed with macros, which in turn can be stored on tablet menus. These mechanisms are ideal for training and initial operations. A simple selection from a tablet menu can turn complex sets of layers off or on. Operating smoothly with drawing layers becomes automatic after a period of using CAD systems.

Drawing layers on a CAD system are more efficient and easier to use than overlay drafting materials in a manual environment. Many more layers can be handled at the same time, allowing finer distinctions between graphic objects. Drawing layers are easier to manage, since they are accessed by simply turning them on and off. For instance, they can be assembled into subsets for plotting with a simple sequence of commands.

Layers are also useful when coordinating the output from the CAD system with traditional and overlay drafting methods. Many projects still use these methods extensively along with CAD drawings. The architectural background is often plotted and sent off to the consultants as a basis for manual drafting.

In the final analysis, drawing layers are an administrative device. They enhance the coordination of design information, both on the CAD system and between various design professionals working on the same project. They enable a single drawing to contain more than would be manageable with traditional drafting mediums. For example, sections and elevations, each on separate layers, can be combined in the same drawing, but plotted separately. This use of layers increases the accuracy of architectural documents—one of the significant benefits of CAD.

Chapter

6

Groups

"When problems occur with the operation of a CAD system, the difficulty is not always found in the hardware or software. Often, the problem is just a screw loose at the keyboard."

A SYSTEM MANAGER

In traditional drafting, line work is connected because one line is contiguous to the next on the drawing. The order in which the lines are drawn does not matter. With practice our brains recognize the design elements symbolized by the drawing, making the connections obvious. Graphic objects can intersect, overlap, be parallel, or have any other conceivable geometric relationship. We understand the meaning of the shape because we recognize it.

Whether contiguous or not, lines exist in a CAD system without being associated in the visual sense that we understand so well. Each line is understood by the system as a distinct entity, part of a graphic data base for a drawing. A CAD system recognizes objects based on how they are described in graphic display files. Nevertheless, for some procedures the system operates as if some lines were graphically related to each other.

A CAD convention called "groups" is used for this purpose. One line is associated with another when an operator sets a connection between them, making them into a *group*. Each line or object becomes part of a list which represents the entire group. Operationally, graphic objects, such as lines or text, are grouped by selecting one object after another. They can be selected individually, or the operator can designate everything within a rectangle to be a member of the same group. The operation will vary depending on the system in use.

Once defined as a group, graphic procedures can then be performed on the collection of graphic objects as a whole. This is the basic reason for assembling objects into a group in the first place. The group can be moved, rotated, copied, erased, enlarged or reduced, filed, and retrieved. All members of the group will be affected at the same time. *Symbols*, as the term is used in CAD drafting, are groups that have been named and filed in a central library for convenient transfer from one drawing to another and for other purposes when lines must be treated in association (see Fig. 7-6).

Entirely new relationships between graphic objects are possible with groups. It is not necessary that the members of a group be connected in the visual sense. Unconnected lines, objects scattered over the drawing, can be associated into a group. Notes are objects which can be members of groups, and on CAD systems where deep groups are allowed (see Table 3-1), groups can include other groups. Objects that are from different layers of the drawing can also be connected into a single group. Thus the same symbol can appear in different forms on different drawings (see Fig. 7-2). As we shall see, text information can also be attached to different parts of a group for different reporting purposes (see Fig. 13-2). With groups, parts of drawings can be connected in ways that are not visible until the connection is required for some design function. For example, a pattern of fire sprinklers showing the extent of spray from each nozzle can be assembled into a group. The group of sprinklers can be moved around the floor plan until optimum coverage is achieved. Extra sprinklers can then be deleted. The extent of spray need not be shown on the final plot.

The Structure of a Group

The structure of a group is based on how many members are in the group and the order in which they were added. The structure forms a strict hierarchy that can be described with an inverted-tree diagram (see Fig. 6-1).

A simple, shallow-tree group structure includes only a set number of tiers, typically three. A complex, deep-group structure has many members, including subgroups within the major group. Much of the discussion in this chapter applies to systems which allow unlimited recursive grouping of this type. For elementary graphic functions, such as moving collections of objects around on a drawing, the structure of the group is of little consequence. However, for more advanced operations, such as replacing a member in every copy of a group, the structure of the group will determine whether the operation can be done globally.

Members of a group are identified by their relative position in this structure, or family tree. As in family trees, genealogical terms define the structure. At the lowest level are the primitive graphic objects, or "children." When each group is created, a control and geometry record is established at the top level of the structure. The geometry record, which includes the list of children, is considered the "mother" of the group. A mother may, in turn, be a child of a larger group. The top level within the group structure is referred

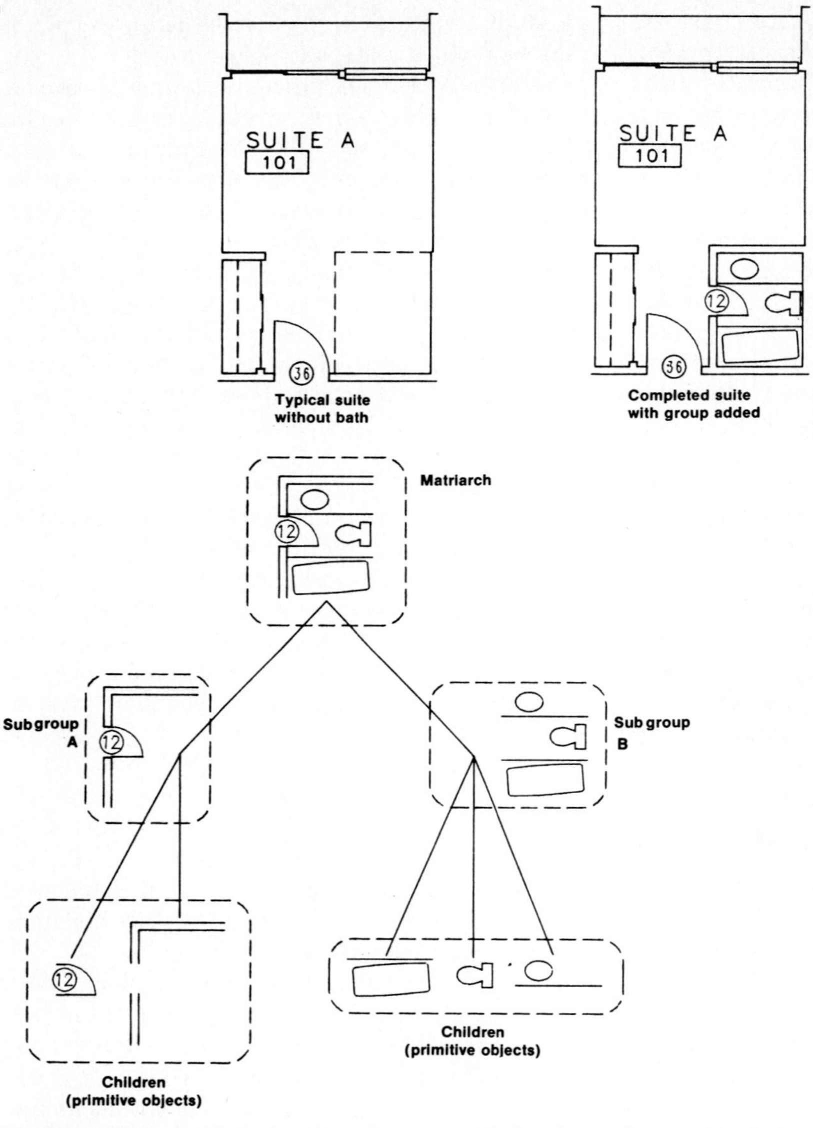

Figure 6-1 The inverted-tree structure of a group applied to design elements for a bathroom. The matriarch of the group is organized into two sub-groups based on the related nature of the design elements involved: This subdivision facilitates later revisions to the drawings.

to as the "matriarch" of the group. Although there can be more than one mother in a group, there can be only one matriarch for the group as a whole.

Note that the origin of the group is the origin of the first graphic object picked at the group's highest level. Carefully locating the origin of graphic objects yields advantages for placement and sometimes affects drawing object counts (see Fig. 7-8).

On CAD systems which support unlimited, recursive grouping (see Table

3-1), groups can include several levels within the same structure. If all members of a group are added one after the other in the same operation, the group has a simple structure with only two levels, including the primitives and their mother. If a group includes other groups, or if complete groups are added to an existing group, the group has a multilevel structure.

Once a group is created, operations can be performed on the group as a whole. Realize, however, that when you select the group, the matriarch or the highest level of the group is being selected for most graphic operations. Although separate system utilities make it possible to insert, extract, or move members within a group, most CAD systems select the matriarch and operate on the group as a whole. On certain systems, however, it is possible to select a specific member at any level within the structure of a group. For instance, a child can be selected and moved without affecting the entire group. This mechanism allows you to select a group member and "walk," or move up or down within the levels of the group structure. This capability is useful for analyzing group structure as well as for modifying the members of a single group. Other techniques, described in the next section, can be used for modifying every copy of a group.

The treelike group structure, with its levels, overlaps—but is a distinct concept from—the layers (often referred to as "levels") that organize the drawing. Admittedly, the use of the term *level* in this parallel context is somewhat confusing. However, the structure of groups is intertwined with drawing layers. For example, the drawing layer that is in use or is active when group members are selected designates the layer for that group. The group itself thus has a specific drawing layer. The separate children, or subgroups, may be resident on several different drawing layers. However, their matriarch exists on the layer on which the top-level group is created. A complex group can include members on several different drawing layers. For example, the primitive graphic objects, the children of the group, can be grouped on layer 14. If, however, the last member of the group is added while drawing layer 40 is active, the matriarch will reside on layer 40. In most cases, managing the levels within the structure of the group is most convenient when objects on the same layer are also grouped on that drawing layer (see Fig. 7-3).

Composing groups into a hierarchy, including primitive objects, subgroups, and, finally, a matriarch, enables us to operate on subsets of objects within the group. As we know, many objects have associations that bridge drawing types. Yet everyday CAD procedures are made easier if these objects are handled as a group. For example, the plan for a bath will be used by several different consultants. By grouping the plumbing fixtures on a separate level from the walls and door, changes can be made to the subgroup for the fixtures without affecting the walls (see Fig. 7-13).

Group Integrity

When copies of a group are made, all the information in the graphic data base that describes the group need not be copied as well. Some of the information is reused by each copy thus conserving drawing memory. Copying a group generates a new record in the graphics file for the drawing. This record includes such information as the location of the copy and a pointer to a new record of nongraphic information for the copy. However, the copy does not require a new record of its geometry. Its geometry describes the shape of the group, and the copy looks the same as the original; the record for each copy merely refers to the geometry record of the original group. The copy uses the same geometry record, and *group integrity* refers to this sharing of a single geometry file by copies of a group.

Two key benefits derive from maintaining the integrity between copies of a group. First, by relying on a single geometry record, drawing memory is conserved. Second, since each copy refers to a single source for its geometry, changes can be made automatically to every copy by changing the source. Changes can be propagated in this way to every group which is an exact copy of the one you are working with. In fact, it doesn't matter whether an operation is performed on the original group or one of its copies. Since they share a common geometry, changes to any copy affect the single geometry record for all the others. Consequently, the effect can be spread to a selection of other copies or all other copies. It can also be restricted to the particular group that is being modified.

When a group is modified without spreading the effect to any other copy, the group no longer refers to the original source for its geometry. It becomes unique and requires a separate geometry record of its own. In many cases, a new version of an existing group is required. However, if a copy no longer refers to the original geometry record, it is impossible to make global changes to a copy that has been modified from the original source. Changes must now be made directly to the new version. If the common reference to the same geometry record is broken, the integrity with the original source is incomplete.

Certain design problems require the use of new versions of an existing group. For example, the same group of furniture items can be used in several offices. A subset of two or more offices, however, may require an additional item of furniture, such as a terminal. In such a case, it is easier to add a member to the group of typical furniture than to create a new group from scratch including the additional member. The result is a unique new group which is then copied to create the two or more exceptional cases.

However, many design, as well as drawing management problems, can be solved by working with copies that share integrity with a group as a single source. For example, something as simple as an incorrect pen number can be globally modified in every copy of a group. Delete the group member with the incorrect pen number, re-create the member using the correct pen number, add it to the group, and spread the effect to every copy of the group.

For a more dramatic example, it is possible to replace every copy of a group in a single operation. The steps in this procedure must be applied to the matriarch, or the top level of the group, rather than to any other level within the group structure. First, the replacement is added to the existing top-level group. The original group can now be removed and the effect spread to every copy. This will leave the new group in place of the original.

Judicious use of this procedure can delete every copy of a group throughout the drawing without putting anything in its place. A scratch layer, on which everything can be deleted, must be set aside. First, create a dummy object on the scratch layer. Then add it to the group. Delete the original group members and spread the effect. The only thing left of the group will now be the dummy objects on the scratch drawing layer. All that remains is to delete all objects on this layer. This procedure of replacing every group with a modified group is also the normal method of spreading an effect on a system which has shallow-tree grouping (see Table 3-1).

Integrity between the copies of a group indicates their connection to a single source. This integrity is a powerful aid when drawing changes, always inevitable, are required. The ability to make global changes, which depends on integrity, increases the value of creating and working with groups. Since only one copy need be changed and other copies will then reflect the change without further work by an operator, this type of change is the fastest and most efficient available on a CAD system. Group integrity should be guarded like a special design technique that provides an edge over the competition. Chapter 7 includes illustrations and a description of a procedure where symbols, which are distributed among several copies of a group, are globally replaced.

Recommendations for Creating and Using Groups

When creating drawings on a CAD system, correct group structure and group integrity are central issues. The structure and integrity of groups is not obvious without testing; copies of a group can look the same and yet be disconnected from their original source. Drawing memory, drawing organization, and speed of performance are all affected by how well groups are put together and how they are used. Remember that how groups are created will determine how easily they can be changed later. The following recommendations for creating and using groups are based on the principles described in the previous section:

1. Avoid unnecessary groups, groups that are created for temporary drawing convenience only. Do not group items unless they need to act together for some definite reason. Grouping will consume drawing memory. More important, if another operator edits an object which is unnecessarily grouped, other component objects may be needlessly deleted or copied.
2. As a corollary to item 1, do not leave unnecessary groups on a drawing. If it is necessary to group a series of objects which are not otherwise related for movement or transfer, ungroup the collection after the operation is complete.
3. Group objects on the appropriate drawing layer. Objects that are on the same layer will always appear together and can be grouped on that layer. When grouping objects from different layers, chose a distinct layer for the matriarch of the group as a whole. Preferably, the group layer should

correspond to a designated layer for objects that relate to a specific design discipline, such as for architectural, mechanical, or electrical drawings.

4. Locate the origin of the group for convenient manipulation of the group as a whole. The origin can be used to align the group with a line or grid intersection. Establish a convention for the location of origins with every group. An origin that is always located at either the center or the lower left corner will facilitate finding the origin as well as picking the group. Picking, moving, and placing a group by its origin is more precise than performing these operations using a random point on the group. When focused on critical areas of alignment, a view of the entire group may be impossible. Locate the origin with this in mind; with certain systems, the origin of a group is determined by the origin of the first member of the group. The origin can be relocated with a utility for modifying groups.

5. Group objects in the correct order. The first member of a group can determine certain automatic graphic functions such as gapping lines. Also, certain plotters draw objects in the order in which they were grouped, and thus drawing appearance can be affected. For instance, selecting crosshatch lines as members of a group before selecting any perimeter line allows it to be drawn last, producing a neater final appearance.

6. Plan the structure of a group so that later editing will not destroy the integrity of copies of the group. Identify objects that make up the simplest entities, and group these as children at the lowest level within the structure of the group. Objects that are common to all copies of the group—objects that are the least likely to change, such as the outline—should be treated as children. Conversely, group objects that are likely to change at the top of the group structure. Elements that vary from copy to copy and are likely to change include: the serial number, add-on parts of a shape such as a desk return, and additional members of a family such as subgroups of furniture and equipment within the walls of a room. Grouping such objects at the top makes it easier to modify versions of the group while maintaining the integrity of each copy. This technique is important for systems that support deep-grouped objects as opposed to shallow-tree structures.

7. Create an original control version of the group and store it, perhaps just outside the drawing border, separate from the line work of the actual drawing. Make all changes to the control version of the group and spread the effect to the copies within the drawing. To make new copies of the group, return to the control or preferred version rather than to groups that are already located within the drawing. This technique applies to systems that support local symbols as well as systemwide symbols.

8. Be aware that the CAD system will automatically create groups for certain operations whether you want them or not. For example, in order to change scale or rotate an object, certain systems will create a group out of an ungrouped object.

9. When adding an object, or a group, to an existing group that is already distributed throughout a drawing, do not create a new group. This will needlessly consume additional drawing memory. Rather, use what utilities are available to insert the object, as a new group member, into the existing group. This does not apply for shallow-tree groups.
10. Test the group; in particular, see that changes to copies of a group are satisfactory. If many copies of the group are anticipated, try a few likely operations, such as an alignment or addition to the group, before starting actual work on the final drawing. Remember, the structure of a group and the integrity of its copies are not revealed with a simple visual inspection. Although many techniques are available for revising graphic objects, working with copies of groups that enable global changes to be made will save a great deal of time. However, it is imperative that groups be constructed correctly in the first place so as not to inhibit global change. Testing is an essential step.

The structure of a group determines how easily the group can be changed. The recommendations outlined above are intended as guidelines for creating groups that are rational as well as versatile. Anticipating the degree of change that drawings will require is not always easy. However, as designers and architects, we know from experience that certain drawing elements are relatively stable, and others are likely to change again and again. When creating groups, this kind of thinking should prevail.

Final Observations about Groups

For those with little exposure to CAD, the concept of a multilevel yet disembodied group of graphic objects may seem quite abstract, even foreign. Analyzing groups reveals some fundamental differences between drawings as they are perceived by humans and drawings as they are perceived by computers. Normally, a design element can be defined with a collection of lines that we recognize and associate based on observation combined with experience. A designer intuitively understands the meaning of lines on a drawing. Line work can be crossed, overlapping, unconnected, curved, or straight, yet, we have no difficulty recognizing an abstract collection of lines as a distinct part of a drawing. The visual relationship between lines is all that is necessary for human recognition. A single line and an arc represent a door in plan, for instance. A separate number and a circle represent what we refer to as a reference symbol for the door. Taken together, we understand these separate elements to represent a door because they look like a door.

If the system had to recognize objects based on the composition of their line work, it would require fairly sophisticated analysis. In fact, pattern recognition problems are a subject for future artificial intelligence. The relationships between lines, such as the ones that represent a door, must be made explicit and unambiguous to the current systems with a direct mechanism. Fortunately, groups are understood by the system as a list of objects. The system does not need to know anything about the geometric relationship between the members in the group. The objects only have to be included on the list assigned to the group. With a list, the system can recognize all the members of a group and act on them in concert. Finally, if we understand, as the system does, that copies of groups all refer to the same geometry record, we can see how it is possible to change one object and spread the effect to every copy. The copies are merely different versions of a single original. In the final analysis, groups are a simple logical concept.

Chapter

7

Symbols

"If I had done it right, it would have worked."
CAD OPERATOR SLOGAN

Chapter 7 begins with a brief look at how symbols are used in traditional hand drafting. From this perspective, the chapter describes the multidimensional character of symbols as they are used in intelligent drawings. Currently, symbols are the most developed component of intelligent drawing; they make use of several automatic data processing design aids at once. In a CAD environment, symbols are particularly versatile.

Symbols bring entirely new capabilities to the drawing process. Not only are they complete graphic versions of a design element, in certain CAD systems they can modify existing line work on the drawing, for example, adding door jambs when a door symbol is inserted in a wall. Design application software is available that uses symbols to automatically create plan and elevation views of rooms or exterior elevations (see Chap. 10). Also, symbols can be connected to written design information, such as schedules, notes, specifications, and cost estimates. On a CAD system, symbols share characteristics with traditional symbols as they have been known and used in hand drafting. However, there are significant differences. Most important, symbols can be modified or replaced in global operations. No longer just a guide through the drawings, symbols are powerful actors in interactive graphic procedures.

The Familiar World of Drafting Symbols

The use of symbols has a long history in architectural drawings. They originated as visual aids that coordinated different parts of the drawings. A symbol on one drawing refers to another version of a design element, such as a detail, on a separate drawing. Although drafting symbols are illustrated in architectural graphic standards, as a technical concept they are not precisely defined. We understand them based on widespread common use: "Symbols are the architect's signpost. They guide the document reader through the drawing set." [POP80]

Standard symbols are always included as a guide to the staff in the office manual of a design firm (Fig. 7-1). Reference books on architectural drafting show symbols used as a kind of graphic shorthand for many different types of information shown on architectural drawings. With traditional drafting mediums, symbols are used to indicate any of the following:

1. Abbreviations for certain words, such as angle, centerline, penny.
2. Designations for materials, such as glass, concrete, earth.
3. Location keys to different parts of the drawings, such as sections, elevations, and details.
4. Reference keys to schedules for doors, windows, finishes.
5. Representations of plumbing, mechanical, and electrical fixtures.
6. Furniture and equipment.

In the following sections, we concentrate on symbols used to establish location and cross-reference and to represent design elements such as fixtures

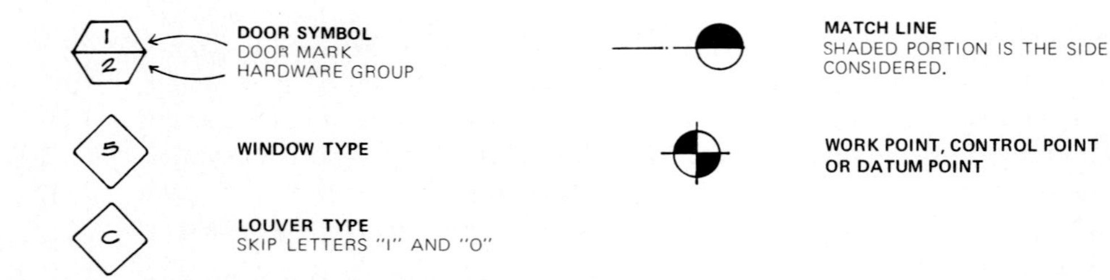

Figure 7-1 A selection of typical architectural drafting symbols. Prior to the introduction of CAD, symbols were essentially limited to this type of reference key. (*Courtesy of Northern California Chapter of the American Institute of Architects. Task Force on Production Office Procedures.*)

and equipment. The term *reference symbol* here designates both the location keys and reference keys described above. Similarly, a *footprint symbol* designates symbols that represent design elements such as plumbing, mechanical, and electrical fixtures or furniture items. Symbols used for these two purposes have been developed into rich complex mechanisms on CAD systems. The principles described in the following sections, however, can also be applied to symbols used for abbreviations and material indications.

If we look outside of architectural drafting, we find a wide proliferation of other examples of symbols, and more uniformity in their use. In the field of electrical engineering, for instance, an extensive symbol library is used, which is built from a vocabulary of indications for basic electrical functions, and the meaning of the symbols is widely agreed upon. The American National Standards Institute (ANSI) 1981 catalogue of *Electrical & Electronics Graphic Symbols & Reference Designations* includes more than 1500 distinct symbols.

Architectural symbols are not derived from a central vocabulary of common shapes. As a result, they are not as uniform in appearance throughout the profession. Variations based on regional preferences are tolerated. This tolerance is a by-product of the individuality that distinguishes the design work of one office from the next. Another factor supporting a general lack of uniformity among architectural symbols is the enormous variety of possible combinations of both material and space. Architectural drafting does not lend itself to the degree of graphic standardization seen in electrical engineering. Instead, common use within general standards of professional practice has been the rule. To illustrate, the reference symbol for a door number may include a circle in one office and a square, hexagon, or ellipse in others. Regardless of shape, however, the reference symbol appears, in all cases, with the door on the plans and it always includes a reference to the door schedule. We do not see any reason to deviate from this principle of common use. As we shall see, computer systems are an environment for an even richer variety of symbol types and use. Rather than standardization for its own sake, experimentation in the form of redesign and creation of new symbols is to be encouraged.

In the realm of traditional drafting, symbols are created that use the entire spectrum of drafting techniques and mediums. Symbols can be traced with the help of templates, copied onto the drawing from pages of specially designed transfer type, or included on their own sheet in a set of overlay films. Regardless of the drafting medium, however, a well-designed symbol must satisfy the following criteria:

1. Easily identifiable.
2. Reproduce simply.
3. Unique.
4. Share common use throughout any single profession or discipline.

These criteria serve the requirements of traditional drafting quite well. To capture the full potential of symbols in a CAD environment, however, other requirements must be added to this list: to be correct, the symbol must have a structure that is recognized by the CAD system; to be complete, a symbol must be connected to written information as well as different parts of the drawings such as schedules, notes, and specifications.

In a computer environment, the power of traditional drafting symbols is amplified. Their new capabilities allow us to automatically manipulate design elements for quantity takeoffs, reports, sorting, and connections with other documents. All the functions performed by drafting symbols, including the role of graphic shorthand, are still available. However, a symbol on an intelligent drawing performs and then expands these functions with new powers that are complicated, novel, and sometimes spectacular. CAD symbols are as different from traditional symbols as a traffic signal that senses cars in the intersection is different from a stop sign.

The Brave New World of CAD Symbols

The fundamental distinction between traditional drafting symbols and CAD symbols is that the latter can be recognized by both a CAD system and the designer. As design projects become more complex, drawings include more information and require more cross-references. Fortunately, we now have a new electronic partner reading the signposts.

Computer recognition of symbols is accomplished by attaching a computer-recognizable flag to the group of graphic objects that makes up a symbol. With such flags, the system recognizes any number of symbols on the same drawing. Properly set flags allow the system to distinguish between different types of symbols and between the different purposes for which symbols are used.

Most important, the system can find and read a symbol without having to inspect its geometric shape. It is very difficult for a computer to recognize an object based on its shape. As of this writing, computer science is just beginning to use pattern recognition in applications such as mapping and robotics, and, in many cases, a computer will take longer to recognize shapes on an architectural drawing than will a human observer. The shape of the symbol remains as a visual signpost for the designer or contractor—the human reader of the drawings. With symbols, however, the computer only has to recognize a flag; it doesn't matter what a symbol looks like.

In fact, the same symbol can appear in different forms on several drawings at once. The door leaf and swing, with its reference bubble, appear on the architectural floor plan. On the background drawings for the work of consultants, only the opening is shown. The opening can be shown or automatically filled in on the drawing for the reflected ceiling plan (Fig. 7-2).

All of this is accomplished when a properly constructed symbol is placed on the drawing. No additional operation is required. In another example, equipment can be shown as an outline on the architectural plan, with required clearances on the facilities plan and as a dotted outline with its electrical hookup on the electrical plan. All these different graphic elements are included in a single symbol.

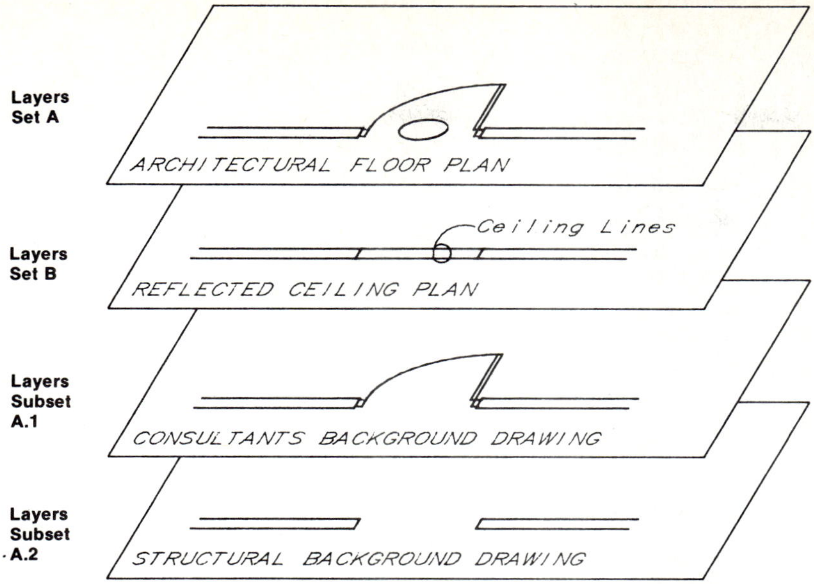

Figure 7-2 Different graphic versions of a single door symbol shown as it appears on separate drawing layers.

Different forms of the same symbol are possible because, much like overlay drafting, the drawing is divided into several different layers or levels. Each layer can be displayed and plotted separately or in combination with other layers. Separate parts of the symbol are created on separate drawing layers and are then tied together in a group (Fig. 7-3). (This may not be possible on systems with shallow-tree grouping structures.) Yet the symbol is stored, retrieved, and placed as a single and complete entity.

Once a symbol is copied onto a drawing, it is moved into a final location with system utilities. The procedure is similar to the use of a template in hand drafting: the symbol is rotated or mirrored and copied any number of times. Like any other graphic object, CAD systems can move symbols around at will. Within certain constraints, the system can automatically place the symbol for you.

Symbols are supplied from three basic sources. The first is CAD manufacturers who include libraries of symbols along with the graphic software. These libraries are starter sets and vary in completeness. They enable you to begin work on actual project drawings soon after training. Of necessity, they are designed for the general case. Be prepared to modify, enhance, and expand on the symbols supplied from this source. The extent to which this is necessary will depend on such factors as the type of work in your office and the relationship between your office and other consulting firms with CAD equipment. Symbols from CAD manufacturers are not immutable. Change them to suit your own needs.

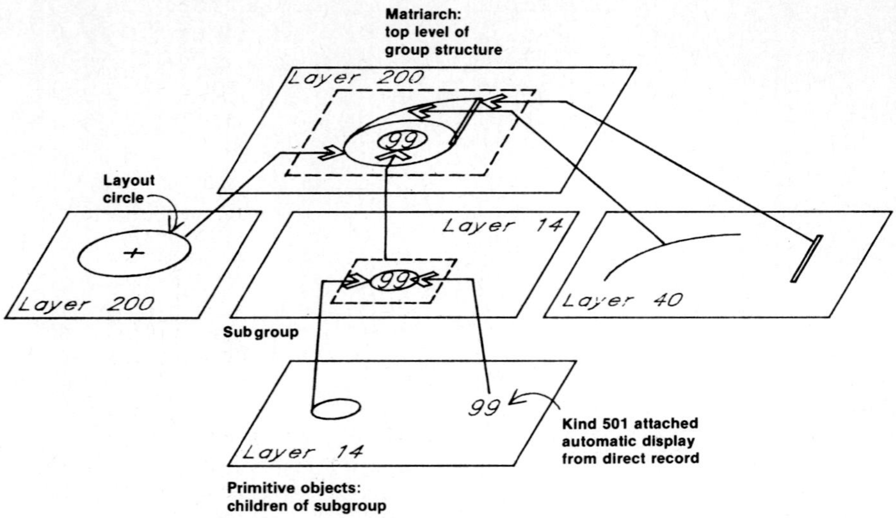

Figure 7-3 The grouping structure of a door symbol also shown with separate drawing layers.

Libraries of symbols are also available from third party suppliers and CAD consultants. These symbols tend to be specialized for a particular design problem, such as interior planning or the design of commercial kitchens. Very large libraries of symbols for furniture are available from the major manufacturers of office furniture, including Steelcase, Herman Miller, and Haworth. As time goes on, third-party symbol libraries will become available on more and more systems.

In the final analysis, the major source of symbols is your own office. Your symbols will be created for the special design requirements of your own clients. They can be optimized to work with procedures for specific drawings and reports.

There is more to creating symbols than meets the eye. Before a symbol can be used, it must be constructed very carefully within the requirements of a particular system. Symbols are not just a collection of lines. They have a nonvisible structure that is used by the system for automatic graphic functions, global revisions, and coordination with files of written information. To take advantage of these capabilities, however, the symbol must be carefully assembled.

Reference Symbols

For simplicity, we have bundled the traditional indications for both location keys and reference keys into a single category, namely, reference symbols. Both location and reference keys address the problem of coordination among different parts of drawings. Reference symbols take the form of simple geometric shapes such as circles, rectangles, or squares (Fig. 7-4). Most include a key or a serial number composed of numbers or letters. The serial number indicates the drawing location of, for example, a complete schedule, or of a related detail, interior elevation, or section. With CAD, reference symbols serve the same purpose they perform on drawings from traditional drafting mediums. They continue to be signposts; only now their capabilities are amplified.

A *reference symbol* is defined as a graphic key, not literally shaped or dimensioned, that connects different parts of the documents and is combined with text information.

Some examples of reference symbols include:

1. Work points, column line or building grid line bubbles, and match line bubbles, which are used to fix the position of design elements in space.
2. Section, detail, or interior elevation bubbles, used to relate different views of the project.
3. Door, window, equipment, furniture, or room keys, which are used to relate a design element to a separate schedule or table. In this example, reference symbols are combined with footprint symbols. See also Fig. 7-5.

Since they perform the same function, reference symbols look the same on both CAD and traditional drawings (Fig. 7-5). Existing standard symbols can be recreated on the CAD system without the need for significant graphic modification. The size and shape need only conform to the requirements of traditional drafting for easy identification and shared use. Recommendations for the construction of symbols that make efficient use of computer memory are described later in this chapter.

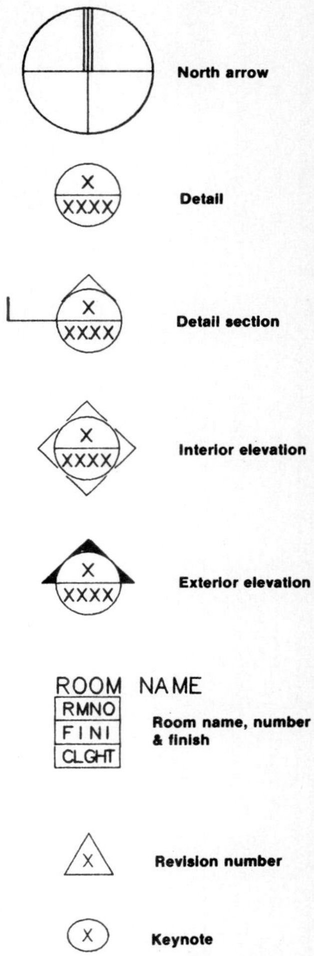

Figure 7-4 Some typical CAD reference symbols.

Finding Our Way around with Reference Symbols

With CAD, project documents are still organized around the traditional system of plans, elevations, sections, schedules, details, and specifications. Since this organization reflects how design work is documented for purposes of construction, designers will probably use the same system well into the future. The need for separating different kinds of information into different documents is unchanged. On a CAD system, however, reference symbol capabilities make coordinating this information easier—in some cases automatic. As a result, the use of reference symbols improves the accuracy and reliability of final documents.

In a manual environment, coordinating and checking design information in different locations throughout drawings requires a considerable effort. First, you must locate a reference symbol and read the serial number. Then, while remembering the number, you search from drawing to drawing. Finally, when the correct schedule or detail is located, you check the information. This is a crude physical search combined with mental recall. It often requires moving back and forth several times between a reference symbol and another drawing. The drafters know where everything is on the drawings, but they do go home for the day.

Reference symbols can automatically connect different parts of the doc-

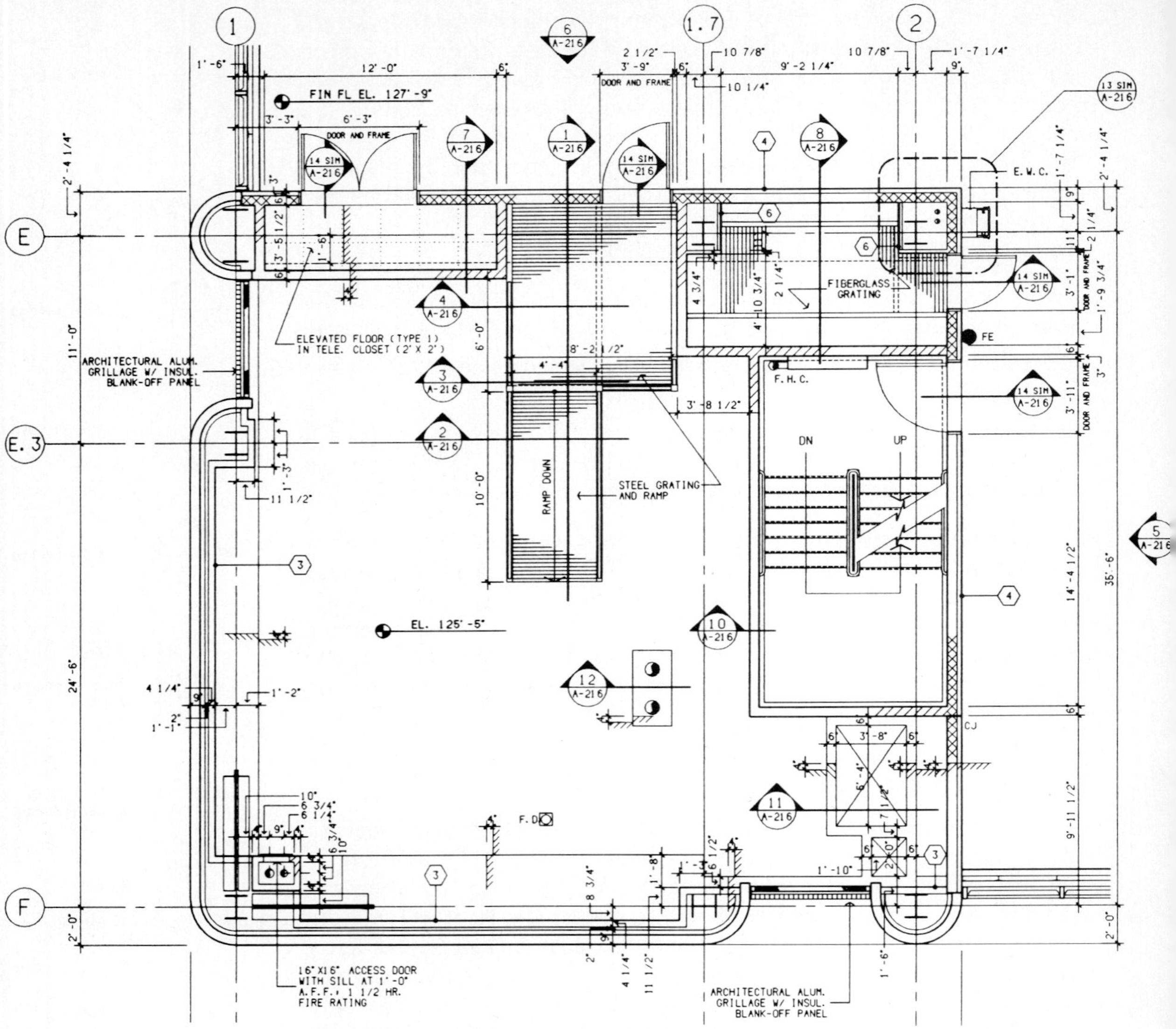

Figure 7-5 Reference symbols shown on an enlarged-scale floor plan. (*Courtesy of Skidmore, Owings, and Merrill, Houston, TX.*)

uments. They do the searching for us. More than simply guiding the human reader with numbers and letters, reference symbols guide computer recognition.

The most straightforward method for connecting reference symbols to schedules is the use of automatically created reports. The key, as with traditional drafting, is the serial number in the reference symbol. It identifies a design element, such as a door, in relation to other design elements of the same type. Initially, the serial number appears on the drawing as a string of dummy text. There it is part of the group of objects which represents the reference symbol. Later, the dummy string is replaced with an actual serial number (see Fig. 13-5). It is also recorded in a direct nongraphic record of text information associated with the symbol.

The serial number is used in combination with automatic report-writing software. The system first scans the full-scale drawings. It finds the reference symbols and reads the serial number. As it reads each symbol, the name of the symbol and its location are written to a temporary, or scratch, file. In sorting and summarizing the scratch file, the system creates a schedule or report automatically. The resulting report includes the serial number and related nongraphic information from other text files. The report can also list the drawing or file where the information was found (see also Fig. 14-2). The system can compare current with prior temporary files and will indicate which objects have been changed since the last report.

This procedure is repeated after each round of modifications to the drawings. By reporting on the drawings, we are asking the system to find out what is included. The connections between design elements and reports are established by using key fields, which contain an alphanumeric key. If reference symbols are built correctly, including keys that are stored in records attached to the symbol, coordinating design information is easy.

The ability to automatically coordinate different parts of the drawings provides two essential benefits. One is improved speed of access—the system requires less time to search through the documents and find all the correct versions of a design element. More important for limiting the liability of the designer, installing the automatic connections ensures that references between design elements and reports and schedules retain their integrity. The detail is referred to by the correct reference symbol; the room number is associated with the correct records in the finish and furniture schedules. During the design process, schedules and details will change. However, the system cannot make the mistake of reading the serial number in one reference symbol and retrieving information related to a different symbol. The result is improved document accuracy.

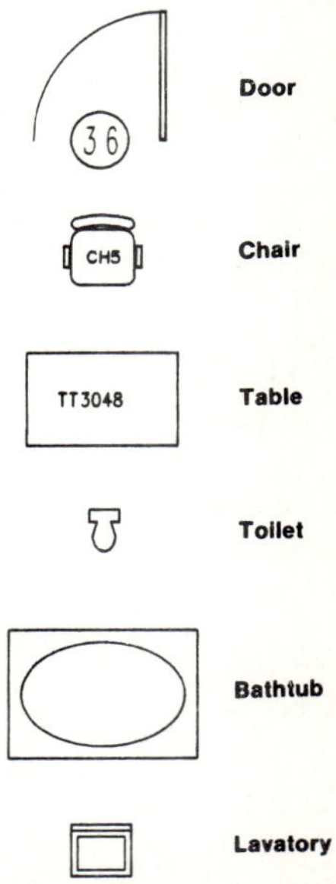

Figure 7-6 Typical "footprint" symbols.

Footprint Symbols

The concept of a symbol as a signpost must be expanded beyond the traditional location and reference functions described above. Entire design elements can become symbols (see Fig. 7-6), and thus symbols in a CAD environment become radically different from symbols used in traditional drafting. Symbols are more than simple guides. "Footprint" symbols, as we call them, look like drawing elements that are copied using paste-up, transfer, or overlay drafting techniques. In fact, the same principle for the reuse of a graphic copy of a design element is applied.

Any design element that can be drawn unchanged from one project to the next is a candidate for becoming a footprint symbol. Although it describes a design element, perhaps even an entire part of the project, a symbol is not specific to any one project. It can be reused on project after project.

Since footprint symbols describe specific design elements, such as doors, equipment, and furniture, they are dimensionally accurate. Once they are copied onto a project drawing, footprint symbols represent part of the design of the project itself. As such, they must accurately fit the surrounding design conditions.

A footprint symbol can include a reference symbol. We used to refer to the box or circle around a door number as a symbol—specifically, a reference symbol. Now, the line work for the entire door along with this reference symbol is one complete symbol (Fig. 7-6).

Footprint symbols, like reference symbols, are important elements in the office standards data base. Created before work on project drawings begins, they are filed in special drawings or symbol libraries. Copies are retrieved by name for use on project drawings.

A *footprint symbol* is a literally shaped object, which represents a design element, that is grouped, connected to text information, and stored separately from any project drawings. Footprint symbols are used to represent:

1. Doors and windows along with their reference keys.
2. Furniture and equipment.
3. Plumbing, mechanical, and electrical fixtures.
4. Complete room plan and elevation templates.
5. Stairs, elevators, and other building core elements.

It is possible to design symbols that require some additional line work once they are located on the drawing. Where a symbol must adjust to a variety of different conditions, modification is appropriate. Footprint symbols can be used as flexible templates that are transformed slightly for different design conditions. Entire rooms, including standard plans or elevations, can become symbols. These are stretched or shrunk to fit the project after they are placed on the drawing. In many cases, the system will automatically modify parts of the drawing when the symbol is moved into place.

Automatic Drawing Modification

When a symbol is placed on a drawing, some CAD systems can modify the drawing graphics that are related to the symbol. The simplest example is the removal of wall lines where a door or window symbol is placed. Any lines that are overlapped by the symbol, such as the pair of wall lines, are removed. The system can also automatically add new line work to the drawing, for example,

1. Sill lines for windows and doors.
2. Door jambs to a specified width and thickness.
3. Above-door wall lines that appear only on the reflected ceiling plan (referred to as "ceiling lines").

Such line work does not have to be recorded as part of the original group for the symbol. The system automatically creates the line work when the symbol is put in its final location on a drawing (see Fig. 7-7).

Of course, if a symbol is removed, such as a door symbol, the original wall lines are automatically restored. When one door symbol replaces another, some CAD systems automatically adjust wall lines to the size of the new opening.

Symbols as Graphic Design Information

Symbols are a form of permanently recorded design information. Both graphic and nongraphic information can be stored with a symbol. For example, symbols can be located on a drawing automatically according to spatial requirements that are stored with the symbol. Design elements, such as fixtures, equipment, or furniture, can be located automatically at a specific distance and orientation to a reference line, such as a wall. With CAD functions for placing symbols, certain utilities can be used to locate and copy the symbols according to specific design parameters. For instance, the number of copies, spacing, setbacks, and orientation to other elements in the design can be specified. Openings, such as doors and windows, can be automatically located at the center of the wall or at a specified minimum distance from a

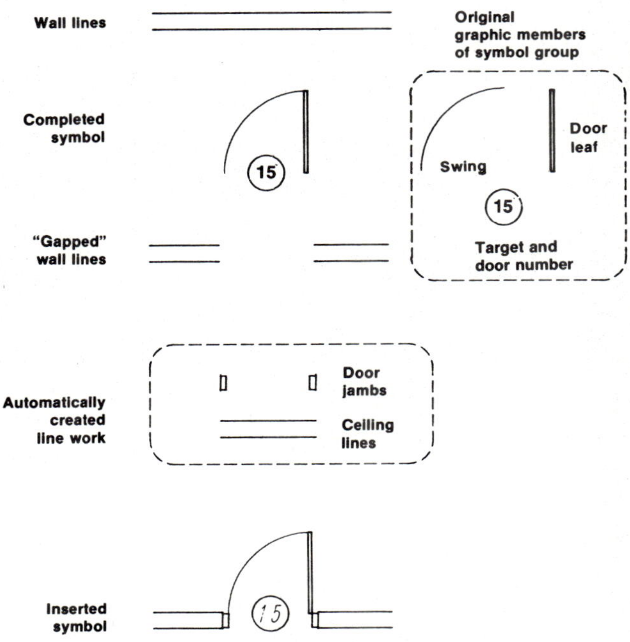

Figure 7-7 Representation of drawing modification resulting from an automatic insert-symbol operation. *(Courtesy of CalComp, Anaheim, CA.)*

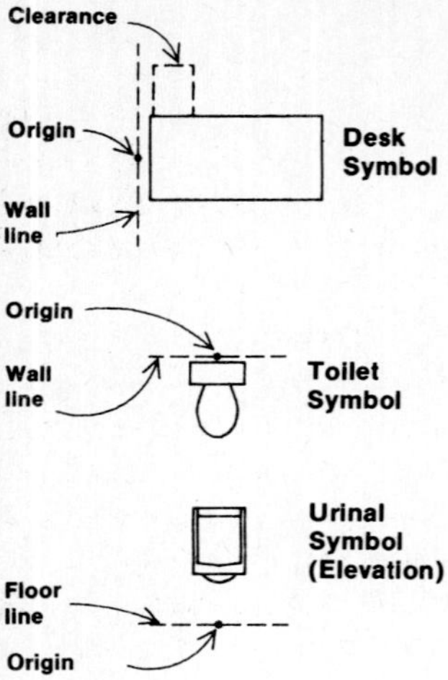

Figure 7-8 Origins used with symbols. By including an origin at a preassigned offset with each symbol, they are automatically set back from walls, floors, or other design elements when placed on a drawing.

corner or point along the wall. Several of these requirements can be combined to reduce the procedure for placing symbols to a one-step operation. Symbols can become miniature graphic robots. They know which way to turn and where they should be located as they are placed.

In the world of manual design, the instructions for locating design elements on drawings propagate in a variety of ways. They are indicated on sketches and sometimes included in office graphic standards. More often, they are understood as rules of thumb (or secret knowledge privately held by a semispiritual designer caste). Such requirements, however, tend to be reused with little or no modification on each new project. The robe hook is centered on the door, 70 in high, every time.

Design requirements of this type can be recorded as graphic information with a symbol. Reference points are included in the group for the symbol along with the line work (Fig. 7-8). The reference points are placed at specific distances from the edge of the symbol. The system places the symbol such that the reference point is located on a designated line. Thus, the symbol is located at a preassigned offset and orientation from a wall or other reference line.

By default, the origin of a symbol group establishes the reference point of the object for spacing. Reference points are displayed when the operator is checking or moving the symbol. They are recognized and used by the system to locate the object. Otherwise they are not visible. Guidelines, which can indicate alignment or height, can also be grouped with symbols. Guidelines and reference points need not appear on the final plotted drawing. They can be assigned to a drawing layer designated for that purpose. Finally, clearances or setbacks can be shown with symbols for furniture, equipment, or cabinets. Again, such indications need appear only when a certain drawing layer is used. On some CAD systems, guidelines and reference points are unique data types that are shown on the CRT screen but are not recognized by the system for plotting.

Recording design information with symbols reduces the time required for instructions to drafting staff. With most symbols, the designer does not have to instruct the operator concerning every detail of their location. Everyone on a project uses the same symbols. Graphic standards are applied by the system from information carried with the symbol, minimizing time spent checking every relationship or minor offset. As a result, the designer is free to concentrate on exceptions to the standard conditions.

Recommendations for Line Work

The first requirement for an efficiently designed symbol is to minimize its line work. Reference symbols can be created to appear as they do in traditional drafting mediums; the simplest geometric shapes, without patterning or in-fill, are recommended. For footprint symbols, the simplest outline of the object with the fewest possible line segments is recommended. As a general rule, include only the minimum line work necessary for easy recognition by human readers. The symbol is no place to express subtle rendering techniques.

Visual clarity has always been an essential principle for organizing architectural drawings. However, there are additional reasons for keeping line worl to a minimum. Regardless of a system's power or storage capacity, there is always a practical limit to the amount of line work that can be stored with each drawing. As more line work is added to the drawing and more objects included, the drawing will become full. "Full" means more than in the visual sense of a dense collection of lines. You can store hundreds or thousands of symbols on a single drawing. They hop in place very quickly. However, each copy adds to the memory requirement for the drawing. See Figs. 7-9 and 7-10 for examples of symbols which are clear and straightforward.

You will pay a penalty for drawings that occupy large amounts of memory. At the very least, the penalty is slower response from the system. At worst,

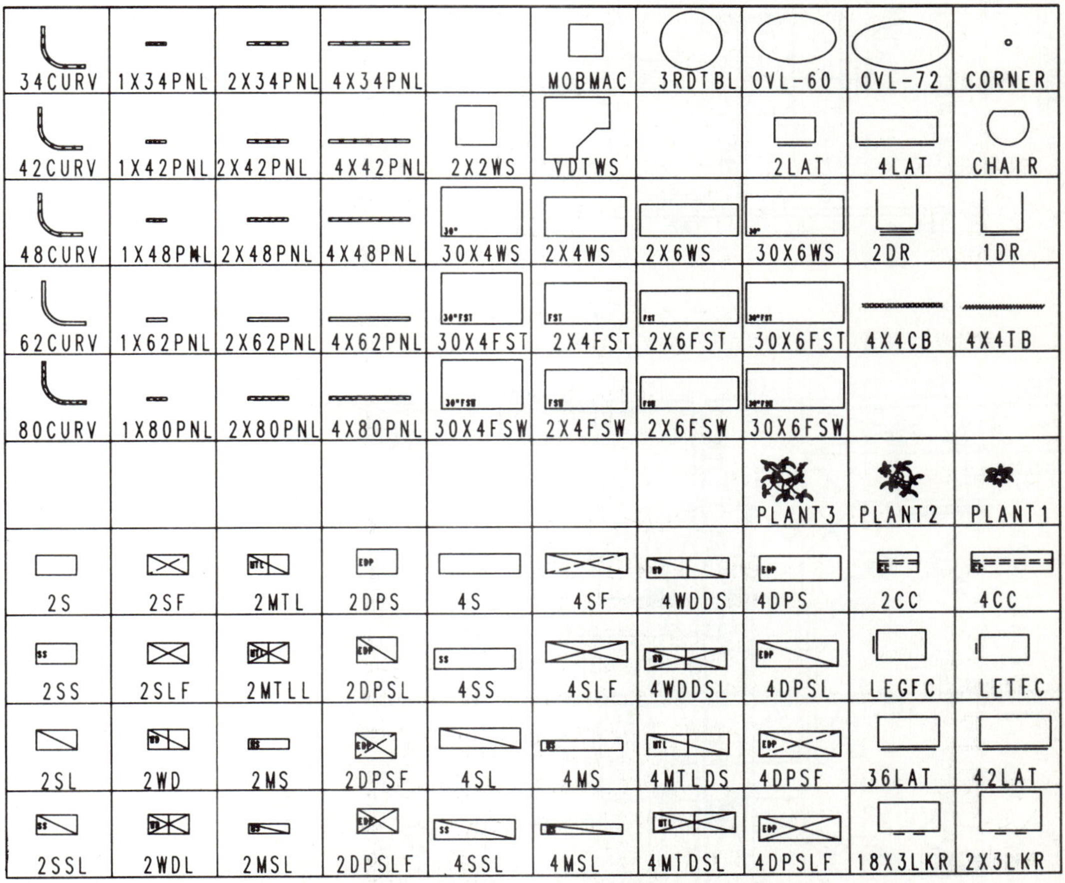

Figure 7-9 Reproduction of the symbol library, along with symbol names, for furniture used to create the partial facilities plan shown in Fig. 7-10. (*Courtesy of Union Mutual Life Insurance Co., Facility Planning, Portland, ME*)

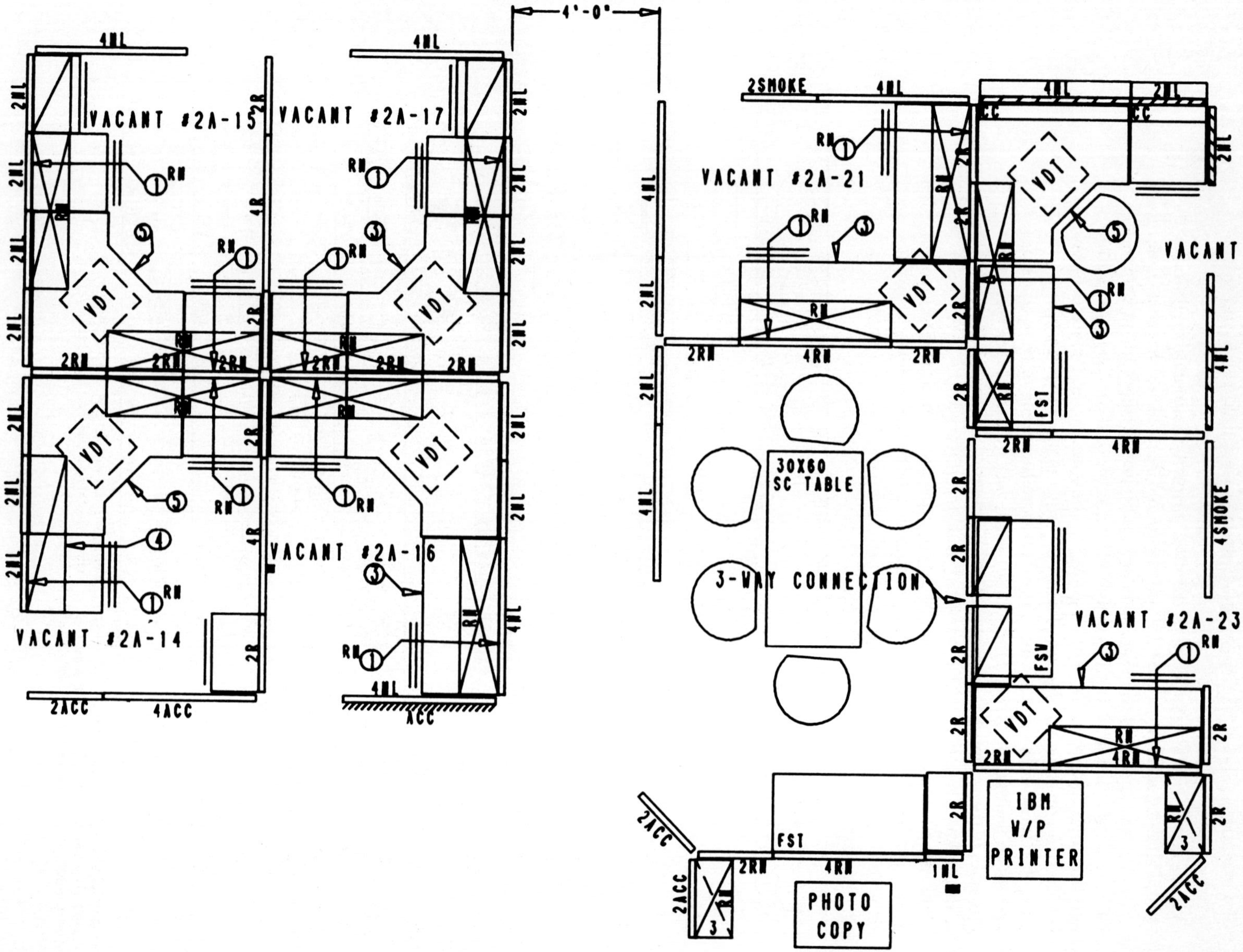
4'-0"
VACANT #2A-15
VACANT #2A-17
VACANT #2A-14
VACANT #2A-16
VACANT #2A-21
VACANT
VACANT #2A-23
30X60
SC TABLE
3-WAY CONNECTION
IBM
W/P
PRINTER
PHOTO
COPY
2SMOKE
4SMOKE
VDT
FST
FSV
2ACC
4ACC
ACC

drawings on systems which use real files rather than virtual files for drawings may fill up, and certain operations may fail to work altogether.

Along with the traditional requirement for clarity, visual brevity is the rule with symbols. Just as important, symbols composed with crosshatch patterns, poche, and special line styles consume more memory than is necessary. The north arrow or the scale, which appear only once on a drawing, are not of concern here. Consider how many times, however, symbols for doors, windows, and plumbing fixtures are going to appear. Footprint symbols, unless drawn with a minimum of line work, are more likely to be memory hogs than reference symbols. Since they consume precious memory, discourage subtle renderings that only serve as the signature for the work of the office. Let the quality of the design work itself perform that function.

Remember that symbols can be recognized by the computer with the use of an invisible flag. The system does not care what the symbol looks like. By expecting the system to faithfully reproduce and use the same graphic techniques developed for traditional drafting, we are simply imitating hand drafting. When reading and coordinating design information on a CAD system, many visual clues that served the manual process, such as poche, can be minimized or retired. The human reader of architectural drawings is assisted with entirely new tools, such as automatic reports, electronic files, and data base management utilities. Like cats, CAD systems see in the dark.

Scaled vs. Unscaled Symbols

The size of a symbol when it is copied from a symbol file onto a drawing must correspond to the scale of the drawing. There are two opposite approaches used to control symbol size in relation to the drawing scale, and they depend on whether the CAD system is drawing-oriented or project-oriented (see Table 3-1).

In a drawing-oriented system, the scale at which the symbol was originally created is compared to the scale of the drawing. Then, the system applies a scaling factor to the size of the symbol before displaying it. Such symbols are referred to as "scaled" symbols. As we know, the graphic size of an object depends on the scale of the drawing where it is used. For example, a door is drawn smaller on a drawing at a scale of $\frac{1}{8}$ in = 1 ft than on a drawing created at $\frac{1}{4}$ = 1 ft. With the use of this scaling mechanism, a symbol can be created at one scale and subsequently used on drawings of different scales, thus reducing the total number of symbols that need to be created. Designating symbols as scaled is particularly appropriate for footprint symbols.

The size of a reference symbol, on the other hand, usually does not depend on the scale of the drawing. The size of a north arrow, for instance, remains the same regardless of the scale of the drawing. Symbols that are always

Figure 7-10 Excerpt from an office facilities plan created entirely with symbols. Note: well-defined graphics and keynotes clearly indicate arrangement of furniture, including elements overlapping each other vertically such as drawers, shelves, lights, and bulletin boards. *(Courtesy of Union Mutual Life Insurance Co., Facility Planning, Portland, ME)*

drawn at the same size are referred to as "unscaled" symbols. When a copy of an unscaled symbol is reproduced, the scale of the drawing is ignored, and no scaling factor is applied by the system.

With CAD systems that are project-oriented, however, automatic procedures for scaling symbols are essentially reversed from those described above. In this case, footprint symbols for objects such as doors are placed at full size on drawings regardless of drawing scale. In contrast, reference symbols are scaled either up or down depending on the scale of the drawing.

Although these two approaches seem contradictory, the concept underlying them is the same. Somehow, the size of a symbol must correspond to two factors: scale of the drawing and its use as either a footprint or a reference symbol. Each approach represents a different way of looking at the same thing.

From the point of view of a drawing-oriented system, the operator can designate a symbol as either scaled or unscaled when a symbol is initially created and filed. This designation applies to the entire symbol group. Consequently, any lettering that accompanies the symbol is also designated as either scaled or unscaled.

As we know, lettering is often located within part of the line work for a symbol. For example, the serial number for a door is usually shown within a bubble that accompanies the drawing of the leaf and swing of the door. To be readable, however, lettering usually appears at the same size regardless of the scale of the drawing.

As of this writing, most CAD systems do not have the capability to designate different parts of a single symbol as both scaled and unscaled, and this poses a problem for lettering.

Two possible solutions to this problem exist. First, duplicate symbol files can be created and maintained for drawings at different scales. In fact, this is a standard solution for CAD users. It is usually necessary to display greater detail or line work that is more complete with design elements that are shown at a larger scale. For example, enlarged plans of bathrooms are often included with the small-scale plans of a complete floor. The plumbing fixtures may be drawn as simple outlines at the smaller scale, whereas fittings and drains are shown at the larger scale. In this case, it would be necessary to use different symbols at different drawing scales for the same plumbing fixture or to create the fittings and drains on a drawing layer which will not be displayed at the smaller scale.

If the CAD system can create drawings from a data base of building components, any duplication of symbol files can be managed quite easily. Here, a numbered code is used to retrieve symbols. Before the system retrieves a copy of a symbol, however, it checks the scale of the drawing. The system then copies the symbol from a designated symbol file that corresponds to the scale of the drawing.

The second alternative is to divide a symbol, say, a door, into two separate symbols, one for the door line work, and another for the reference symbol, which includes the serial number and the bubble that surrounds it. Thus, the symbol for the line work can be designated as scaled and the reference symbol unscaled.

It would be ideal if different levels within the structure of a group could be designated as either scaled or unscaled. Both the bubble and serial number could remain unchanged, and the line work for the door would respond to the scale of the drawing.

Creating and Testing Symbols

Designers have been using drafting symbols for a long time. In typical hand drafting, the outline of a symbol is traced from a template, usually made from a thin sheet of hard plastic. Perhaps even easier are rub-on copies of symbols or decals from preprinted sheets of transferable film. These analogies, however, give a deceptively simple impression of the requirements for building original symbols on a CAD system.

CAD symbols require a structure of their own (Fig. 7-11). Creating the correct appearance on the screen, or even on a single drawing, is not enough. A simple visual inspection will not reveal any of the special graphic capabilities or connections to text information that are essential to intelligent drawings. A design element may appear to be drawn correctly, but not satisfy all the requirements for a symbol. New criteria for completeness come into play. Before they are used on a project drawing, symbols must be tested. This is a new problem that did not exist in traditional drafting (it was hardly necessary to test a template).

Requirements for their correct assembly can be revealed by describing a series of tests for symbols. (See material on creating groups on Chap. 6.) The

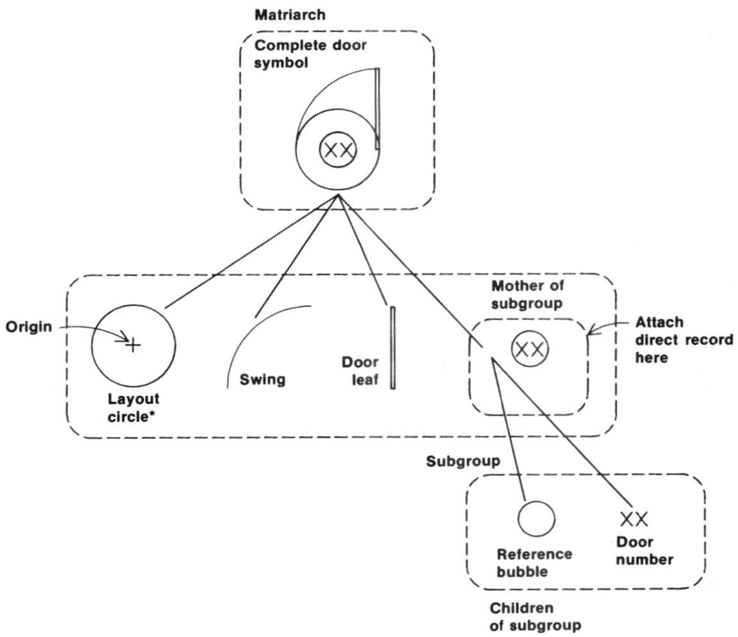

Figure 7-11 Inverted-tree grouping structure of a door symbol.

following is a list of specific tests that will determine the structure and capabilities of a symbol.

1. Inspect each line, or primitive object, to see that it is assigned the correct color and pen number.
2. Inspect each part of the structure for the group, both the primitive objects and any subgroup within the symbol, to ensure it is on the correct drawing layer.
3. Check the group structure of the symbol as a whole. On certain CAD systems, the area gapped by a symbol is determined by the size of the first member of the matriarch of the group. See that the correct object is the first member of the group. Also, see that the matriarch of the group is on the correct drawing layer.
4. On certain CAD systems, pen number or color can be assigned to a group. This will override the pen and color assigned to the members of the group. If necessary, confirm that the pen number and color for the matriarch of the group are set to 0. Other CAD systems automatically preclude this possibility.
5. Check that the origin of the group is in the right location, for example, in the middle of the graphics or in the lower left corner.
6. Check that any required flags (see Chap. 4) are associated with the correct object within the group, including those at the top level of the group as a whole.
7. See that dummy text strings are included and that a flag or kind number, if used for the automatic display of text, is assigned to the string.
8. See that the text strings are represented by a matching record in a direct file (a property or attribute file) that is associated with the symbol. The direct file must also be associated at the correct level within the group structure.
9. File the symbol in a designated symbol library or drawing for symbols only.
10. Retrieve the symbol onto a sample drawing.
11. Double-check that the symbol is on the correct level and that the direct file is still attached.
12. Test the automatic graphic capabilities of the symbol by moving it into a final location.
13. Test the automatic display of text by entering text in the direct record for the text string.

These tests are a formidable procedure. Symbols that meet these criteria, that pass all these hurdles, are valuable, representing a real investment in time on the part of the office that creates them. Once they have passed, however, each symbol becomes a powerful worker that can replace entire steps in the assembly of design documents.

The difficulties implied in a procedure this complex are many. Obviously, a symbol, or any part thereof, created on the wrong drawing layers, won't even appear on certain drawings. More subtle is a missing special flag or a missing reference to a nongraphic record. Since it cannot be seen, this type of omission can go unnoticed until it is time to create a report. Unfortunately, by then it may be impossible or too time-consuming to install the necessary record or flag with every copy of the symbol on the drawings.

The Use of Groups with Symbols

Symbols are groups that are named and stored in a central library, or file, which is separate from project drawings. In a way, a symbol is a specialized example of a group. Since symbol are groups, however, the mechanisms that determine the structure and integrity of groups are essential to the power of symbols. For example, certain automatic graphic functions depend on the order in which the line work for a symbol is assembled into a group. Because symbols are often included in larger groups, global operations on symbols are possible. A symbol can be replaced in one group and the effect spread automatically to all other copies of the group.

Symbols are stored in electronic files on the CAD system. As they are stored, each one is given a unique name. A system command, such as Retrieve from Symbol Library can be used to move the symbol out of the file and onto a drawing. In fact, only a copy of the symbol is retrieved. The symbol in the central file remains unchanged regardless of how many times it appears on the drawings. Since the same symbol is used on project after project, symbol libraries are part of the office standards data base. When a symbol is retrieved from a library and placed on a drawing, it becomes part of a project data base.

The order in which the objects are filed into a group is important to the special graphic capabilities of symbols. The system understands the order as a structure for the group. By the convention of certain CAD systems, the first member of a group is used to define what is referred to as the "extent" of the group, or symbol. The extent is simply two points, located on the perimeter of the line work for the group, which include the maximum and the minimum *X* and *Y* values of any object in the group. In the case of symbols, the extent defines the box that surrounds a symbol (see Fig. 7-12). By designating a rectangle which encloses the symbol, the operator defines the extent of the symbol. The corners of the rectangle define the extent. The block that defines a symbol on personal computer CAD systems performs this same function.

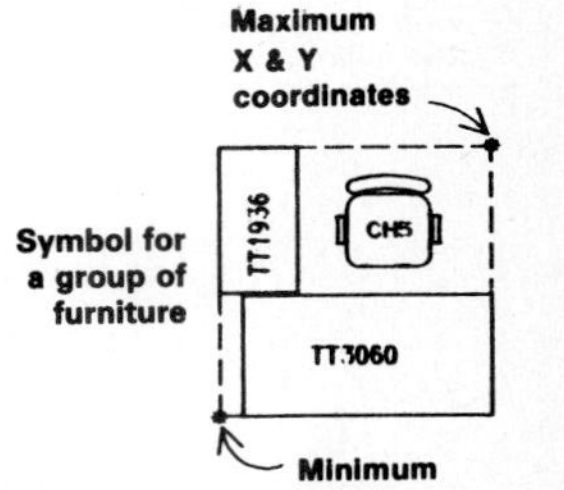

Figure 7-12 A representation of the extents, the minimum and maximum *X* and *Y* coordinates, of a group of furniture symbols.

Conventions are developed on many CAD systems whereby the first member of a group is used to control automatic graphic functions. When a door symbol, for example, is located on a plan, the size of the opening in the wall is determined by the size of the first member of the group. In a related example, the first member of a group is used to define an area where any existing line work on the drawing should be removed. For instance, a part of a tile pattern, within the outline of a piece of furniture, or a plumbing fixture, is removed by placing the symbol over the pattern.

Since a symbol is a group, a symbol should be designed to take the fullest possible advantage of all the capabilities a group has. For example, on a system that supports local symbols, using copies of a single symbol which has been retrieved from a symbol library is more efficient than retrieving copy after copy from the symbol library. Making copies of a symbol that is already on the drawing conserves drawing memory. More important, because a single symbol on the drawing is the source of other copies, each copy has a shared integrity with the source. Consequently, the copies can be modified by changing the source and spreading the effect of the change to all copies.

For the purpose of placing or duplicating entire sets of objects, symbols are frequently combined into larger groups. For example, the plumbing fixtures in a bathroom can be grouped along with the wall and door that enclose the bath. This bath can, in turn, be used in a variety of different apartment configurations. The group for the bath can be copied several times into any number of different apartments on the plan. This procedure is an efficient way to produce the major elements of a complete floor plan.

If we explore this typical case further, we can illustrate how symbols, within copies of a group, are modified by working on the initial configuration of the group as a single source for each copy (Fig. 7-13). Note, however, that the symbols must first be included in the group in the correct order.

Assume that the same plumbing fixture in every bath must be changed once copies of the bathroom have been distributed throughout the drawing.

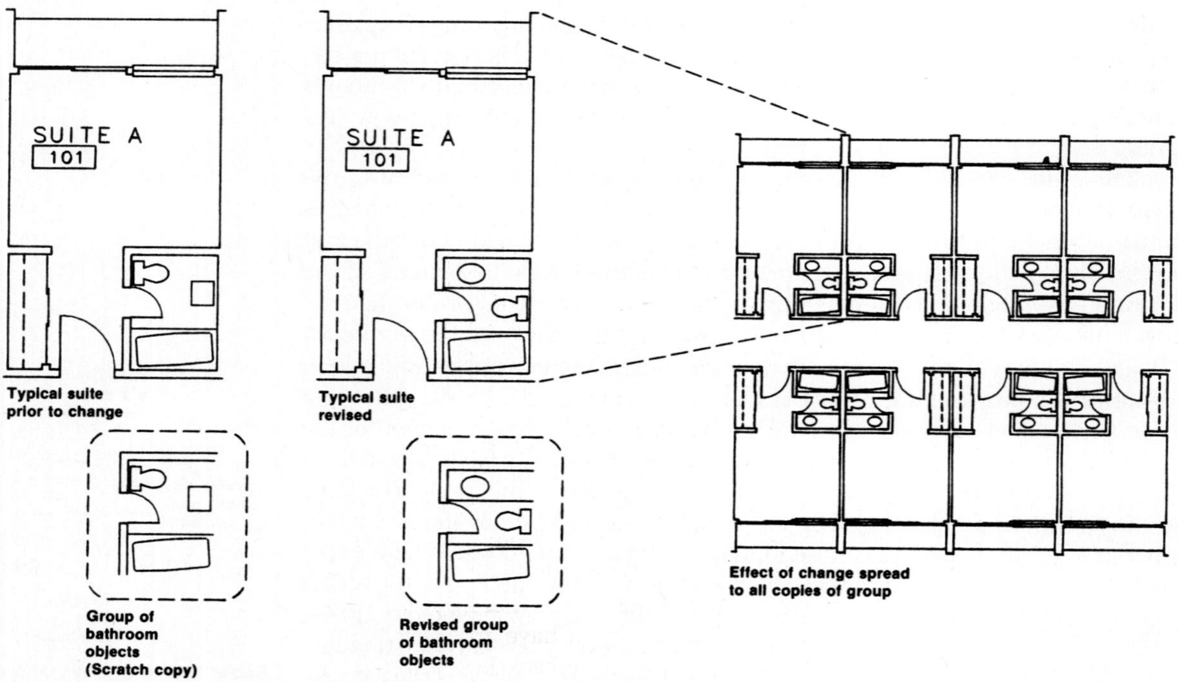

Figure 7-13 Use of a group structure, organized by room, enables revisions to all copies of the group in a single global operation.

The change could be as simple as relocating the fixture or as dramatic as replacing it altogether with a new plumbing fixture. The procedure for this type of change follows.

1. Select any copy of the bath. As stated in Chap. 6, a reference copy of the group should be stored outside of the boundary for the drawing. Use this reference copy preferentially.
2. Relocate the fixture as a member of the group, or, if it is to be replaced, delete the fixture from the group. Notice, CAD utilities for these operations are not the same as those used for operations on graphic objects that have not been grouped. Utilities that work directly on the members of a group must be used.
3. If the fixture is to be replaced, insert a symbol as a new member into the group. Again, it is necessary to use system utilities that work on the group as a whole, rather than the primitive graphic objects themselves.
4. Instruct the system to revise all copies of the group wherever they appear on the drawings, thus reflecting the change in other bathrooms.

Since we are working directly on the source for each copy of the group, the change will automatically appear each time the group appears on the drawings. No further operations are required. Although it appears to be the case, in fact, every copy has not been changed; we have only modified the central source which each copy reflects.

This example illustrates how a room can be used as a practical organizing unit when considering how to assemble groups. Group symbols within a room, such as furniture or equipment, on one level within the structure of the group. Group walls, doors, and windows in a separate subgroup from the group of symbols. Group tile patterns and other finish indications again as a separate subgroup. All these subgroups are then grouped under the same matriarch. In this way, the members of a major group are divided into rational subgroups. Consequently, operations can be performed on separate subgroups and their members without destroying the integrity of the group or its subgroups. By carefully combining symbols into subgroups under a single matriarch, a structure is created that enables us to efficiently manage changes to a drawing. If, on the other hand, symbols are combined into simple groups with only two levels to their structure, certain changes will have to be made to each copy of the group, one at a time.

Final Observations about Creating Symbols

Creating symbols that are highly efficient requires planning as well as cooperation among all those who use the CAD system. Personnel from all levels within a design firm must participate. Someone must have an in-depth understanding of the CAD system and be able to communicate that understanding to others. Equally important, someone must understand and be able to explain the content and purpose of the project documents—not just the drawings themselves, but their interrelationships. Usually, a CAD operator cannot be expected to supply the in-depth knowledge required in both of these vital areas. When designing symbols, the requirements of the entire project, as well as of the system, must be considered.

Development and testing of symbols takes time and patience. The development of a complete library of symbols that are tailored to the requirements of a particular office represents a considerable investment. Considered in this light, symbols are expensive. Fortunately, the payback is significant. Symbols do much more than just speed up the assembly of drawings. A wide variety of reports, schedules, and tables can be created automatically if the right symbols are in place. Even checking the drawings is simplified with a well-designed report. In many cases, manual procedures can be virtually eliminated. For example, the procedure for counting furniture can be reduced to a single step.

Once symbols are on a drawing, they also can serve as a conduit for capturing written design information. Written information resides in nongraphic files and travels along as symbols are placed on drawings. Such files can be designed to satisfy all at once several different reporting requirements, such as schedules, cost estimating, furniture and equipment takeoffs, and outline specifications. Symbols act like wiretaps; they eavesdrop on the design process.

Symbols are more than just parts of a drawing; they are tools for creating drawings and reports. In fact, they carry design information in a new form. Consequently, they are a reusable form of design document. New proprietary considerations emerge from this capability. For example, many real estate development organizations include architectural staffs, and CAD systems are being installed to assist these in-house design staffs. If design documents are supplied from a consulting firm on a machine-readable medium, are clients free to reuse symbols from such documents without further consideration? In this circumstance, it is time to revise the standard contract for services.

Chapter

8

Names and Numbers of Objects and Records

"If one analyzes the numerical work in a typical structural design, it is surprising to find how little is actual computation. The major part of the effort is in collecting and organizing the numerical data in preparation for mathematical operations for display and evaluation. In other words, much of what is normally called design is in reality bookkeeping." [LOGC70]

The most strategic piece of written information associated with a graphic object is its name. The name of an object is the pivot between graphic information shown on the drawing and nongraphic files, as well as other software applications; everything rests on it. Names designate specific graphic objects, which in turn represent design elements. Thus design elements are identified within either files of similar objects or files of written information. Names also designate specific records in nongraphic files. In many cases, the names of objects are stored in these nongraphic records.

Names of objects and records are used during many procedures for creating architectural documents on a CAD system. Copies of symbols are retrieved by name from files or libraries of symbols. A name such as DR36, for instance, identifies the symbol for a 3-ft-wide door. This uniquely identifies the particular lines, arc, and lettering that represent a door of a specific size and configuration. The same name combined with a serial or version number identifies the door when the system scans the drawing to create a door schedule (see Fig. 14-2).

Names of objects and records also coordinate design elements for different software applications. A software application may be written to recognize a set of names and pick those objects for specific kinds of analysis or graphic operations. Applications such as projections, three-dimensional modeling, facilities planning, mechanical, electrical, and structural design all refer to the same windows, walls, doors, columns, and furniture shown on the architectural floor plans. For example, on the two-dimensional floor plan, a name is used to retrieve the symbol for a window and place it in a wall. A three-dimensional image, however, will require line work that is different from the two-dimensional abstraction of a window shown on a plan. The plan drawing is simpler. The line work for the symbol must be replaced with the more complex symbol in the three-dimensional model. However, since the symbol for the window is named, the system knows what it represents. The system also knows where the window is located in relation to other graphic objects. With an operation referred to as "model building," the symbol name is compared with a list of corresponding three-dimensional graphic objects. The correct object is thus retrieved to replace the two-dimensional window symbol.

Although usually named with an alphabetic character string, graphic objects are also identified with numbers. For example, a graphic object stored in a data base of construction components is identified with a seven-digit number based in part on Construction Specifications Institute (CSI) specification numbers. With such a data base, the line work that represents an 8-in masonry wall is created by first entering a number, such as 08400.08. This identification number retrieves a specific pattern of lines, including a width and a pattern of crosshatching. This same number is used to identify the wall when we create an outline of specifications. It is used to create a construction cost estimate. Such a component number serves the same function as the name of an object.

Names also identify specific records and fields of nongraphic data. Nongraphic, or written, design information is located not by the data itself but according to the name of the record and field where the data is stored.

Names for graphic objects and names for nongraphic fields are also used in combination. In a typical nongraphic record, a field is set aside for symbol name or component number. This field is a *key field*. Names for key fields should be tracked in an officewide data dictionary. When the name of an object appears in a key field, it indicates that the written data in the record pertains to any graphic object with the same name. Thus, key fields which store names of objects serve as the connection between drawings and nongraphic files. Key fields allow information to be transferred between CAD drawings and a data base of indirect files or even between files remote to the CAD system.

The Importance of Naming Conventions

Although they are entered by operators, the names of objects, records, and fields are most commonly used by data processing equipment, not the human reader of design documents. The purpose of the name is to identify an object or set of objects within the computer system, and to allow items in files of similar objects to be sorted and tracked. As long as each object has a unique name, the order in which it is stored in a file does not matter. If the file is modified or if new objects are later inserted, the system can still find the correct object or record according to its name.

With manual filing systems, items tend to be stored by category: accounting in one file, drawings in another, and specifications in another. When a file is retrieved, the entire category is retrieved. Items in the file may be organized by date or in alphabetical or numerical order. Often, every item within a category is in the order that it was added to the file, in other words, in a random order. To retrieve an item, one scans through the entire file visually until the item is found. As long as the file is relatively brief, this method is satisfactory.

With computers, however, we have to be more explicit. The criteria for the search must be specifically defined ahead of time. Many operations require that the system locate a subset of design elements, e.g., a complete list of all the furniture items along with their pertinent written records. In this case, the names of the objects have the strategic role of telling the system which set of graphic objects to look for on the drawings, and the record and field names tell the system what pertinent nongraphic data is required. Names of objects and fields indicate the desired results of a selection process.

To perform such a search, every graphic object, record, and field must have an identifier that is not repeated with any other object, record, or field. Assigning a unique name to each graphic object and to every written record in a project data base is a significant undertaking. This should be an officewide process that involves the data base administrator. If the names and the initial records are designed with repetitive use in mind, the system can use one set of names to organize file after file. Once names are in place, the system can do more than simply find one item at a time.

The format of an object name or nongraphic field name affects the speed and convenience of information management. Consequently, the format of names must meet special requirements. For the design professional, these requirements are a relatively new problem. In the realm of traditional hand drafting, graphic objects are not named. The pair of lines that represents a wall, for instance, only exists on the drawings. They cannot be stored and retrieved; separate from the project, such lines are not graphic objects. Paste-up drafting systems, where decals of often-used drawing elements are stored and reused, are a possible exception. Even in this case, the names of such decals are usually not stored on a computer, and they cannot be connected directly to a file of written design information. Names of objects are not required outside of drawings on a CAD system.

The Format of Unique Names

The name of an object is composed of letters, numbers, or both. The rules for assembling the letters and numbers, their particular composition and meaning, are defined in a *format*. The format affects most of the data processing procedures with CAD documents. There are three basic requirements for the content and format of names used for an object:

1. Content must be unique to each object.
2. The name must be recorded with the object.
3. The field must use only characters or numbers with a distinct beginning and ending.

A name must not be repeated with any other graphic object; it is used only once. A reference to a graphic object can in turn be repeated any number of times throughout a project. In fact, the same graphic object can represent more than one distinct design element. A symbol for a desk can represent any number of different types of desks depending on manufacturer, finish, and color, for instance. However, to find each symbol and combine it with other data, the symbol must have only one name. When data fields are combined with the object, the complete version of a design element is described by extracting information from the nongraphic records.

By being stored in a nongraphic record associated with the object, the name is permanently connected to the graphic object. Without this connection, the symbol is only a collection of lines on the drawing, merely primitive objects, vectors, and points. Although the lines may make sense to the designer, for anything but the most elementary graphic procedures, such as move, copy, and delete, lines alone cannot be recognized by the system. To the system, primitive objects without a nongraphic record cannot be combined with other text files.

Finally, the name is a defined field with a specific number of characters. The system must know how long the field is and recognize its beginning and end. The particular content of the format is determined by the type of design element and by its use in the project. Requirements for names of door symbols are different from those for names of room boundaries, for instance. The capabilities of the data processing system in use will also affect the format of names for objects and fields. Anyone can enter names, but the system must be able to recognize them.

Brevity and Elegance

The name of an object or field not only must be original, it must also be brief. Although it represents a design element, the name does not have to completely describe the design element. The name should contain no more than the minimum number of characters required to identify a graphic object, field, or record. The fewer characters the better. There are several reasons for this recommendation.

Although unique names are primarily used by the system, the system is operated by humans. Usually, the operator is working with a series of similar graphic objects or records, not just a single object in isolation. All the door symbols, for example, are placed on the drawing in a single operation. As a result, symbol names are frequently listed in columns or tables. Symbol names are used extensively not only for creating drawings, but also for extractions, schedules, and reports. They are recorded many times throughout the files in a project data base. For example, the architectural space program, a furniture inventory, specifications, a cost report, and the update file use the same symbol name. Consider the problem of reading hundreds, perhaps thousands, of names in search of only a few. The format of the name should be considered in this context.

The format should be designed to reveal patterns within a list (Table 8-1). Organize names into subsets or families within a larger group. A pattern makes it easier to recognize a subset within the list and to detect errors and exceptions.

Use a one- or two-letter abbreviation to indicate, for example, the version or style of a design element. Combine abbreviations with one or more numbers to indicate the size or type of the element. For instance, the symbol for a 36-

TABLE 8-1 Typical Symbol Names

Symbol name	Description
	Doors
DR24	2′-4″ door
DR24E	2′-4″ door, elevation view
DR24S	2′-4″ door, section view
DR36	2′-6″ door
DR36E	2′-6″ door, elevation view
DR36S	2′-6″ door, section view
EG78	Double egress door, 7′-8″
FP30	Folding partition, 3′-0″ panels
FP40	Folding partition, 4′-0″ panels
PR50	Pair of doors, 5′-0″
PR70	Pair of doors, 7′-0″
SL40	Sliding door, 4′-0″
SL50	Sliding door, 5′-0″
	Plumbing Fixtures
DF14	Drinking fountain, 14″ × 11″
DF15	Drinking fountain, 15″ × 15″
LS20	Square lavatory, 20″ × 18″
LS24	Square lavatory, 24″ × 29″
LV19	Oval lavatory, 19″ × 16″
LV26	Oval lavatory, 26″ × 18″
TB60	Bathtub, 60″ × 32″
TB66	Bathtub, 66″ × 32″
WC1	Water closet, wall-mounted
WC2	Water closet, floor-mounted

in-wide door can be designated "D36" or "DR36"; a 36-in-wide window, "WN36." If letters are used in the first two or three positions in the field, the system can sort the list of names according to the alphabet into subsets of door, window, and other symbols. Such a list can be sorted in either ascending or descending order and broken down into logical families. To ensure correct sorting, only letters or only numbers should occur in the same position within a field.

Succinct names are also easier to enter. An operator is less likely to make a mistake when entering a name if it is brief, five characters or less. When entering data, the number of errors increases with the length of the field. The combination of two or three letters and two or three numbers can generate unique names for thousands of distinct graphic objects. For many frequently used graphic objects, a simple name of five characters or less can be remembered easily and entered without having to be looked up each time. Long names, eight characters and over, are difficult to read or remember and take longer to enter.

Remember that when the system sorts, searches through files, and combines various records of nongraphic data, the field names are the most frequently processed items of information. Files of long and complicated names require more processing time. Keep names for objects and fields as brief as possible. Within their own context, they should be elegant in the clarity and order they establish.

Finally, when assigning a series of names, provide some breathing room. Leave space so that additional items can be named and inserted at intermediate points as demand arises. It is not necessary to use an uninterrupted sequence of numbers or letters. Gaps or blank spaces can be left in the list between names for one family of objects and the next. If every number in a sequence is used, the list can be expanded only at the end. This assumes that the family or subcategory is complete.

ASCII Files

The format for names of objects and fields must be valid for operating systems and software other than the CAD system in use. In this regard, avoid the use of special characters and punctuation since systems and software may differ in how they sort items containing special characters. (Special characters include #, $, %, *, [or], / or \, > or <.) Special characters that are accepted on one system may not work on another. For example, DR/36 may be an acceptable symbol name on one CAD system. However, another system might ignore the / and identify this name as DR 36, DR36, or merely DR. None of these match the symbol name used on the drawing. When information about this door has to be transferred back and forth between systems, a conversion step will be required to translate one version of the name into the other. The problem can snowball as networks are developed that require data to be transferred between a greater variety of systems. However, conversion will be unnecessary if the names for objects and records are restricted to formats that are common to most systems.

In many systems, certain punctuation marks, such as periods, are also considered delimiters and are perceived as a mark for the end of the field. Some systems do not even allow punctuation in key fields.

Fortunately, almost all systems support the American Standard Code for Information Interchange, called "ASCII." With this code, information such as names of objects and nongraphic fields can be exchanged between separate computers. ASCII is a standardized 8-bit pattern for representing characters. Essentially, it represents the letters, both upper and lower case, the numbers and the punctuation found on the keyboard of a standard typewriter.

Although a system may support ASCII, it will likely work with another internal operating code altogether. ASCII includes the punctuation marks and special characters commonly used in the United States. Note, however, that the command syntax for punctuation marks and special characters varies with different internal codes—another reason to avoid the use of special characters. ASCII applies to data in text files rather than to software-specific internal operating codes. Character information can be exchanged between systems as long as each system can convert a file of text into ASCII. A file that has been converted is understood by any other computer system that supports ASCII.

Commas, periods, colons, and semicolons are easily mistaken for each other; once incorrectly entered, distinctions between such punctuation marks are hard to recognize and tedious to correct. Whole letters and numbers are easiest to read and transcribe.

Serial Numbers

Numbers that accompany design elements, such as door and room numbers on architectural drawings, are serial numbers. They can be thought of as a "street address" within the project. The *serial number* identifies a design element on the drawings in relation to similar design elements within the project.

A serial number serves a purpose different from that of the name of an object or nongraphic field. The serial number serves as an address of a design element within the set of project documents. It comes into being only after a graphic object, such as a symbol, has been retrieved by name and placed on the drawing. The serial number is an item count or schedule number; it can be a simple number or letter in ascending order. Serial numbers are used primarily in the context of the construction documents, that is, on drawings and in schedules. They are project specific data and are sometimes used in key fields in related nongraphic files. Since the serial number is not the primary identifier of a graphic object within the system, its format can be defined using existing graphic standards. Conventional techniques developed for traditional drafting—including abbreviations, keynotes, standard room names or numbers—are appropriate.

As in traditional drafting, the serial number can be filled in any time after an object is placed on the drawing. However, when an object is first created and filed as a symbol or component, and before it is used on a drawing, a field must be provided for the serial number in the nongraphic record attached to the object. The field can be empty and accompany a string of dummy letters that are grouped with the line work. It is important, however, to have the field for the serial number provided with the object before it is included on a drawing.

Unlike the name of an object, the serial number is not unique. It is more like a street address number that can appear again on the next street. In fact, the same serial number is found on different design elements.

Characteristically, the serial number is variable; it is likely to change. The choice of serial number depends on the position of a design element in relation to similar design elements. When the design changes, the serial number must change. For example, as modifications are made, rooms are often renumbered. Room 110 will become room 114. Because the serial number identifies a design element within a project, it is also less stable than the name for a graphic object.

Since it is variable, keeping track of the correct serial number on a drawing is a problem that does not lend itself to a single operation with a completely automatic data processing procedure. If the doors change, all the door members will have to be found and checked. To some degree, the correct serial number must be maintained with ordinary visual procedures for checking drawings. However, by finding and listing the objects on a drawing with the use of names for each object, the system provides significant help for finding and monitoring serial numbers.

The problem of coordinating a change can be simplified by limiting the family of design elements that a serial number applies to. For example, the door number can be assigned to match the room number. Room 100 has door number 100 and so on. For rooms that have more than one door, the door number is appended to the room number. Room 100 can have doors numbered 100.1, 100.2, etc. When a room is changed with this numbering system, only those doors that are part of the room, not every door on the floor, need to be found, checked, and renumbered.

Fortunately, several automatic techniques are available for changing serial numbers. The number for every copy of a symbol can be replaced with a global change. Serial numbers can be changed with the use of direct files that are part of the drawing. If the serial number is displayed on the drawing from nongraphic records, it can be revised indirectly by changing the nongraphic record.

Chapter 9

Boundary and Location

"That's the beauty and the power of computerization: ease of creation of original, potentially reusable data, convenient storage of reusable data, ease of manipulation of that data, and convenient retrieval. That's what systems are all about, and computers are the quintessence of systems." [STIT84]

On architectural drawings, boundaries are essential design information. Space is defined more precisely by boundaries than by walls, floors, or ceilings. Such physical elements must correspond to the structural forces in a building; boundaries are not so constrained. The boundary of a department can leap walls, even span several different floors.

A boundary is the geometric perimeter of an area. It is not the same as the area, but it is used to determine areas. Since a boundary is also a graphic object, it is given a unique name. A boundary's name is as important as its geometry, since it associates the boundary with an administrative designation, such as a room or department name. Typically, on CAD systems, the boundary of a room or department is selected so that the system can calculate an area. Areas are required when determining material quantities, an analysis referred to as "quantity takeoff." Areas are used explicitly in quantity takeoffs to estimate costs of floor, ceiling, and, when combined with ceiling height, wall materials. Boundaries serve administratively in quantity takeoffs to name the area being surveyed.

Boundaries are not often shown or drawn explicitly on the final plans. Nonetheless, they are used by virtually every design discipline. In space planning, a typical office building is organized into departments, each defined by a boundary. Mechanical design depends on an analysis of heating and ventilating zones, again defined by boundaries. Zones are also used in energy analysis, lighting design, and acoustical design. The same boundary may or may not serve more than one of these disciplines. Separate sets of boundaries are often required on the same plan.

Boundaries are used extensively in the fields of facilities and property management, which depend heavily on architectural drawings for determining boundaries. The net rentable area of a project is derived from boundaries that carefully distinguish between tenant areas and common areas. In some cases, such as condominium ownership, the boundary coincides with the distinction between the structural and the finish layers of material on walls. Vertical boundaries between multiple use spaces where structural elements must penetrate the spaces below, such as over a public right-of-way, can be very complicated and difficult to describe.

Fundamentally, boundaries define where design elements are located within a project. Only when objects fall within certain administrative boundaries is their location defined in terms other than *X* and *Y* coordinates. This is the main reason for designating boundaries and including them as components of an intelligent drawing.

Boundaries as Derived Information

Boundaries are implied by the location of design elements such as corridors, stairs, vertical shafts, columns, and walls. A single boundary can span many of these elements. Boundaries are derived from the line work of other graphic objects. For the most part, graphic objects represent distinct design elements, such as walls or columns, and thus a wall may or may not imply a boundary. In practice, graphics serve largely to verify the location of a boundary.

In general, the line for a boundary does not represent a design element nor does a design element represent a boundary; the boundary represents an administrative decision about what is included within a designated area. As a result, boundaries must be created on a drawing with additional operations other than those used for drawing the floor plan. After all, even the perimeter of a floor is usually not drawn separately and therefore is not available as a graphic object. A room becomes a positive space only when the walls have been drawn around it. The perimeter is perceived as complete after the walls, columns, and openings, which are located side by side along the perimeter of the floor, are all in place. Like the perimeter of the floor, boundaries are interpreted from the plan by visually inspecting the design elements and then superimposing a line on top of these elements. Practically, boundaries are added as named graphic objects after the walls are drawn.

Mechanisms for Drawing Boundaries

A casual inspection of the graphic capabilities available on CAD systems might lead one to expect a system to draw boundaries during the operation used for laying out walls. However, as outlined in the discussion above, the layout of a boundary is derived from the existing graphic aspects of a plan and from administrative decisions. As of this writing, CAD systems used commercially for production drafting do not recognize the boundary of a room as a distinct graphic unit unless it is drawn separately. A room derives its identity as a specific space from a collection of separate, preexisting design elements.

Once a floor plan is completed, several procedures can be used to create boundaries. When selecting a procedure, the purpose for which the boundaries are defined as well as the complexity of the plan should be taken into consideration.

The most direct approach is to trace over the existing line work on the drawing. At each wall, a decision is made as to whether the boundary is located on the face of, or at the centerline of the wall. At openings for doors and windows, the line spans the gap, corresponding with the face of the wall, the sill line, or the centerline. Finally, penetrations such as columns and shafts can be either traced in outline or spanned as required. This simplistic approach is usually the most efficient procedure for complex boundaries that include several spaces. It is also most appropriate when decisions must be made regarding what should be included within the boundary.

Graphic functions are available for creating trace lines from existing line work without having to redraw each line. Such a trace can be used as a boundary. Using one trace mechanism, an operator merely selects existing line segments. As the operator progresses, the system automatically spans the ends of any two selected lines where no line currently exists. This can be used to subdivide open spaces, such as lobbies or corridors, or to jump from one side of a wall to the next. Finally, when the initially selected line is reached, the boundary is closed. The operation is thus complete; the system has generated a new line coincident with each of the line segments that were selected. The new line is available as a boundary. This semiautomatic procedure is appropriate for boundaries that include several spaces where the perimeter coincides with design elements in a straightforward configuration.

Alternately, the system can generate a new line by tracing the perimeter of a room with a more automatic operation (see Fig. 9-1). Here, an operator indicates the room by either selecting a wall or merely indicating a point within the room. The system then traces the line work along the interior perimeter of the room. It turns in a clockwise direction at each intersection of two lines and thus automatically selects the next line. The trace does not turn when it reaches an opening. Gaps for doors and windows, if under a prespecified size, are ignored, and the line spans the opening. When the system arrives at the beginning point, the operation is complete. Again, the system has generated a new line. Finally, the system attaches a nongraphic record to the boundary line including a field for the boundary name. This mechanism

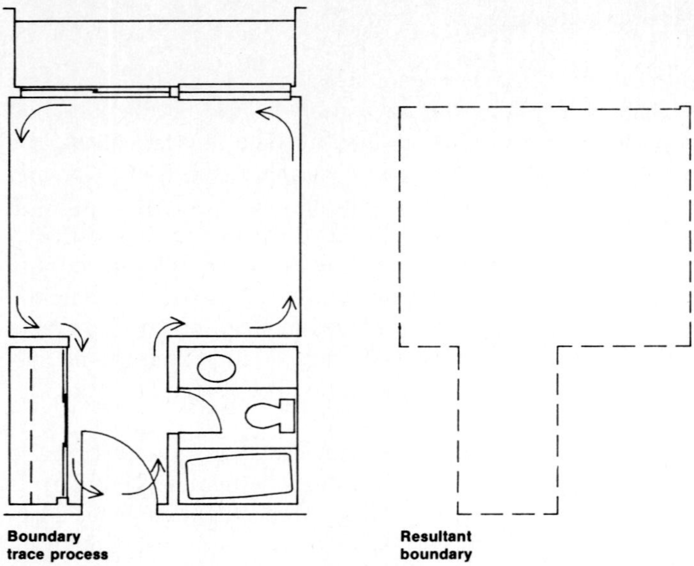

Figure 9-1 A representation of an automatic boundary trace operation and the resultant boundary.

is appropriate for the boundaries of spaces that have a straightforward and unambiguous configuration, such as individual rooms. No system is yet able to automatically trace the boundary of a suite of rooms or department in the same manner.

Regardless of how a boundary is generated, once it is complete, it should be possible to modify a segment of the boundary without disconnecting the segment from the adjoining lines that make up the boundary. This accommodates the inevitable revisions to a plan.

Whatever procedure you use, draw boundaries on a drawing layer designated solely for this purpose so that the layer can be suppressed when not needed. Since boundaries coincide in most cases with existing line work, color and pen number should be assigned so that boundaries are revealed in sharp contrast. Once a boundary is completed, attach a direct record to store nongraphic information. The record enables the boundary to be named and recognized by the system.

Once a boundary is in place on a drawing, the system can recognize the boundary and determine which objects are located within it. The ability to locate and count objects on drawings is the fundamental reason for installing boundaries. The task of creating boundaries is a relatively simple one compared with manually locating all the objects on an existing floor plan. Even the crude approach of tracing over existing line work can be done very quickly with basic CAD utilities for drawing lines. Determining objects' locations by hand is a time-consuming and omission-prone process. Moreover, design modification may call for reports for furniture or equipment inventories to be generated again and again. The ability to report automatically on the location of objects within boundaries will depend on the data processing mechanisms installed with both the boundaries and the graphic objects.

Automatic Nongraphic Records for Location

On some CAD systems, a new nongraphic field type that has a software mechanism for locating objects is included in records associated with any object on a drawing. These location fields, sometimes referred to as "positional properties," are examples of trigger fields which can direct the system to perform an operation on a drawing.

Location fields do more than simply indicate the *X* and *Y* coordinates of an object. Coordinates supply the system with an object's location, but an architect or facilities manager needs to know where objects are in terms of a project, that is, according to the administrative name of the space. Therefore, objects must be located not with cartesian coordinates but with designations such as room number, department name, cost center, zone, floor number, building wing, even building number or site.

If two requirements are satisfied—that named boundaries exist and that objects have records with location fields—the system can automatically determine locations and associate this information with objects on the drawing (see Fig. 9-2).

First, of course, the drawing must include boundaries. Graphically, a boundary is a continuous line that defines the perimeter of an area. The name of a bounded space, such as "Accounting Dept.," designates the admin-

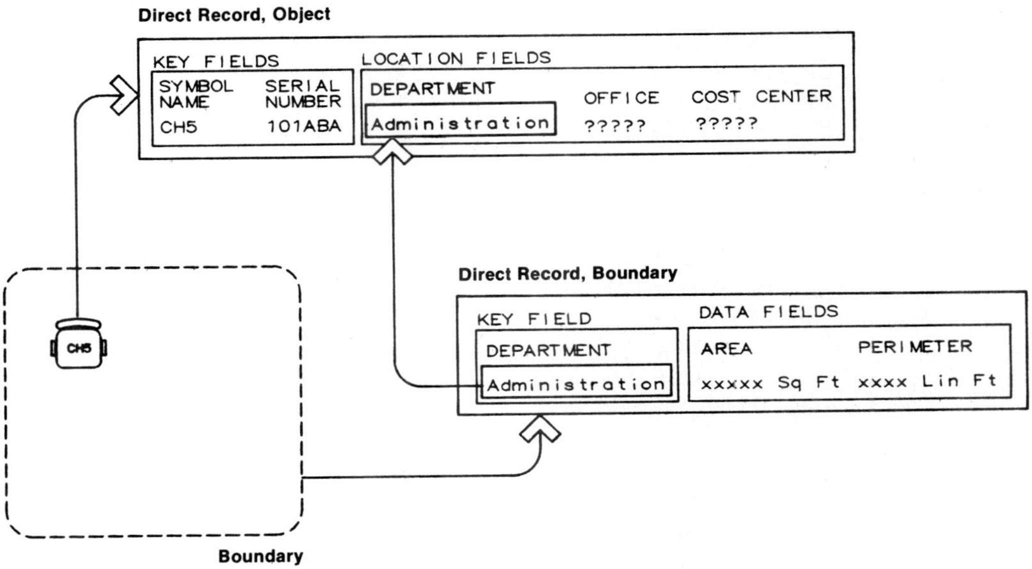

Figure 9-2 Direct nongraphic records attached to both a furniture symbol and a surrounding boundary illustrating the automatic transfer of the name of the department from the boundary to the symbol.

istrative location of objects that lie within it. Consequently, the line for the boundary must have a record attached carrying this nongraphic information in a field. The name of the field itself corresponds to the type of boundary. For instance, the record attached to a boundary includes a field that is named "Dept." The actual name of the department, in this case "Accounting Dept.," is stored in the field as a text string.

Notice the field's name, which can be modified by the operator, is distinct from the information it contains: the system searches first for a specific field name and only then for the information in the field. The advantage of this simple differentiation is that since the information in such a field is expected to change—when a department is relocated into an area that has a boundary named for another department, for instance, the differention allows the system to change the information in the field rather than the boundary itself. In another example, the organization of the facility may change—items that were originally located by installation contract group, such as by manufacturer or owner, are later designated by maintenance group. In this case only the name of the field need be changed to reflect the new administrative designation. Thus the same boundary line, an existing graphic object, is reused by simple but strategic renaming. Allowing the name of the field and the information it contains to be manipulated separately accommodates a broader range of change.

Remember that to determine locations automatically and to associate this information with objects on the drawing, a system must have both named boundaries and a second requirement. The second requirement applies to the graphic objects, such as symbols, that are to be located. As with boundaries, each object must have a nongraphic record. In this case, however, the record includes one or more trigger fields for location. Each trigger field is given a name that matches the name of the field associated with a boundary. In the boundary example above, a typical symbol for a desk would have a location field that is also named "Dept." Notice again, this is the name of the field only. These trigger fields contain no data at first. In fact, before the system searches for a boundary, location fields are empty until the automatic operation is completed.

The record attached to a boundary, by contrast, does not have to include a location field. However, names of both fields, one with the object and the other with the boundary, must match. Thus, the system knows what field to look for when it finds a boundary.

Once objects and boundaries that satisfy these requirements are assembled on a drawing, locations are determined by instructing the system to perform a search of the drawing. The search is triggered by inspecting, or querying, the nongraphic record that is associated with each object. When the search is triggered, the system creates a window around the object. It searches until it finds a boundary line that surrounds an object on all four sides (see Fig. 9-3). It then inspects the nongraphic record associated with the boundary. The system looks for a field name that matches the name of the location field associated with the object. When it finds such a field, the information stored therein is copied into or displayed in the location field

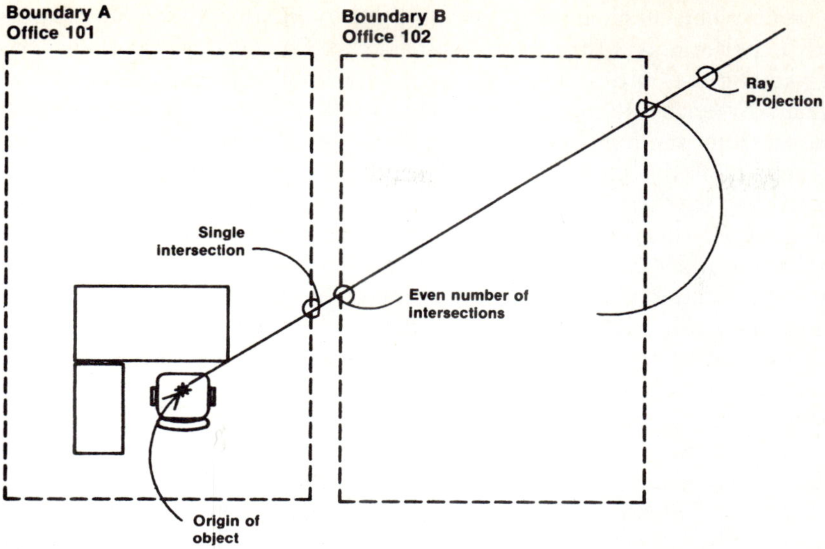

Figure 9-3 A ray projection from a furniture symbol confirming the location of the symbol within a particular boundary. Notice the single intersection with the surrounding boundary compared with the double intersection of a boundary that merely adjoins the one enclosing the symbol.

associated with the object. Thus the name of the location that was originally stored with the boundary, such as the department name "Administration," is associated with each object contained within the boundary.

Because the location is not a permanent characteristic, unlike other nongraphic information, such as manufacturer or color, it is not necessarily stored with the object. It is best displayed in the location field with the object but it should be stored elsewhere. With systems that retrieve the location from the boundary each time it is requested, location remains stored with the boundary. This technique of permanent association and temporary display, rather than permanent storage, is an extension of the concept of logical records which display information that is stored in an indirect file.

Once this information is associated with each object, reports can be generated listing objects and the names of boundaries where they are located.

Additional Capabilities of Location Fields

Storing the designation for location with the boundary rather than with the object has two advantages: objects can be relocated without modifying the nongraphic records, and boundaries can be renamed very easily.

As we know, objects are often relocated during the design process. They are relocated even more often once the project is completed—during the ordinary operation of a modern facility. When an object is relocated, or a new one is added, the record for location does not have to be modified in a separate operation. Since the information is displayed from a stable source, the boundary, adding objects or moving them to the new location will allow their records to perform as if they were automatically updated. The record displays the name of the current boundary once the modification is completed.

The advantages lie in the ease of revising a designated location without altering either the line work for the boundary or the record associated with each object within the boundary. In a simple example, office 110 may be renumbered to office 111, and any symbols located in office 110 are now in a new location. However, the furniture or equipment in the room can be located without actually having to move the objects or change their records. Since the location field reflects the name of the current boundary, simply change the name stored with the boundary and the objects will be identified with the correct location. A single change to one record can be reflected automatically with as many objects as necessary.

Since each location field refers to one specific boundary, more than one location field may need to be associated with each object. Consequently, objects can be located within several boundaries if each location field is given a name that corresponds to a separate boundary. While searching for a boundary, the system checks for other boundaries. For example, a desk can have location fields for room number and cost center as well as department. As a result, the same desk will appear under different subtitles when reports are sorted by different criteria such as room number, cost center, or department.

Boundaries also overlap. A heating and ventilating boundary will include several rooms but may overlap two or more department boundaries. In this case, an object may fall within some but not all of a series of boundaries. Still, no additional mechanisms or operations are required to determine the relationship of the object to the overlapping boundaries. While searching around the object, the system expects to intersect the same boundary on all four sides of the object. If any particular boundary is not found on all four sides, it assumes that the object lies either beside or outside of that particular boundary and the name of the boundary is not reported as a location for the object.

Any type of graphic object can be associated with a record that includes location fields. Not only symbols for furniture and equipment but boundaries also can have location fields. Boundaries are often included within other boundaries. Rooms, for instance, are usually included in larger boundaries, such as cost center, department, floor, wing, or even building. The location of these boundaries within each other is determined by including location fields in the records associated with each boundary. Thus, a report can be generated listing which offices are included in a certain department or which departments are included on a certain floor.

In conclusion, location fields are a specialized mechanism that use nongraphic information associated with boundaries to locate objects. The administrative name of the location is stored with the boundary and automatically displayed on demand with the objects. As a result, locations within a given boundary do not have to be stored or revised one at a time with each object. Also, since boundary names are stored as text records of variable length, the names are in a form that is meaningful to both designers and facilities managers.

Chapter

10

Parametric Design Functions

"A skilled design team will trace this maze of decisions to a satisfactory solution more quickly than an unskilled one. They will do this because experience has taught them to ask the right questions in the right order so as to limit the field as rapidly and as completely as possible. But insofar as this is true, both their questions and the order in which they are asked can be codified in the form of an algorithm. To this extent the design problem is algorithmic." [HEAT70]

Certain architectural elements are used on production drawings for project after project. Some CAD systems include utilities that create drawings for these elements as a whole according to parameters supplied by the designer. Doors, windows, even stair plans, interior elevations, and parking layouts can be drawn with parametric design functions. As we know, every construction project has doors, windows, and bathrooms. Most have stairs and elevator cores. From project to project the design of any one of these elements may vary considerably. However, in drawing such design elements, the same components are used regardless of variation. In a simple example, a 3'-0" single-swing door is drawn with an arc for the swing and a line, or a narrow rectangle, for the door. A single swing door of the next size requires only an arc and line of a corresponding radius and length.

Currently, two general techniques are available for creating frequently used drawing elements such as doors and windows. Most commonly, doors and windows are drawn at typical sizes, grouped, named, and stored as symbols. Thus, they can be copied and reused on one project after another. Another technique available on CAD systems, including personal computer CAD systems, is the parametric generation of the line work for doors and windows. Rather then copying existing line work in the form of a symbol, the system creates lines each time a door or window is requested. A parametric routine prompts the operator to enter the size of the door or window and indicate a location. The system then draws the line and arc for a door or the glass line and sills for a window.

With this latter technique, the system creates line work based solely on dimensions for the shape of the design element. The operator enters the size of an object, and the system draws it as directed. When applied to more complex drawing elements, this technique has been expanded to include functions that will create drawings for bathrooms and stairs, based on their dimensional parameters.

Parametric design functions, such as the stair and room layout functions illustrated in the following sections, are also referred to as "generative graphic procedures." With such procedures, the system creates the major part of a fairly complex drawing element in a single operation. The parameters are input ahead of time, in the form of a script. However, except for initiation of the procedure, the operator turns graphic operations over to the system, which executes them automatically. After the initial graphics are generated, additional editing is required to complete the drawing. See Chap. 16 for another example of a generative graphic procedure.

Two cases of parametric design functions, or generative graphics, are illustrated in the following sections. In the first, the system combines the parametric generation of line work with prerecorded symbols. The symbols are placed automatically in the same operation that generates line work around the symbol. Plan and interior elevation views of bathrooms are created with this operation. In the second case, the system creates all the line work for either plan or section views of a variety of stair configurations.

The Use of a Script for Parametric Design

In both examples, the parameters for the design are entered in a script. Scripts can be as simple as instructions to the system that are recorded in a macro. At the other extreme, a script can be the description of a procedure which is converted into software by programmers or systems analysts. In the examples in this chapter, the script is completed by filling in the blanks on a CRT screen menu. The completed screen thus makes up a script (Table 10-1). The system faithfully creates the drawing according to the dimensions, symbol names, pen numbers, intensities, and drawing layers that are specified in the script.

Creating drawings from a script uses an operation that is very different from those which would otherwise be required. Normally, a drawing such as

TABLE 10-1 Design Parameters Arranged in a Script[a]

Configuration		Handrails	Action
10 NARROW "U"			
11 FLR TO FLR HEIGHT = 10.00′	25 SEP = 8.00″	32 WDT = 1.50″	39 DRAW PLAN
12 FLIGHT WIDTH = 44.00″	26 LND = 3.00″	33 HGT = 32.00″	40 DRAW SECT
Risers	**Treads**	**Nosings**	**Stringers**
14 MAX = 7.50″	21 MIN = 10.00″	28 DPH = 1.00″	35 WDT = 1.50″
15 ACT = 7.50″	22 ACT = 10.00″	29 THK = 1.00″	36 HGT = 10.50″
16 QTY = 16	23 THK = 1.50″		

[a] Note: These parameters were used to automatically generate the stairs shown in Fig. 10-4. (Table supplied courtesy of CalComp, Anaheim, CA.)

an interior elevation would require several different CAD operations, including Draw, Move, Copy, Repeat, and Retrieve Symbols. Although each operation is fast, these operations are usually distributed among several different CAD functions; in other words, each is accessed through a series of separate screen menus. Thus not only does each operation take time, but moving between functions also requires separate steps and more time. In contrast, when the system works from a script the final results are created within a single function.

Specialized CAD functions that generate drawing elements faster than basic CAD graphic utilities are particularly valuable. What is even more important than their speed of operation, however, is that the parametric graphic functions that use scripts have value as design tools. Once a script has been completed, it becomes a preliminary design record. Scripts can be stored, recalled, and used over and over. Not only can a script be reused, it can be reused with minor variations. In contrast to standard CAD procedures, which take advantage of repetitive drawing configurations, parametric design procedures address unique, or nonrepetitive, drawing elements. Drawing elements, such as interior elevations, can include a considerable amount of line work. By editing the script one increment at a time and rerunning it, a great variety of interior elevations, each with subtle variation, can be explored.

Interior Elevations and Room Plans from a Script

In the first illustration of a parametric design function, the system combines the placement of symbols with the automatic generation of line work. Here, a script is used to record the dimensions between plumbing fixtures and the size of the counter, mirrors, and toilet partitions. Either plan or elevation views can be selected as output from this function (see Figs. 10-1 and 10-2).

Many rooms, such as commercial kitchens, institutional bathrooms, and laboratories, include a collection of equipment, fixtures, or accessories that are located in relation to each other. Such design elements are very often configured into rows, one beside the other. The room layout function illus-

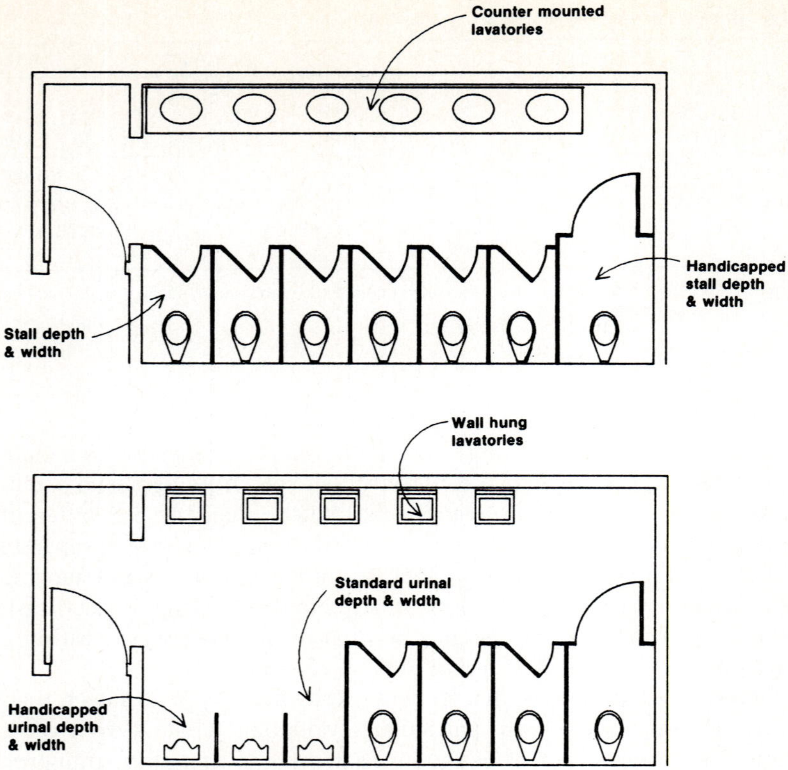

Figure 10-1 Plans of a men's room and a women's room created using a parametric design function. The walls are created separately, and each item noted can be modified from a script of design parameters. (*Courtesy of CalComp, Anaheim, CA.*)

trated here draws the elements in a room one wall at a time. First one row of elements is specified and laid out, then another. Symbols for the design elements are named, and the spacing between them is entered. Several symbols are included in the same script at once. The system then locates the symbols along a line in the drawing, such as a wall, which is specified by the operator. The location of the origin (see Fig. 7-8 for an illustration of an origin used with symbols.) of the symbol in relation to the rest of the symbol's line work determines both the spacing between symbols and the height of symbols shown in elevation views. Along with placing prerecorded symbols, the system creates new line work for the counters, mirrors, and toilet partitions according to the dimensions specified. The height and size of each of these is entered in the script.

Such a room layout function is versatile. It can be used for a variety of design problems: to generate parking configurations by first creating the parking stripe and bumper as a symbol and then specifying the distance between the parking stalls; to generate exterior elevations by working with symbols for windows, columns, and fenestration. Certain interior elevations, such as bath and utility rooms in a hospital, include a dozen or more accessories. With the use of a script, a system can locate and show each accessory in relation to other design elements in the room more easily than if the accessories were placed on the drawing one at a time (Fig. 10-3).

Drawing interior elevations that include many objects is time-consuming. Several cabinets, accessories, and fixtures have to be precisely located on up to four different elevations for each room. By editing and reusing a script, however, different versions of an interior elevation are easily created with minor variations from a basic configuration. Editing is accomplished either by entering new points for the start and end of the layout or by entering a new dimension for any of the parameters. Thus, an optimum design can be achieved without the tedium of placing and adjusting many objects one at a time. Exceptions to a standard room plan or interior elevation, which are caused by an unusual condition, such as a column that only occurs in a few cases can be generated as a temporary modification to the script for the basic room.

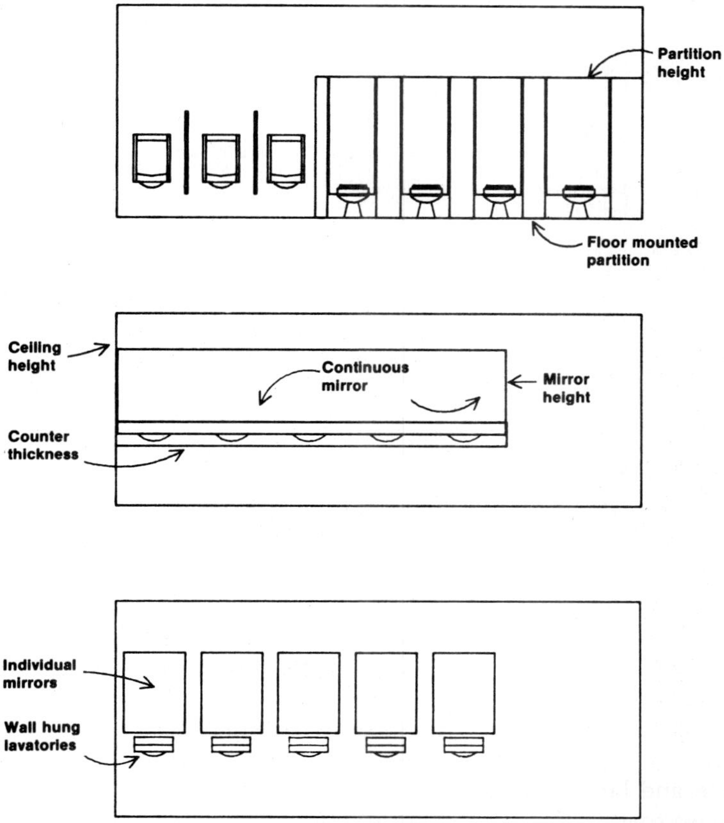

Figure 10-2 Alternative interior elevations created with a parametric design function. Items noted can be modified from a script of design parameters. (*Courtesy of CalComp, Anaheim, CA.*)

Accessory Location Table

	SUB UTILITY	NURSES STATION	PATIENT TOILET	WHEELCHAIR TOILET	NURSES STATION	SOILED UTILITY	NURSES LOUNGE	NURSES TOILET	CPR/CARDIAC TRTMNT
TPD			A4K	A4K				A4K	
PTD	D4C	D4E	L2J	D2J	D4E	D2E	D2E	L2J	D8E
PTD/R									
FND									
FNR									
SD	K3H	K4H	K1H	D3P	K4H	K2H	K2H	K3G	K8H
SCD			L1D	D3D				L3D	
MIR/S			J1A					J3A	
MIR/C									
MIR/WH				D3A					
GB-1			C4L						
GB-2				C7M					
RH			H6B	F6B				H6B	
TB									
SOAP									
GB-3									
GB-4									

Accessory Abbreviations:

TPD	Toilet paper dispenser
PTD	Paper towel dispenser
PTD/R	Paper towel dispenser/receptacle
FND	Feminine napkin dispenser
FNR	Feminine napkin receptacle
SD	Soap dispenser, N.I.C.
SCD	Seat cover dispenser
MIR/S	Mirror with shelf, 18x24"
MIR/C	Mirror, size as noted
MIR/WH	Wheelchair mirror, 18x36"
GB-1	Grab bar, straight, 48" UON
GB-2	Grab bar, "L" type, 54" UON
RH	Robe hook
TB	Towel bar, 30" long UON
SOAP	Soap dish
GB-3	Grab bar, straight, vert. 24"
GB-4	Grab bar, "L" type, 18x24"

General Location

1 North wall
2 East wall
3 South wall
4 West wall
5 1 per stall
6 On door
7 West & South walls
8 East wall, each sink
9 See elev. per A5. 10
10 North & East walls
11 North & West walls

Vertical Location

A+24" to Center Line (CL)
B+28" to TOP
C+33" to CL
D+40" to BOTTOM
E+42" to CL
F+54" to CL
G+60" to CL
H+70" to CL
J+74" to TOP
K 4" CLR, above LAV. or SPLASH
L+52" to BOTTOM
M+44" to TOP
N+56" to TOP

Horizontal Location

A Center on lav. or sink
B Center on door
C Center on wall
D Center on toilet
E CL 18" to RT of lav. CL
F CL 18" to left of lav. CL
G CL 9" to RT of lav. CL
H CL 9" to left of lav. CL
J CL 14" from fixture wall
K CL 40" from fixture wall
L 6" CLR. from fixture wall
M Corner mounted
N CL 24" from fixture wall
P CL 12" to RT of LAV. CL
Q CL 12" to left of LAV. CL
R See elev. per A5. 10
S CL 28" to left of sink CL
T CL 24" to RT of sink CL

Figure 10-3 A schedule of accessories for hospital utility rooms. Note: Organization and information content are similar to that used in Table 10-1; interior elevations similar to those in Figure 10-2 could be generated by automating such schedules.

Parametric Design of Stairs

As in the automatic creation of the graphics for a door, the plan or even section drawings of stairs take form according to dimensions entered in a script (Figs. 10-4 and 10-5). Unlike the comparatively simple drawing for a door or window in plan, however, more parameters are required for a stair. Some of these are entered directly, some are calculated by the system, and still other parameters are derived from a file of values reflecting the requirements of a building code.

For the stair drawings shown, the floor-to-floor height, the tread width, and the tread depth are entered. The number of risers and the actual riser height are calculated by the system according to a standard formula for the relationship among tread depth, floor-to-floor height, and riser height. Finally, the handrail height and thickness are entered. Several different stair configurations, such as straight, L-shaped, wide or narrow U-shaped, even circular or

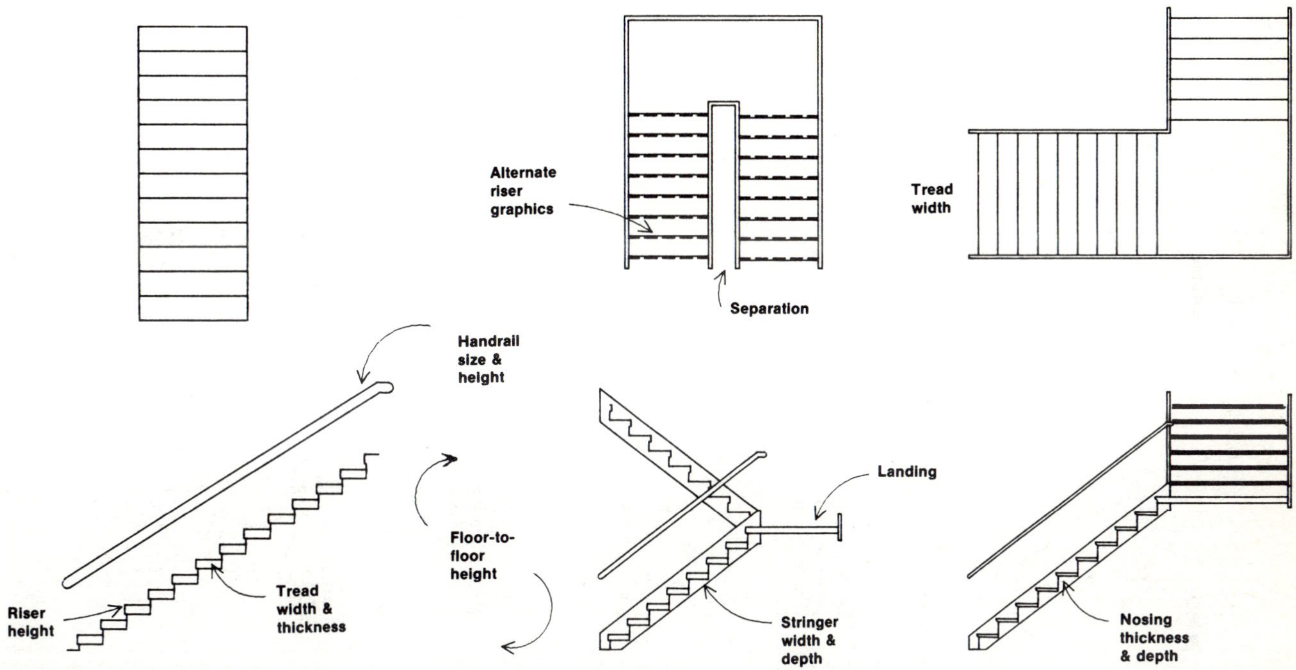

Figure 10-4 Alternative stair configurations created with a parametric design function. All the parameters labeled can be modified from a script of design parameters (see Table 10-1). (*Courtesy of CalComp, Anaheim, CA.*)

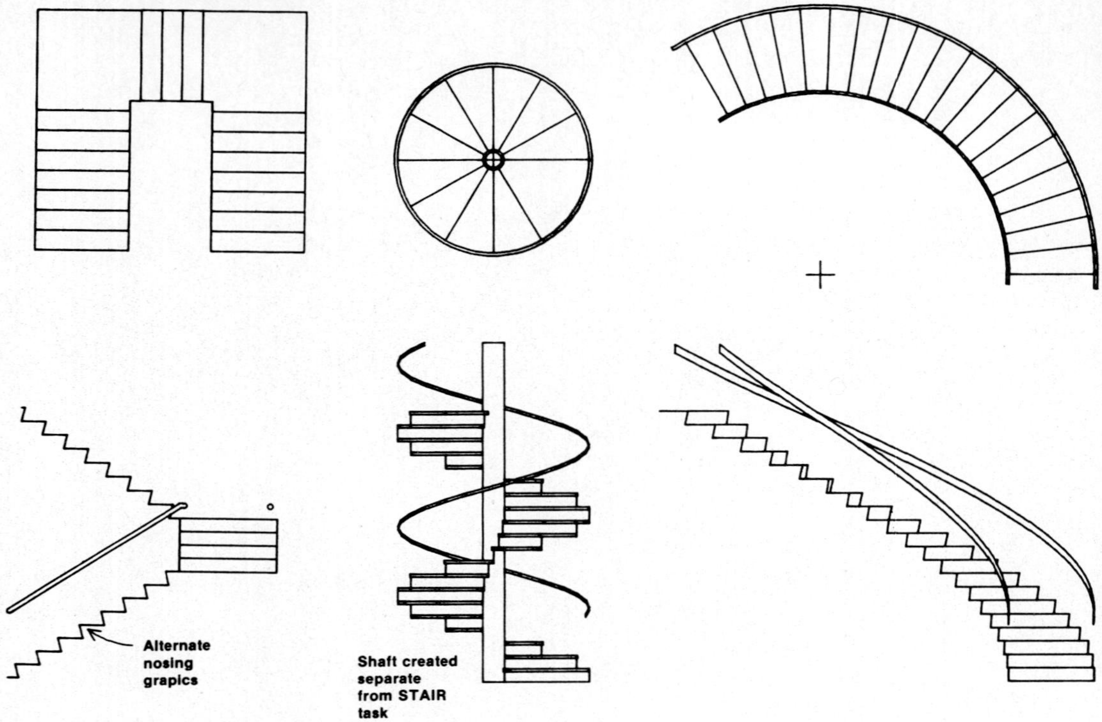

Figure 10-5 Alternative stair configurations created with a parametric design function using the same script of design parameters used for Figure 10-4—only the stair configuration is modified. (*Courtesy of CalComp, Anaheim, CA.*)

winding, can be drawn using minor variations to the script. Also, section drawings are created from the same script. The operator has only to select the drawing type and initialize the process.

The design of a stair must satisfy requirements specified in building codes. Stairs are both an essential safety device and, if poorly designed, a conspicuous hazard. The parametric stair design function shown here uses the system to test the safety of the stair by comparing the dimensions in the script with allowable dimensions that are stored in a preexisting file. Maximum and minimum values for the sizes of different parts of the stair are defined and stored ahead of time in a file of code requirements. Riser height, nosing and tread depth, distance between landings, even handrail height, are checked by the system before the drawing is created. If dimensions entered by the operator fall outside of the allowable range, an error message is displayed, and the system will not generate any graphics until the dimension has been corrected.

In this example, the requirements of several different building codes were recorded in the file. As we know, different geographic locations use different building codes. Moreover, different requirements apply to buildings with different occupancy loads. A stair that serves a building with ten occupants could be unsafe in a building with hundreds of occupants. Therefore, separate records are used in the building code information file to store a series of requirements for differing code specifications. The location and the occupancy load determine the relevant record. Regardless of how the script is changed, the system refuses to draw a stair whose dimensions exceed those specified in the relevant code record.

The automatic design of stairs points toward a liability issue. In this example, the system is being used to test the validity of a design according to specific code requirements. Nonetheless, the operator has general control over the design of the stair. Except for the simple formula which relates floor-to-floor height, tread depth, and riser height, no algorithms are used to create the drawing of the stair. Since the operator controls both the file of code specifications and the dimensions that are entered on the script, liability for the resulting stair design remains with the architect. The system serves as a mute drafter that checks the input yet follows the operator's commands.

Parametric Design—Where Can It Lead?

It is intriguing to consider where the development of parametric design functions might lead in the field of architecture. Given the current state of computer development, only certain design problems lend themselves to commercially practical automated solutions. Since they include the predictable reuse of a limited number of design elements, bathrooms, stairs, and parking lots are obvious applications for parametric design functions. However, if several scripts could be strung together, the possibilities would be boundless. A series of scripts could generate drawings for building elements even more elaborate than stairs: procedures for the layout of entire rooms full of equipment, such as hospital rooms or laboratories, could be described and automated.

The use of parametric design functions points toward the development of artificial intelligence in architecture. It has been demonstrated, for instance, that a computer can lead an operator through a series of questions about the design of the fire safety system in a building. The answers result in a recommendation by the computer for a fire safety system, such as a sprinkler system. The solution could be drawn automatically if the questions included dimensional parameters of the space.

This example can be carried further. An operator could be led through a script about an entire floor plan. Using the operator's responses, the computer could generate the basic configuration of the building as well as each of its systems. With this development, floor plans that are partially complete could be created in a semiautomatic procedure.

However, the practical application for this development may be in the area of facilities management rather than in the design of new buildings. There is a growing need for plans of existing facilities, called "as-built drawings," which are resident on a CAD system. Usually, having an experienced design professional prepare as-built drawings for buildings that are long since complete is too expensive to be practical. Facilities staffs do not always have the capability to perform this task. For example, junior drafters may not have the experience to recognize what building components need to be drawn and which can be ignored or simplified when recorded.

A parametric design function which addresses complete building systems could conceivably draw entire floor plans automatically. A question-and-answer script for each major system in a building could be composed according to generally used principles of design. A script that is based on the overall dimensions of a building and the material and age of its structural system, for instance, could be used for the layout of structural elements such as columns and load bearing walls. Similarly, circulation systems, including corridors, stairs, and elevators, could be defined in response to questions about the occupancy and size of the facility. Each subsystem, such as the lighting, mechanical, communication, and fire safety systems, could be explored in a similar manner. Different scripts could apply to different types of buildings.

The script would be composed so that only key dimensions, not extensive measurements, need to be verified in the field. Based on the response to questions, the system would produce drawings that would be largely complete. The result would be floor plans that portray a configuration of elements within the building that is highly probable based on generally used principles of design. The remaining tasks would be to confirm conditions in the field and to correct the basic drawing output from the system.

The drawings that result from such a procedure do not have to meet the standards of construction documents. Drawings that satisfy the operational requirements of facilities management are simpler than documents used for construction. Moreover, if the major part of an as-built drawing could be created in this way, facilities managers would have the drawings needed without the expense of reproducing the architect's labors or the tedium of field-measuring every item in the building.

Section 3

Written Design Information

The first half of Sec. 3, specifically Chaps. 11 through 14, focuses on computer-aided design (CAD) systems which support addressed attributes, are data base–oriented or are interfaced with data base management systems, and include distributed processing (see Table 3-1). (Admittedly, this combination of capabilities is not available with all CAD systems.) Together, these capabilities enable nongraphic information to be not only connected to objects on drawings but also transferred between the CAD system and related data processing equipment such as personal computers and word processors. Chapters 15 and 16 include illustrative cases derived from architectural space planning. Section 3 discusses how CAD systems can work in concert with data base management and communication tools.

Chapter

11

A Structure for Written Design Information

Architect: "How does the system know if the wall has a window in it?"

Programmer: "Simple. The computer assigns the same number to both the wall and the window."

Architect: "How does it know what number to use?"

Programmer: "It stores the next number in a record associated with a line."

Architect: "What line?"

Programmer: "Don't worry. It's associated with a line that has no color and a length of 0 created automatically in the middle of the drawing."

As a parallel to the visible and nonvisible structures of a graphic object, intelligent drawings include visible and nonvisible structures for written information. Some of the structure can be seen directly on the drawings. Most written design information, however, is stored in files that are organized according to data base principles. Two aspects of the data processing environment determine how written design information is organized: first, how the information is connected to a drawing; and, second, where the information is stored.

Conceptually, written design information is connected to a graphic object on a drawing in one of two ways:

1. Written design information can originate on a drawing and exist as lettering like any other line work.
2. Written design information can be associated with a graphic object in a data base of direct and indirect files (see Fig. 14-1).

As we know, different versions of written information appear in different locations among design documents. With automatic graphic processing, information may be associated with project documents in several different ways. Written information can be stored either on the CAD system in use or on other computer systems that are connected to it. Four basic locations in a data processing environment that can be used to store written design information are:

1. On a drawing, grouped with the actual line work, like traditional lettering.
2. In a direct file that is part of the drawing.
3. In indirect files that are not part of the drawings but are stored on the CAD system.
4. In files that are transferred from other systems and are stored separately from the CAD system in use.

After a discussion of written design information, data bases, and data capture, this chapter explores the advantages and disadvantages of storing written design information in these different locations.

Reading the Drawings—A Tradition

Despite of the predominance of drawings as construction documents for planning and assembling buildings, questions arise that only a written description can satisfactorily answer. How much space is needed? What is the building made of? Where is each design element located? What size is it? How is it installed or connected? And even, how is it maintained? To answer these questions, the construction design professions have developed a variety of written documents, along with written information on drawings, that convey what is essentially nongraphic design information. Architectural space programs, drawing notes, door and hardware schedules, specifications, furniture or equipment inventories, construction cost estimates, and a variety of other documents are all written descriptions of a project. With the drawings they explain a project for the purposes of planning, approval, construction, and occupancy.

Written information can be as simple as a scale or as complex as a construction specification. Without it however, drawings are incomplete. Unless each design element shown on a drawing is accompanied by a dimension and a complete description it is just a collection of lines. In fact, designers identify lines with text. For instance, to be unambiguous, property lines include a written compass bearing and length. Similarly, every part of a building, from the entire footprint to the smallest detail, must be named and dimensioned;

every room, window, and door must be numbered. Without written design information, the drawings cannot be read for purposes of approval, bidding, and construction.

As building projects become more complex, and as they include more systems, more materials, and a wider variety of construction techniques, more written information must be provided along with the drawings (see Figs. 11-1 and 11-2). The increased complexity of design documents makes it more difficult to hold the correlations among documents in our heads.

In the field, drawings explain where the parts of a project are laid out and how materials are assembled. On the job site, the drawings must more or less stand on their own. Therefore, a balance must be struck between information that is presented on each drawing, both graphic and written, and information that must be looked up in other parts of the documents.

In order to be understood and used conveniently, architectural drawings must be uncluttered; they must not include too much written information. After all, the essential information on drawings defines the spatial relationships among various design elements. Architectural drawings indicate where things are located and how they fit together. Therefore, information that is not concerned with location, such as descriptive information, should be as brief as possible. To satisfy this requirement, drawing notes are composed with incomplete sentences which make extensive use of abbreviations. They have been developed into a special syntax for construction drawings, keeping the amount of writing on the drawings to a minimum.

As a general rule, drafters try to avoid redundancy when adding notes to drawings. As drafters, we learn that each item should be noted only once in the correct place. For example, for horizontal surfaces, the rule is that dimensions and notes are shown on the plans; dimensions and notes for vertical surfaces are shown on elevation drawings. However, this rule is an oversimplification, because a thorough and well-organized description of a construction project requires that design information be repeated in different versions throughout a set of documents. With each door, for example, only the door number is shown on the plan. The number is repeated in the door schedule. There it is combined with a description of the door that includes information about size, material, finish, frame, and hardware for the door along with further references to door details. Some level of redundancy is required to coordinate these different versions of information. *Keynotes*, the substitution of a number for an entire note on construction drawings, are, for written design information, the ultimate form of brevity. The keynote number is used as an index to a more complete table of notes shown elsewhere. Keynotes suggest the automatic connections that are possible in a computer environment. As with keynotes, design information is often expanded in another part of the construction document set.

Written information can be streamlined on drawings if more complete information is provided somewhere else. A complete description of a design element emerges by combining these separate descriptions. The door schedule, for instance, does not make sense without the plan indicating where the doors are located. Door schedules are usually included as part of the draw-

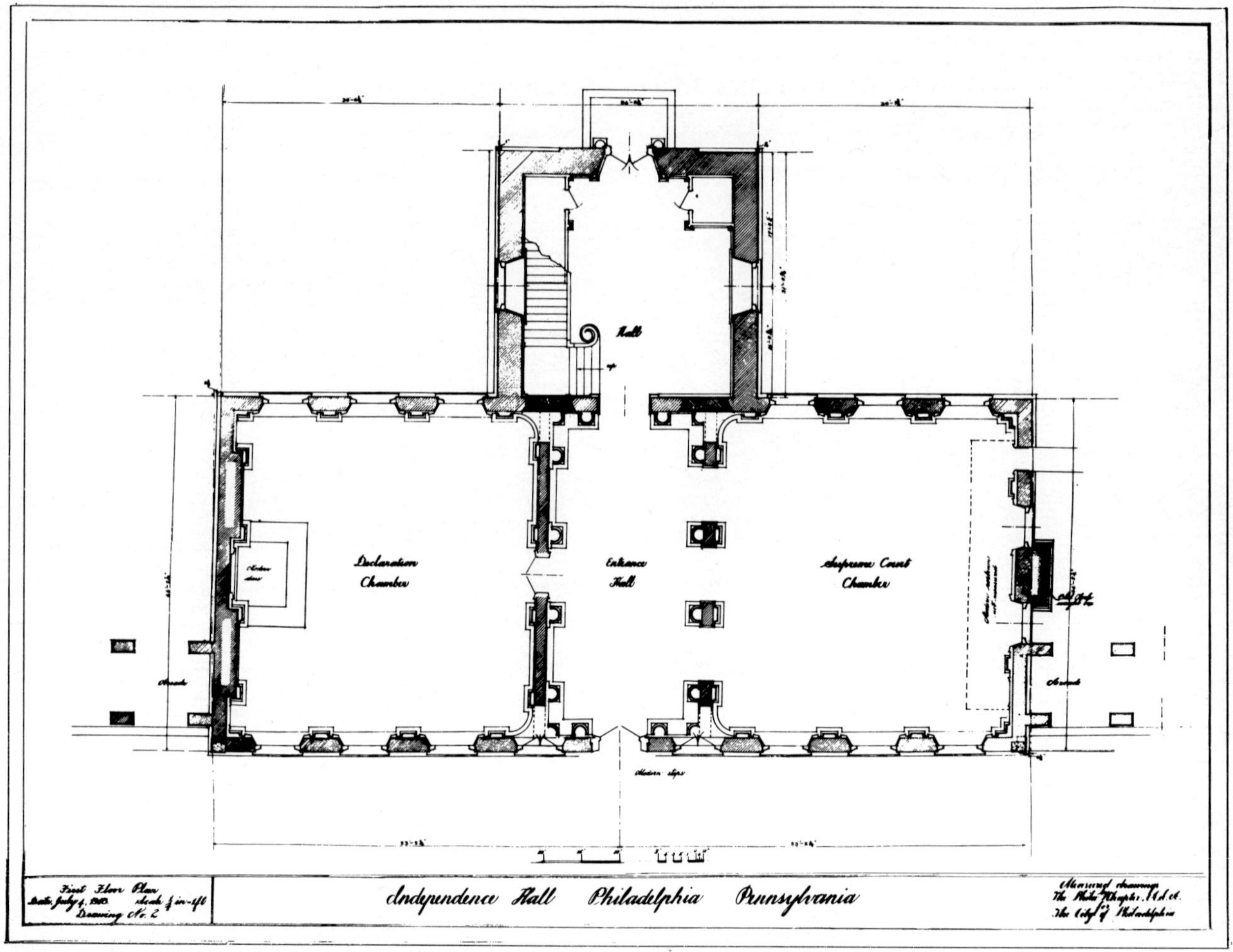

Figure 11-1 Floor plan of Independence Hall showing the absence of symbols and the scarce use of non-graphic information on architectural drawings in the last century. (*Reprinted with permission of C. Gray and J. Boswell,* Blueprints, 1981, Simon & Schuster, NY.)

ings. Architectural space programs, specifications, cost reports, and furniture inventories are another matter. Information in an architectural space program, for instance, is rarely referred to on the architectural design or construction drawings. However, the space program both names and describes design elements, such as rooms and furniture configurations, that are shown on the drawings. Unfortunately, although the contents of drawings and other documents are always related to one another, the connection between separate descriptions of design elements is purely visual. We rely on the fact that the name of an element, such as a room name, refers to the same thing wherever the name appears. The name, however, is often reentered for separate documents; it is not usually derived from the same source.

Help Reading the Drawings

With traditional drafting mediums, the connection between different parts of the documents, between line work on a drawing and written information, exists only in the human mind. The serial number or name shown with a symbol is repeated on drawings of details and schedules, for instance. In both places, it is interpreted as a reference to the same design element, and thus the connection between documents is ensured. However, this interpretation relies solely on our visual and mental powers—we must remember the connections. With intelligent drawings, however, the relationship between a graphic object on the drawing and text information in other documents can be defined so that these separate items of information are in fact connected. You can create an automatic link between a collection of lines on a drawing and any item of written design information. As a result, information can be transferred from a single document, as a source of information, to other documents.

At last, CAD systems can read the drawings along with us. The purpose of intelligent drawings is to ensure that each reference to a specific design element—in the original space program, drawing notes, schedules, specifications, construction cost reports, and facilities reports—is understood by the system to be derived from the same source. Or, vice versa, we must also be able to find the original graphic version of a design element, such as the symbol for a specific item of furniture, from data stored in fields that are part of a nongraphic file. To accomplish this, all the documents must be connected.

Most CAD systems are supplied with mechanisms that create relationships between drawings and other files. However, such mechanisms usually are not tailored to the documents that are created in a design office. Data processing mechanisms that can be customized by a user are referred to as "hooks." In most systems, the hooks are in place, but the connections are not always complete. Moving information between documents is the objective. Finding the right connection and using it correctly may require additional development work before project work begins.

Such development requires a team approach including the designer and a system manager or head of computer operations. First, a specific relationship

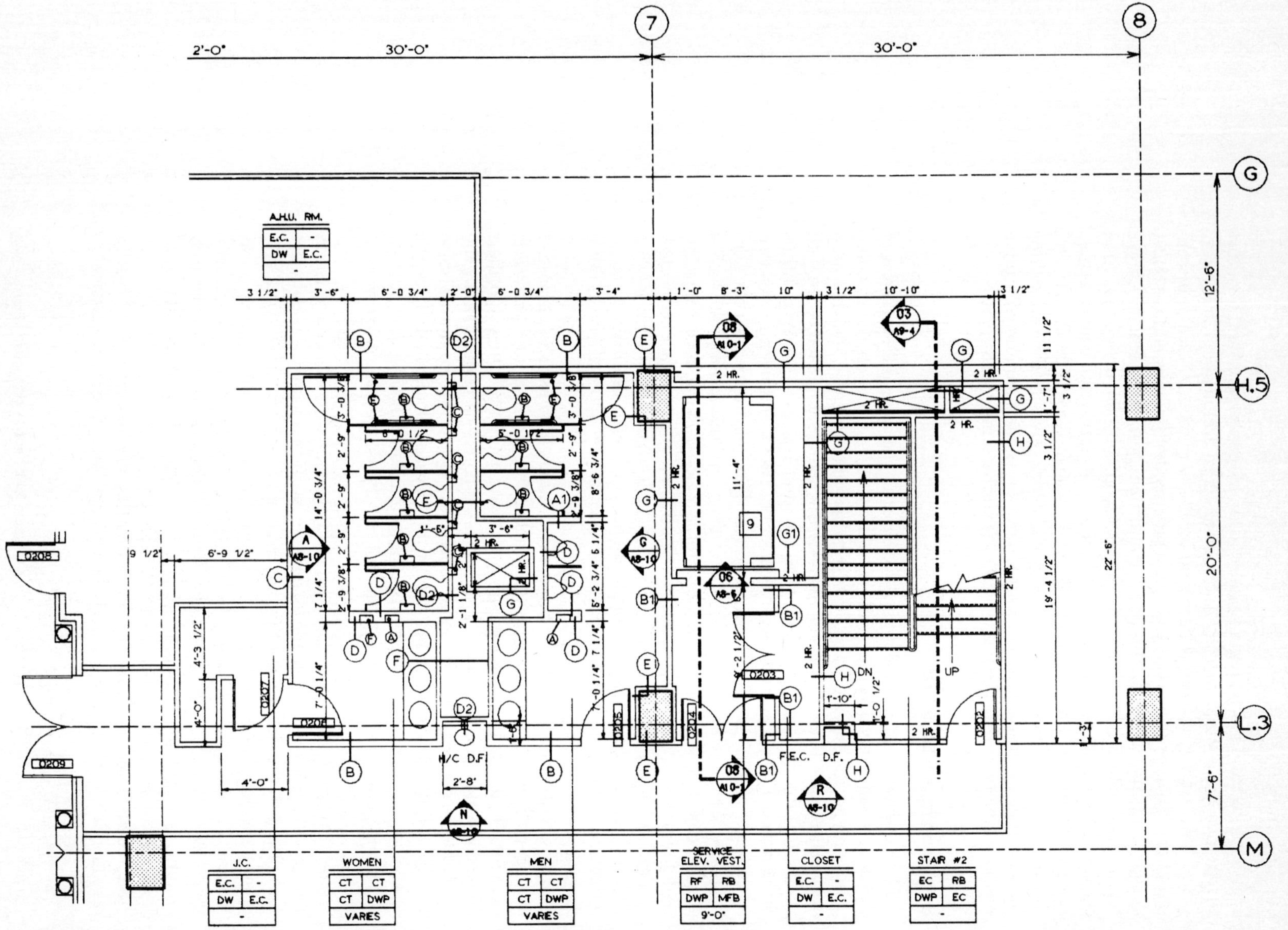

7
8
G
H.5
L.3
M
2'-0"
30'-0"
30'-0"
12'-6"
20'-0"
7'-6"
22'-6"
19'-4 1/2"
A.H.U. RM.
E.C. -
DW E.C.
J.C.
E.C. -
DW E.C.
WOMEN
CT CT
CT DWP
VARES
MEN
CT CT
CT DWP
VARES
SERVICE ELEV. VEST.
RF RB
DWP MFB
9'-0"
CLOSET
E.C. -
DW E.C.
STAIR #2
EC RB
DWP EC
2 HR.
UP
DN
F.E.C. D.F.
H/C D.F.
0202
0203
0204
0205
0206
0207
0208
0209

between design documents must be defined in data processing terms so that it can be performed with the mechanisms available on the computer systems at hand. It is the designer's responsibility to describe the design procedure. Without a complete specification, the system manager or programmer will not know what you are trying to accomplish. Turning hooks into refined connections that serve the design process requires planning, preparation before design project work, and some understanding of data processing techniques.

Capturing Design Information

The entire design process can be characterized as moving from comparatively little information about a project to more thorough and, finally, as drawings and documents are finished, complete information. We start with a sketch on the back of an envelope and end up with hundreds or thousands of drawings and documents. Principles for making connections between written information and drawings are formulated by observing when design information is first created and how it is used later. By focusing on this aspect of the design process, we can decide how best to capture design information in a data processing medium.

During each phase in the design process, new information is generated. It is combined with information from previous phases, and at each step, recorded in the project documents. Some written information exists before the project drawings are started. It evolves and matures along with the drawings. At many points along the way, new information is captured. If the system is set up correctly, the data will already be organized into the right segments for use during succeeding stages in the design process.

If you stand back far enough, you realize that written design information is generated and developed before, during, and after project drawings are created. This process spans a considerable length of time. Early information can be reused in documents that are created later (see Fig. 11-3). For example, space projections are created before design work begins, but they include room names and furniture configurations that must also be used on the drawings. Schedules are created along with the drawings, including information that also appears in the specifications. Complete specifications and cost estimates are finalized some time after the drawings are complete and must reflect graphic information on the drawings. Finally, facility reports and furniture schedules are created after construction has begun, long after the architectural drawings are complete. Once again, these documents reuse information that was originally captured during an earlier phase in the design process.

Many tools are available for data capture: CAD systems, word processing

Figure 11-2 Partial plan of a contemporary drawing for a modern high-rise. Note dense concentration of symbols and references to other documents—contrast this with Fig. 11-1. (*Courtesy of Skidmore, Owings, and Merrill, Houston, TX.*)

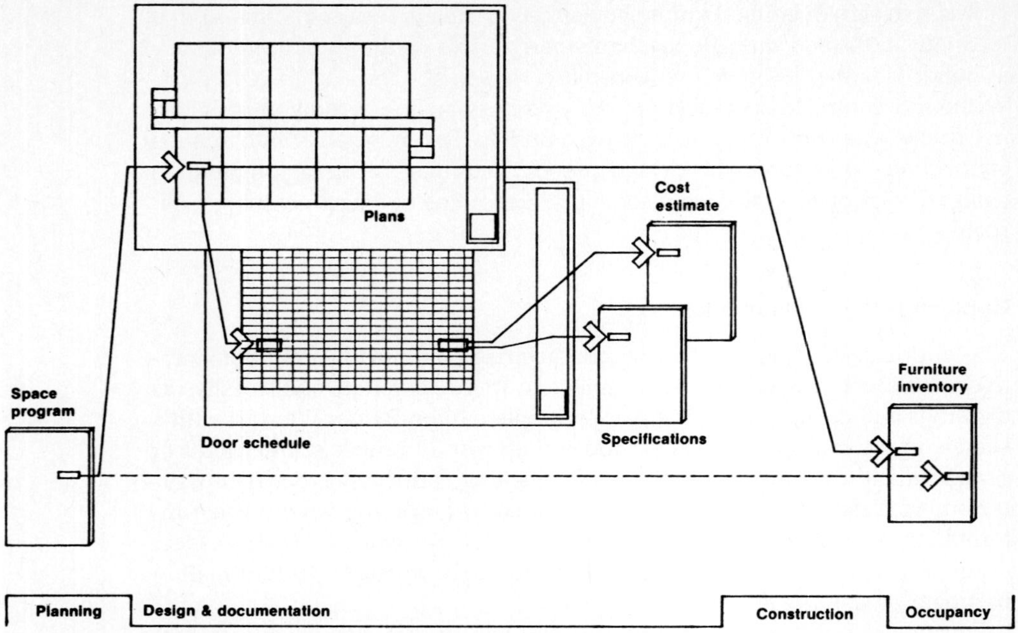

Figure 11-3 A representation of the reuse of nongraphic design information during the life of an architectural project. Note: At different phases the same information, such as the room name and number, appears in several different documents.

equipment, tape recordings, and even video recordings. However, converting information into a project document requires more than just turning on the equipment. Procedures used for capturing information must be as refined as the tools themselves.

The most efficient data capture procedures not only store information, they sort and refine it at the same time. Information must be categorized, labeled, and identified while it is being recorded. The objective is to break down and segment the information so that it can be automatically reused later in the design process. For example, when the architectural space program is first created, it is stored with the use of word processing equipment. If this information is captured efficiently, it is stored with more structure than a simple text file keyed to a room number. Later, parts of it, such as room names and furniture configurations, can be reused on the architectural drawings. (See Chap. 16.) When design information is first generated, it is important to look beyond the original document for possible uses of the information in other documents.

Analyze the task and select the most appropriate method. The procedure must be timely and unobtrusive; it should present the least possible interference with the design process. If done correctly, no additional work will be required during the design procedure and the major content of the document will be conveniently recorded. At the same time, information that is critical to identifying the data must also be stored, and every step in the procedure used for storing the information must be reviewed. For example, when meeting notes are transcribed from tape recordings to text files with word processing equipment, add key words to identify items of information according to different design topics.

Many design documents are created outside the CAD system. In fact, most written documents are assembled neither on the same system that creates the drawings nor by the same person. However, as long as part of the written file includes a reference or hook to a graphic object on the drawings, this separation can be bridged.

When the written information is created, use key fields to reference it to the graphic objects. The structure of the text file is designed ahead of time, and this design must carefully specify the form and character of each record and field in the file. When designing the file, provide space for key fields to accommodate the connections to objects on drawings you have in mind. Once the file and its key fields are specified, design information can be captured and connected to a variety of documents in a single operation.

Meanwhile, on the drawings, connect a nongraphic record containing an identifying name to each graphic object. Commonly, objects to be reached on the drawings are created with their identifying records in place. Most objects are copies from an original and are not unique graphically. The object's identifying name, stored in all key fields along with the records of any written information that pertains to the object, is the pivotal link or hook between the drawing and any text file. As long as the link matches, the drawing is connected to a great variety of files. However, unless it is an exact copy of another object, each graphic object added to the drawings must receive a unique name. The names are stored in a file that is part of the drawing itself. Sometimes referred to as an "attribute" or "property file," this direct file is created with utilities that are supplied with the CAD system. The direct file must be in place and ready to receive records for each object as it is created or copied. Thus, information is captured interactively as symbols and components are created on the drawings.

The objective of an automated process is to capture design information at its inception and reuse it as often as possible. At each project phase, design documents combine information from earlier work with information that is original to the current phase. The same identifying names must be used to coordinate document after document.

Furthermore, information captured in an earlier phase can be used to coordinate information that is added during a current procedure. Names of objects and certain descriptive material are repeated again and again. For example, the room name is the same in the architectural space program, the floor plans, the finish schedules, and furniture reports. Room names that are captured early in the design process can be used as prompts in later phases. They can appear on the screen followed by space for information that must be added during a current procedure.

The following is a summary of the requirements for capturing design information efficiently with data processing systems:

1. Text or nongraphic records must be connected to each reuseable graphic object on the drawing.

2. Such text files must be designed to include reference and key fields.
3. Systematic procedures for identifying as well as storing design information must be followed.

Under the best circumstances, the relation between a drawing and text files already exists before project work begins. This is possible if an office standards data base has been established which includes standard text files and procedures.

Correctly designed files will not require a separate operation for returning to the drawings and installing links to written information. If the key fields and direct files are not in place, however, installing them on drawings that are complete may be time-consuming and perhaps more costly than is practical. Costly, because the link must be stored with each copy of a graphic object that is repeated throughout the drawings hundreds, perhaps thousands, of times. Attach the links to a single original object first. Subsequent copies of the original inherit the links. If the links are not in place, your drawings will not have the intelligence they could.

Lettering

Usually, notes and lettering are like any other graphic object and originate directly on a drawing. All CAD systems provide text entry functions for this purpose. These functions control the size of text, the style of the font, as well as certain editing capabilities. Using a text-entry function is the simplest way to store written information on a CAD drawing.

Lettering that is entered directly on a drawing can also be grouped with line work so that it moves around with a graphic object. If a note is grouped, it does not have to be added in a separate operation each time the object is copied. Any type of drawing note can be created and stored on a drawing in this way (see Figs. 11-4A and 11-4B).

The lettering can be grouped on a designated drawing layer so that it will appear on certain drawings only when the designated layer is displayed. If the outline of the object is stored on a separate layer, the lettering will disappear when only the layer for the line work is shown. For instance, a door number need not be shown with the door symbol on the background drawing for consultants.

Lettering that is created directly on a drawing in this way should be used only for very limited forms of annotation, however, since it is not linked to any files other than the drawing itself. Thus the system cannot read the information in a way that is useful to a project architect. This mechanism is appropriate for building grid lines and dimensions which describe the geometric relations between design elements. This geometric information does not generally appear in other files of written information about the project. As a result, the information is confined to the drawings where it appears. Also, since this geometric information will not be used on other projects, except perhaps as part of a detail drawing, it will not have to be transferred into the office standards data base.

Limited capabilities are available for managing lettering that has been recorded with text entry directly on the drawing. Such lettering can be edited only on the actual drawing. More important, it cannot be reused except as a copy of itself.

Store Lettering in Direct Files

Lettering that is associated with a graphic object should be stored in a record that is part of the direct file for the drawing. It can still be displayed on the drawing as part of the group for the object, but, if it is also stored in the direct file, the text is part of the data base of written information about the project.

Storing lettering in a direct file provides a wealth of data processing capability. You can manage text and notes on the drawing in an entirely new way: Written information can be displayed in preassigned locations from any number of indirect or transfer files. The name or serial number of a design element as well as key notes or even complete drawing notes can be brought onto the drawing from a master file of written design information. (See also Chap. 13.)

Another significant advantage is derived from storing lettering in a direct file: Text displayed on a drawing can be modified without actually working on the drawing. If, as is likely, a symbol has been copied in many places, the lettering that accompanies each one on the drawings can be changed without finding and selecting them one at a time. You can update multiple objects at once by working on the file of written information rather than the drawing. Each copy of the original graphic object refers to the same text file as a source. With a single change in the source file, the change is reflected with each copy of the graphic object on the drawings.

Global change is not possible if lettering is handled like line work and grouped with a graphic object. Although they require planning and additional work before the project begins, direct files can be easily installed. They are built into the graphic objects in the office standards data base before objects are used on a project document. Such files can then be used on project after project. Global change is only one new possibility. If lettering is stored in direct files, other data processing tools, such as word processing, can be used to create drawing notes. When modifying text—even lettering that appears on the drawings—word processing systems can be more cost-effective than the use of the CAD software.

A rich structure of cross-references between design information in different documents can be created. These cross-references allow us to work on a variety of documents with different computer systems while reusing the same written information that appears on the drawings. Furthermore, by storing lettering that appears on a drawing in direct files, cross-references to design elements stem from the drawings themselves. As a result, you are assured that reports and written design documents faithfully reflect the status of the drawings. In fact, this is a degree of accuracy previously unknown to architectural documents unless they were produced by some automated process.

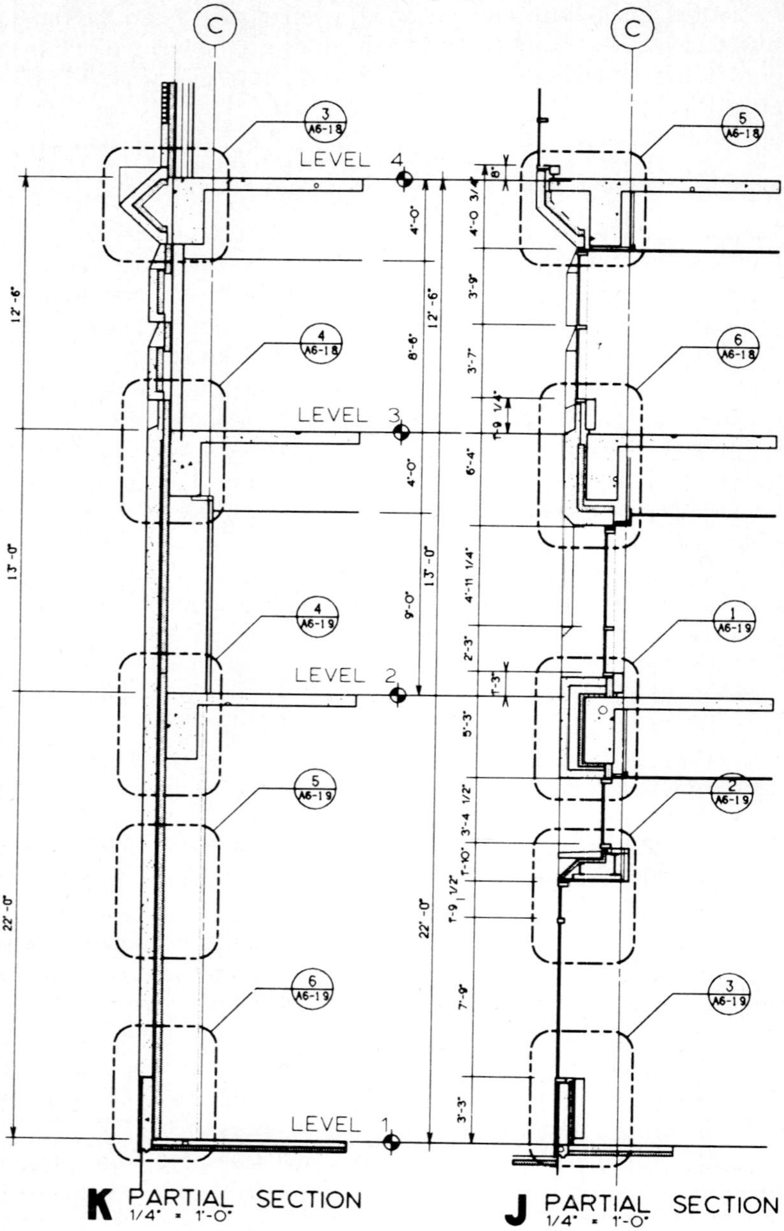

Figure 11-4 Both drawings show dimensions and lettering for elements such as floor heights and material indications appropriately stored only on drawings as text rather than in nongraphic file. (*Courtesy of Skidmore, Owings, and Merrill, Houston, TX.*)

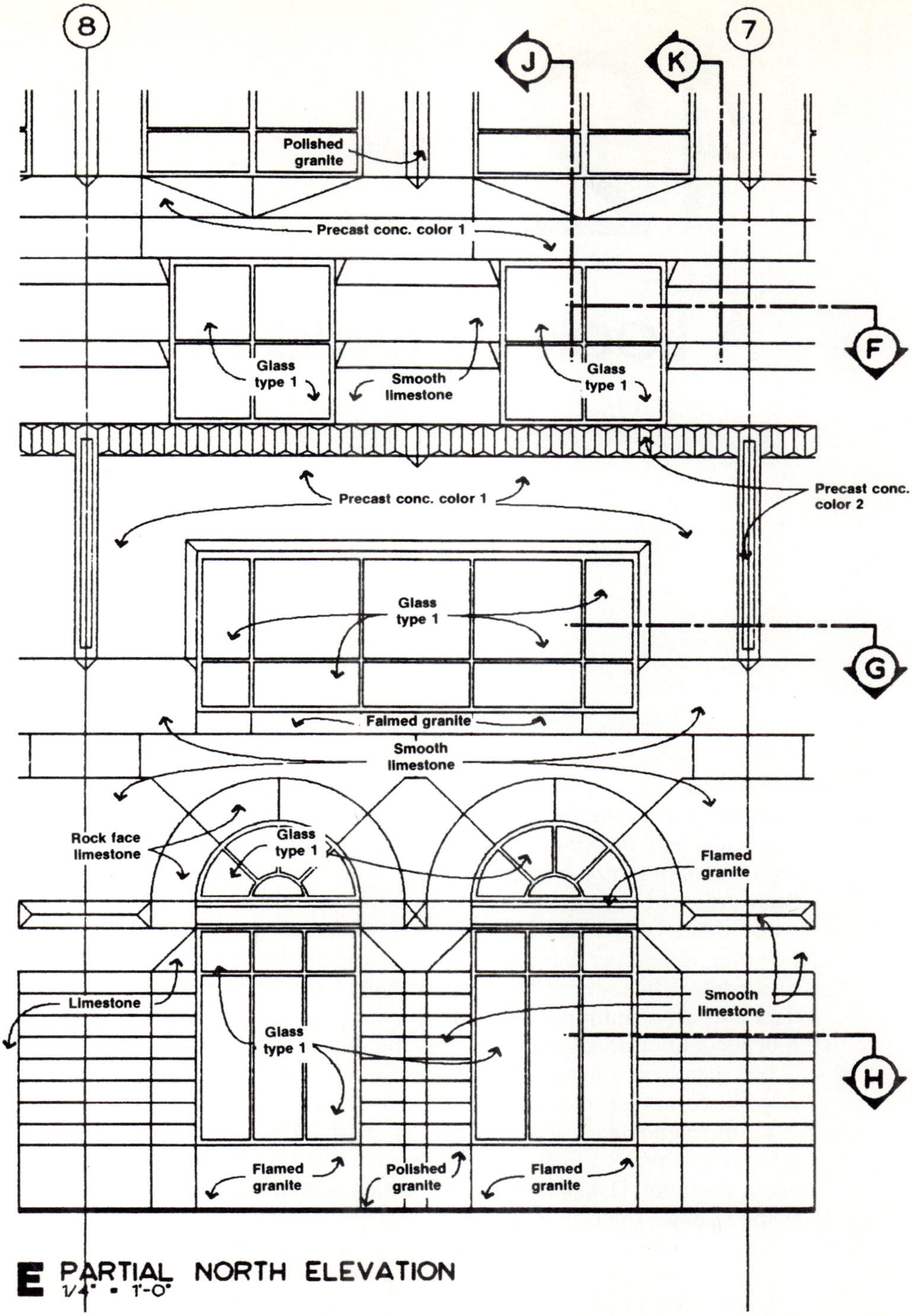

E PARTIAL NORTH ELEVATION
1/4" = 1'-0"

Chapter 12

A Look at Data Bases

"In order to operate, a system requires some, but not all, of its parts."

—A DATA PROCESSING AXIOM

As a prelude to the discussion in Chap. 13 on nongraphic file structures associated with drawings, Chap. 12 briefly describes data bases and how they are used to organize information in a design firm. The term *data base* has been overused and suffers from some misunderstanding. Many people assume a data base is any file composed of records and fields. The following, however, is a proper definition: "A data base may be defined as a collection of interrelated data stored together, without harmful or unnecessary redundancy to serve multiple applications; the data are stored so that they are independent of programs which use the data." [MART77]

In a data base, the same information serves as many software applications as possible, and developing systems to use data this way led to the concept of "data independence." This concept implies that the data, and the application programs which use them, are independent so a change in one does not affect the other. Data independence facilitates multiple associations between items of data. Information is thus used for several different purposes with several different programs, and the information is not repeated for each separate application.

Information is interconnected in a data base in ways that allow searches along different access paths. To achieve flexibility, associations between data items are as important as the data itself.

The following are the primary characteristics of a data base:

1. Data can have multiple uses.
2. Existing programs do not have to be redone when changes are made to the data base.
3. The data base can grow and change without upsetting the current use.
4. The data can be searched in fast and flexible ways.
5. Efficient data storage avoids multiple versions of the same data.
6. The operator gains access to the data in a simple fashion.
7. The data is protected from unrestricted access and from damage or loss.

In the design process, many forms of data, including graphic, written, and numeric, are analyzed and manipulated with many different types of computerized processes, and any one data processing procedure handles only a relatively small volume of design information. When contrasted to the data processing requirements of other fields, such as banking, these two characteristics of data processing in the design field are quite unusual in that they place particular emphasis on data independence. Data independence allows design information to be processed in a form that is accessible to new and varied software applications; this accessibility is important to the successful use of computers in architectural design.

Given these characteristics, a monolithic data base, with application software and files for all types of design information resident on a single system, is impractical. A better arrangement is a collection of files that interacts with several software applications distributed across a variety of equipment where the files are connected with associations and transfer mechanisms. (Chapter 15 discusses the requirements of different data base management systems.)

By applying data base principles to such a distributed system, we can produce a sketch of an organization for a collection of files which, taken together, comprise one or more data bases. We can describe four major types of data bases within a design office.

1. The office administration data base, encompassing information related to personnel, clients, consultants, accounts, and service contracts.
2. The office standards data base, representing the cumulative experience of an office, including reusable project data, design and documentation standards and policies, special studies, or special design techniques.
3. The project data base, including all the information necessary to represent the design and documentation of a specific project for purposes of planning, approval, construction, and occupancy.
4. External data banks, accessed when needed, such as those available for specifications, construction cost estimating, building products, demographic projections, and weather records (note that, although external data bases are not discussed in this book, external data banks such as DIALOG and The Source can also be accessed for public information about clients and are used increasingly for technical research.)

With the exception of data concerning billable hours, the office administration data base operates in a separate realm from project work. It is not within the purview of this book.

Sometimes considered part of an office standards data base are references in the office library, including building and zoning codes, graphic standards, technical bulletins, and product information. Although this information is applied during project design work, in general it is not stored on computer systems. This information is usually of such volume that transferring it onto a computer system is impractical for an individual office. If design information is not accessible with basic software applications such as word processing, for our purposes it is not considered part of the office standards or project data bases.

Office Standards Data Base

Standard or master files tailored to the specific practice of an office make up the office standards data base. In contrast to project documents, such standards are used on project after project. Typically, an introductory set of standard drawings, symbol libraries, and nongraphic files, for door and finish schedules for example, are supplied by a CAD vendor. A design office rarely has the resources to assemble a complete set of standard documents and files before work on a project with a CAD system begins. However, revising the examples provided and gradually adding new ones will expand the data base and customize it over time to the unique requirements of the office. The following list outlines documents and files that would be included in a well developed office standards data base.

1. Standard drawings with title blocks.
2. Symbol libraries or files.
3. An organization of drawing layers.
4. Standard line styles, lettering fonts, and color schedules for drawing line work.
5. Standard room templates for such rooms as bathrooms, stairs, utility rooms.
6. Space planning data such as typical room standards (see Chap. 16).
7. Furniture and equipment descriptions and specifications.
8. Standard drawings along with report files for schedules, including door, hardware, window, finish, equipment, header, beam, and other schedules.
9. Direct and indirect file formats.
10. Digitizer tablet menus.
11. Specialized macros.
12. Drawing checklists.

13. Drawing notation files including allowed abbreviations and keynotes.
14. Libraries of standard building details.
15. Both master and outline specifications.
16. Files of construction cost information.
17. Building code checklists.
18. Architectural topical key words for use with an automated project log.
19. A reference manual of operating procedures.

The contents of the files above are derived from previously completed work as well as existing references and from the accepted rules of thumb for the profession. As outlined in Chap. 8, standard information is always associated with objects on drawings in named fields and records. All the names in use in the office standards data base are defined and stored in a data dictionary, which lists the allowable named fields and their contents.

Although accessible by anyone within the office, the organization or structure of the office standards data base should be controlled by a single individual who understands the needed links between files and is prepared to work with different systems. Such a data base administrator sets up communication protocols, creates transfer files, and reviews the design of individual files to ensure that they are compatible for data transfer. This role is performed by the system manager, production manager, or even the librarian.

Developing an office standards data base is a long term undertaking requiring the participation of the office as a whole. The period between peak project work loads is ideal for progress on this task. The production manager plays a key role in building up the content of the office standards data base. After all, the cost of operating a CAD system makes it expensive to stretch out the drafting work on a project. The production manager should define an ongoing program that takes advantage of slack periods to expand the data base where needed. Nonproject time should be assigned to specific development tasks. Assign tasks to individuals ahead of time, and, when time permits, incremental progress will be made.

As information is developed in project data bases, use some of it to revise and expand the office standards data base. Merge selected fields from project files with standard files, as in the case of standard room type information. When merging files, the project number should travel with the file to indicate its "source." Other office standard information will carry a source such as a building code or building material technical reference. If projects consistently use a different parameter than that stated in the standard, revise the standard.

In the long run, the office standards data base is a specialized resource that augments the power and utility of the CAD system. Work on expanding it is an investment in the resources of the office and deserves job numbers as well as dedicated project managers.

Project Data Base

The project data base contains all the design information collected and used during the life of a specific design project. The contents are drawn from the office standards data base, outside data banks, and new information generated during the progress from one design phase to the another. Initially, the project data base is set up with selected information from the office standards data base, such as project specific checklists or templates, relevant details and specification sections, and typical room plans. At most 20 to 25 percent of its contents are obtained from the office standards data base.

Because of the day-to-day nature of the design process, the project data base is highly volatile. Called upon by multiple actors, the information in it changes quickly and is constantly being revised, tested, edited, and improved. The project data base must therefore be maintained on a medium that provides immediate access and that is dedicated to the specific project. By its nature, the quality and content of a project data base is completely within the jurisdiction of the design team.

Copies of project data that can be reused on future projects are merged back into the office standards data base. However, project files remain in the project data base and are archived when the project is completed. Information originated while working on a project that would not be transferred to the office standards data base includes:

1. Copies of contracts for service.
2. Complete project drawings and schedules.
3. Material quantities.
4. Square footage areas from project documents.
5. Meeting notes including any design decision file.
6. Architectural programming information such as space projections and surveys of occupants.
7. Construction administration information such as change orders.

Combining project data bases with a mature office standards data base achieves ratios of productivity considerably beyond those realized with high-speed CAD drafting alone. Standard building elements, spatial parameters, and checklists provide designers with information which would otherwise be reconstructed for each project and thus eliminate or make automatic entire steps in the progress of design work.

Chapter 13

Direct Files as Part of the Drawing

"Furthermore, in many application programs . . . an 80/20 rule holds: the major portion, say 80%, of the program deals with modeling entities and only 20% with editing pictures of them. In other words, graphics applications tend to be data and processing intensive but not picture-making intensive."
[FOLE82]

Any graphic object on a drawing can be connected to written information. A record, sometimes called an "attribute" or "property record," for nongraphic information is attached to each object. These records are kept in a file of nongraphic information, referred to as a *direct file,* that is part of the drawing itself. The information that we find in each record can be stored in many different fields throughout a data base file system. In fact, information can be connected to graphic objects through a multidimensional system using transfer files and a variety of equipment. In order to coordinate this information, however, certain items of key information must be stored in the direct file that is a part of the drawing.

The direct file can be thought of as an index. With it, the system can find both written information and the graphic object to which that information pertains. A direct file contains subject names and their addresses throughout the entire set of project files. Rather than page numbers, however, this index contains "pointers," which the CAD system uses to find objects on a drawing.

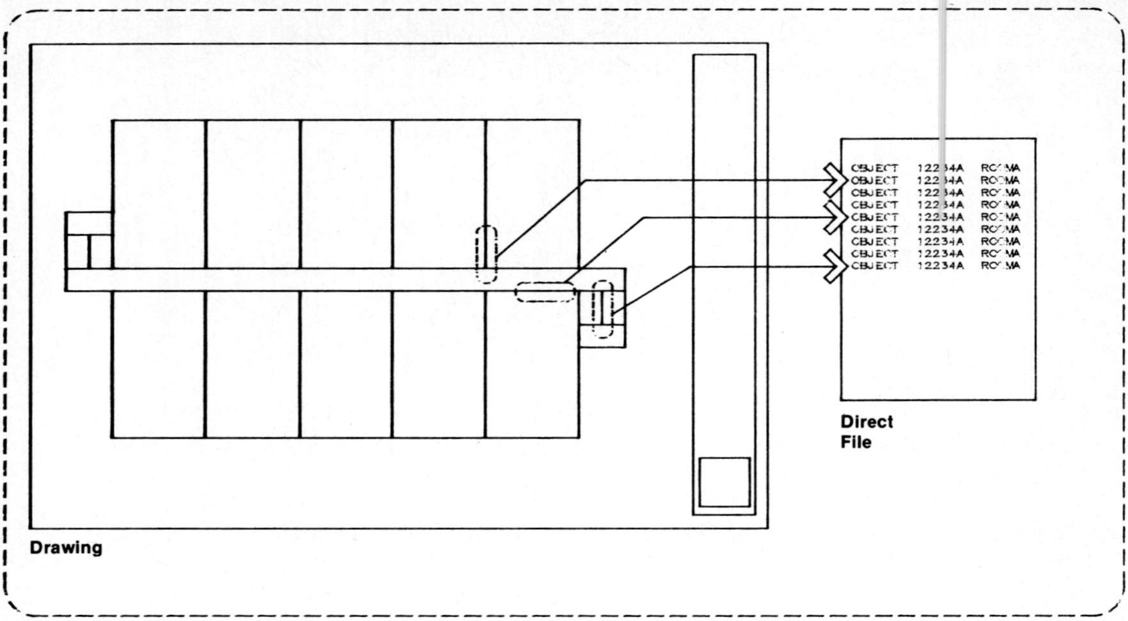

Figure 13-1 Relationship, from CAD perspective, between drawing and file of nongraphic information: Both are seen as different parts of a single file.

As far as the system is concerned, a graphic file for a drawing (where line work is defined as graphic objects) and a direct file are just different parts of the description of a single document (Fig. 13-1). To oversimplify, it is as if you stored the contents of your letter file in the flat file along with the drawings. The system perceives both the letter file and the drawings as pure information.

When a drawing is retrieved from the system's mass storage, an image of its file containing graphic records is sent to the screen. At the same time, direct files of nongraphic information are read into an area for temporary storage in the central memory where they can be called on quickly while the drawing is being used.

Some software applications, such as mechanical or electrical design and drafting applications, are designed to work with specific direct files. In this case, the files are automatically assigned to the drawing when the application is initialized. Otherwise, you select the file by name.

Initially, a record is attached to a graphic object by picking or designating the object and then providing the name of a record. The structure of the record must already exist along with the direct file. On some systems, you can designate any item at any level, such as lines, text, or groups of lines, to have a record attached. The record is connected to a graphic object by a data processing mechanism similar to that used for grouping various lines on the drawing: a pointer is attached to the object by the system. It tells the system the position of a specific record within the direct file. Once it is attached, the pointer is included among the characteristics that describe the object to the system. The pointer is stored with the line work in the graphic data base for the drawing, and it becomes part of the object. It doesn't matter what shape the object is: the system "feels" the pointer, not the shape, and finds the nongraphic record.

Once the system has found the nongraphic record, we can read the information it contains. With the use of this same pointer, we can also store information in the record. More important, the system can do it for us.

Records and Pointers

Once a record is attached, a graphic object can be copied for use throughout a set of drawings. With each copy, a new record is created and entered in the direct file. Information from the original object is also copied with the record. The copied record can eventually contain information that is very different from the original data such as the position of the object on the drawing. Among several copies of the same object, it is the information in each record that distinguishes one graphic object from the next. The symbol for an office furniture partition of any height is the same in plan view; however, we have to be able to tell partitions of different heights apart. The record attached to the graphic object does this by storing the height as nongraphic information.

On systems which allow deep grouping, different records can be attached at different levels within the structure of a group of objects (see Fig. 13-2). For example, one record is attached to the symbol for an item of furniture. This record contains such information as the manufacturer, color, model

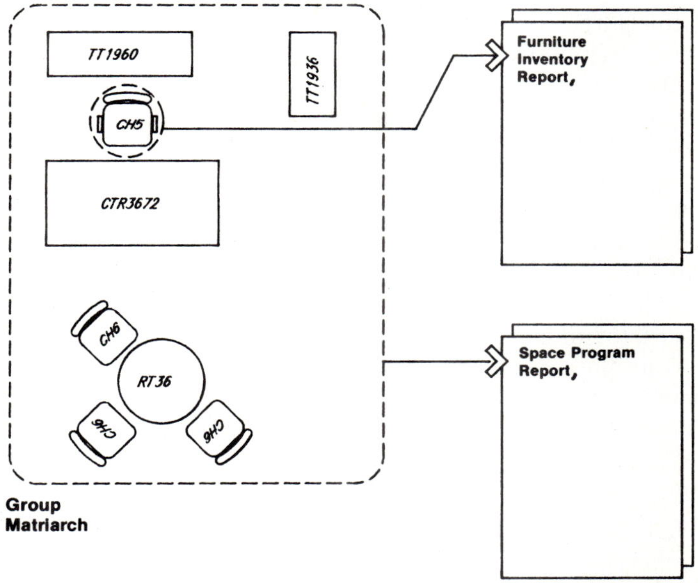

Figure 13-2 Separate reports derived from nongraphic information associated both with the members of a group of furniture symbols as well as with the group as a whole.

number, size, and price. A furniture inventory report is created from these records. A collection of symbols that represents the layout for a typical office, such as a desk, chair, bookcase, and files, is grouped together. If the furniture group is located within a boundary for a single office, attach a separate record to the boundary. Or, with an open office plan that treats the furniture group as a workstation, attach a separate record to the group of furniture. This record contains information about the room, such as room name, office function, department, and cost center. As a result, a facilities program report is created from records attached to the group.

Records can be attached to graphic objects at any time. Symbols usually have a record attached when they are created, before they are used on a project drawing. As the symbol is originally stored, so is the record stored with it. As the symbol is copied onto drawings, so is the record.

Objects that are created on the drawings ad hoc, such as walls, must also have a record attached by the operator or by the system. Even if the object changes shape during the design process, it must retain its connection to written information. If a wall is created from a library of construction components, the record is attached automatically when it is drawn and stays attached even when the shape of the wall is modified.

A Direct File and Its Records

Before a record is attached to a graphic object, however, a direct file must be in place with the drawing. These direct files are called *property files* or *attribute files* by CAD system manufacturers. The schema or field layout for the direct file may have to be created. Use software applications that are specially designed for this purpose. Manufacturers of CAD systems supply some direct files along with graphic software applications; often, the files are already associated with any symbols that are provided. Files, and the records that are included, are designed to store information for typical cases, such as schedules for doors and finishes. Like the symbols, they are designed to satisfy the general case. For many design problems, you will have to create new files in your own office.

Remember that the information stored in a file is distinct from the structure of the file. Information in the file is governed by the requirements of the design profession. The file itself is structured by the CAD system. Direct files, and their associated indirect files have a complex structure defined by the system. They are not as simple as manila file folders but, the information stored in them can be.

Nongraphic or text files are subdivided into records—a record is simply a set of one or more consecutive fields on a related subject (see Fig. 13-3). At the lowest level of file structure, each record is further broken down into one or more fields—a field is a set of one or more characters which is treated as a whole. Within a file, records are organized into rows and columns. Ultimately, separate files are organized, like page after page of tables, into sets of files. With this structure, relationships between information that is stored in different files can be explicitly designated.

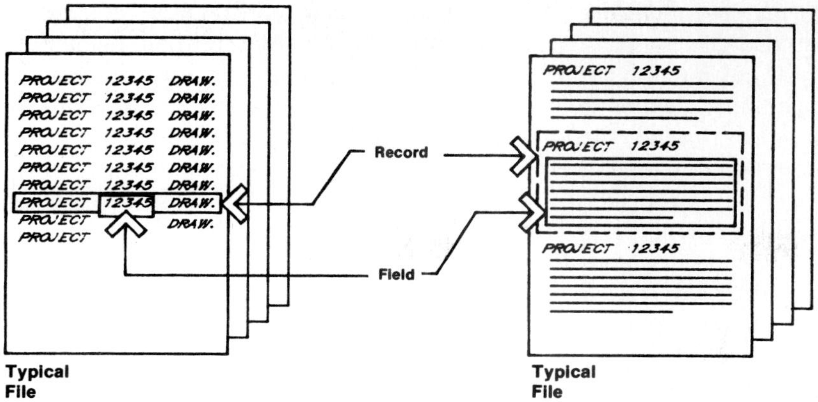

Figure 13-3 Two representations of the hierarchical relationship among files, records, and fields.

The structure of a direct file depends on the CAD system being used. Different degrees of flexibility are available with different systems. A block of space may simply be provided for each record in the file. In this case, information about a graphic object is organized like correspondence: it is written out line by line. Although straightforward, this free format does not include many mechanisms for cross-referencing the information or defining relationships between records in separate files. Without the ability to cross-reference items, information will have to be recorded more than once. For example, a room name included in a direct file for a space program will have to be entered again on the plans and again in a file for the finish schedule. This is inefficient.

Alternately, we can be very specific about the structure of records in a direct file and how they are connected to other files. Direct files are not separate islands of information floating on a CAD sea. In order for direct files to be connected, they must include cross-references or key fields and information must be stored in the right places. Direct files have a multidimensional structure that can be elegant as well as complex.

The structure of a direct file is determined by the records it contains. In turn, the records, which accompany graphic objects, are determined by the fields out of which the record is composed. So, a record for a graphic object can be defined by:

1. The number of fields in the record.
2. The name of each field.
3. The type of data stored in the field.
4. The size of each field.
5. The function performed by the field.

Each field in a record must be named. This may seem obvious, but it is a relatively new requirement. The smallest item that gets a name in a manila folder may be an entire correspondence, a memo, or a contract. Information in a manila file can be organized as simply as the order in which items were last put back into the file. We can find items if we can remember the item by name or date, such as the memo from the July 10th client meeting, but we have to flip through the entire file to find the item. Items in a direct file, however, are designated very precisely. A direct file resembles a finish schedule; each column heading and row is identified.

Data in a record can be either characters or numbers. If a field is numeric or if it is filled in automatically, CAD systems sometimes provide a default size for the field. A great deal of numeric information, such as total count, length, or area, can be automatically calculated and stored by the system. If the size of the field is assigned by the architect, however, it must be long enough to handle any data that is likely to be included.

Finally, the system recognizes different kinds of fields that perform different functions:

1. Direct fields store information directly with a graphic object.
2. Indirect reference fields point to and display information that is stored in indirect files.
3. Trigger fields activate a software process which captures information from the drawing, such as the location of an object.
4. Calculated fields store the result of a calculation, for instance, the sum of data in two or more fields.

Different functions are implemented by using these different kinds of fields.

Information that is stored as input from the operator, like the direct file itself, travels with the objects on a drawing. The direct fields in a nongraphic file are a simple list. The list can contain many different types of information, including names, sizes, drawing notes. Some essential information, however, should be included in the direct records that accompany any type of graphic object. Key fields, such as the name of an object, project number, and serial number, must be included so that the graphic object can be connected to information in other files as these files are developed.

Information in indirect reference fields is not actually stored in the direct file itself. These fields display information from files that are not part of the drawing. Rather, the information is stored in indirect files on the same CAD system. A copy is displayed when the direct file is queried. This kind of field is sometimes called a "virtual field" because it presents information as though it were in the direct file, that is, the operator performs no separate operation to access the information.

Indirect reference fields link different but related files of written information. We can use these fields as a table of contents—they connect a graphic object to entire chapters of written information. In fact, with indirect reference fields, the record attached to an object can be a multidimensional table of contents.

Trigger fields have programmed capabilities that enable them to automatically find certain information from the spatial relationships on the drawing. Rather than storing data, they store the name of a subroutine or macro. When queried, the subroutine performs an automatic operation which extracts information from the drawing. For example, the location of a graphic object is determined automatically with the use of positional or location fields. Also, areas and lengths can be automatically calculated and stored with the use of geometric trigger fields.

When the name, type, size, and function of each field is specified, the record is defined. Different design elements such as walls, doors, windows, and plumbing fixtures require records that include fields which are specific to the type of design element. "Door number," "equipment number," or "height," for example, are not required for every design element. However, certain fields, such as "project name" and "specification section," are common to every design element and should be included in every nongraphic record.

Logical vs. Physical Records

In a typical record, fields are assembled in a series; each field is adjacent to the next. A record arranged in this way is called a "physical record." In a simple case, such as a brief table, all the information for an object might be stored in one field after the other in a single physical record.

More often, however, a single text record contains a subset of all the possible fields of information that are connected to a graphic object. In fact, written information is distributed throughout a set of files. Since the information is in separate files, it is actually stored in different physical records. To pull these records together for a specific report or schedule, different fields are assembled into what is known as a "logical record," which can include fields from many separate physical records. A logical record is defined by the initial field combined with all the fields that are connected to it. A logical record is a conceptual entity that spans more than one physical record. As a result, physical records can be combined into many different logical records.

Logical records specify relationships. With them, the physical record attached to a graphic object is the root of many different records. Since a logical record contains key fields as well as data fields, we can match records from different files (see Fig. 13-4). The relation between logical and physical records allows us to assemble the same design information into many different specific reports.

Logical records are a lot more dynamic than a file cabinet full of manila folders. Imagine opening the file drawer and throwing information into it randomly, but retrieving it with ease. It does not even matter what drawer we use. With logical records, the system sorts the information into the segments we need, and the correct information can be drawn right from the drawers and file folders.

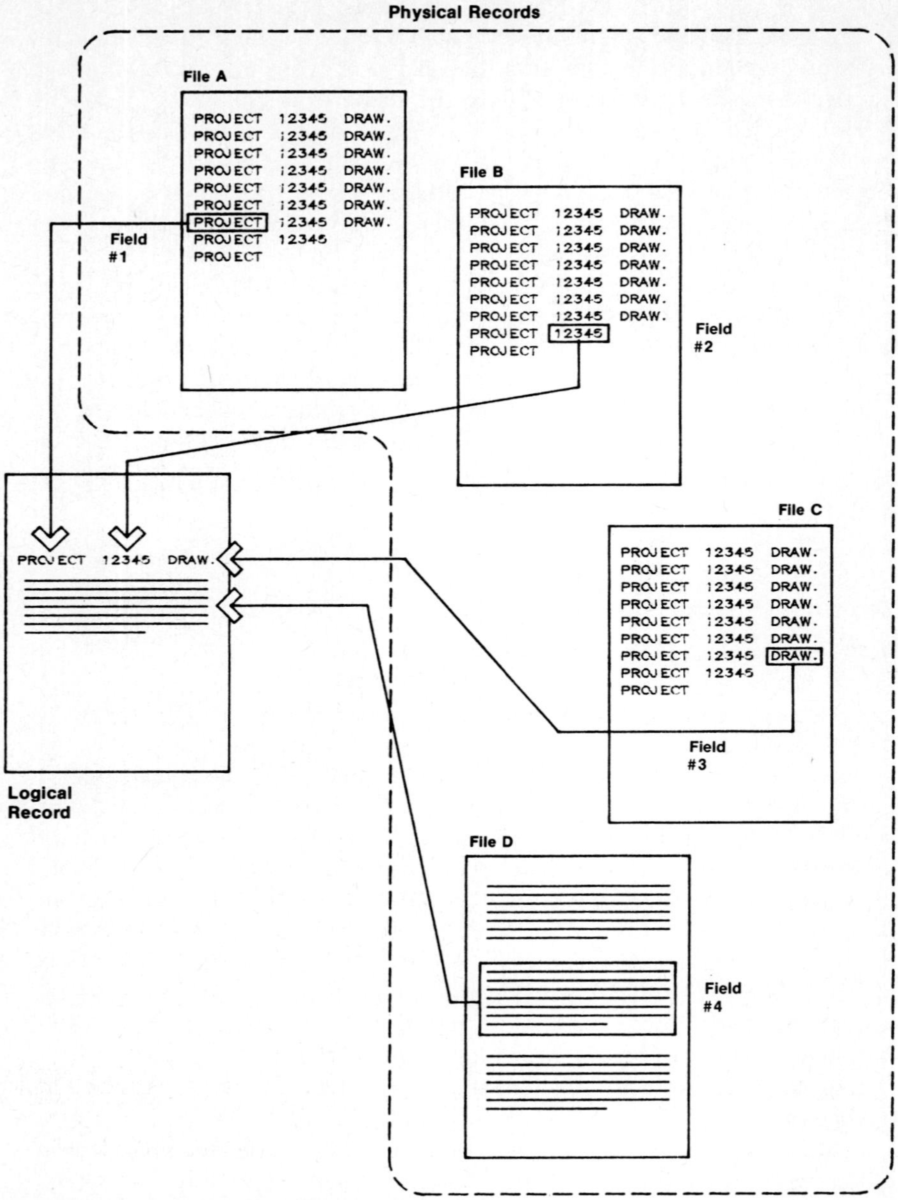

Figure 13-4 Logical record created from information stored in records from many separate physical records.

Recommendations for the Design of Direct Files

Design your files so that only key information is stored in the direct file attached to the objects on a drawing. These fields are either the direct, sometimes called "real property" fields or the trigger fields. (Refer to Chap. 15 for further recommendations on key fields attached to graphic objects.) As mentioned, other information is destined for fields that are designated as indirect reference fields. What type of field to use depends on factors such as the type of information, the speed with which it must be accessed, the number of copies of the graphic object throughout the drawings, and the need to modify the information swiftly and conveniently.

Store most written design information in files that are indirect or separate from the drawings. The volume of design information is so large that storing all of it with the drawing in a direct file is impractical. The file that travels with the drawing does not have to include records for everything you ever want to know about a design element. Remember, you can use logical records to compose many different physical records for use with various documents and reports. We can have many different indirect files associated with the same object. Most information is pointed to with the use of indirect reference fields. Think of the direct file as a card catalogue, an index to an entire cabinet of files. In fact, you don't even have to include a separate field in the direct file for each indirect file that may be associated with the object.

Records in a direct file should contain fields for the following typical items of data:

1. The name of the graphic object.
2. The serial number of the design element.
3. Measurements derived from the drawing, such as area, length, or volume.
4. The location or position of the design element in the drawings.
5. Key fields to indirect files, such as manufacturer number or specification section, that apply to each type of design element.

Include only fields for necessary information. Do not try to shove the entire file drawer into the index card catalogue.

The first and most important field identifies the graphic object. It does not identify a design element per se but rather the collection of line work on the drawing, such as a pair of lines that represent a wall. The identity of a design element is derived from descriptions that are distributed throughout the entire set of documents. The object name is just the index number for a humble graphic object.

Trigger fields are provided for information that is derived from spatial relationships on the drawings. Information such as location and area will be correct only if drawings are examined directly. If this information were recorded in a permanent field it would become out of date. (You can be sure that the drawings are being changed even as you read this.)

Finally, the relationship to indirect files must be indicated by the use of key fields. The word "key" in key field does not indicate that the information in the field is more important than other information. The analogy for a key field is a key in a lock. Information in the key field, such as an object name, is compared to information in key fields in separate records. If the key fields match each other, the connection is complete. Thus, information in an indirect file can be connected to a graphic object.

The fields listed above serve only as an outline for a typical record in a direct file. Organization of the fields will depend on several factors, including the type of design service. For example, the record for an item of furniture can include both the manufacturer's name and model number as key fields. Together, these are used to look up size, color, price, etc., in an indirect file. If the manufacturer and model number are stored in an indirect file, the name of the object, along with the project name, can be used to look up the manufacturer, model number, size, and so on.

Automatic Display of Text from a Direct File

Lettering that is shown with a symbol or component can originate in a direct file and can be displayed automatically on the drawings. It can also be automatically revised from this same file. Numbers or names for doors, rooms, furniture, and equipment, even complete drawing notes, can be displayed and controlled with this mechanism.

First, the text is represented by a string of dummy letters or numbers, such as XXX. This string is grouped and stored with the line work for the symbol or component (Fig. 13-5). The text string depicts the size and location of the final note on the drawing, and the string will be filled in later. It serves as a reminder that the information is not yet complete. This text string must also be designated with a special flag or kind number that the system recognizes. In general, flags are used to trigger automatic graphic functions—in this case, the automatic display of text from a file.

One of three methods is used to create the information that replaces the dummy text string on the drawing.

1. It can be supplied by the operator while working on the direct file.
2. It can be retrieved from an indirect file.
3. It can be created automatically by the system.

The information for display, such as a room name, is not actually stored on the drawing. Rather, it is stored in a record in a direct file that is attached to the graphic object. Once the record is triggered, the dummy string on the drawing is automatically replaced with a number or note from the file. This change can be triggered by either picking the objects one at a time or by instructing the system to update all the text strings on the drawing at once.

For some data, such as an area, location, or serial number, the system can create the information for us. Let's take the example of room numbers. We must indicate the objects, such as symbols for room names, which can be done by picking each symbol in a series. After entering the starting number,

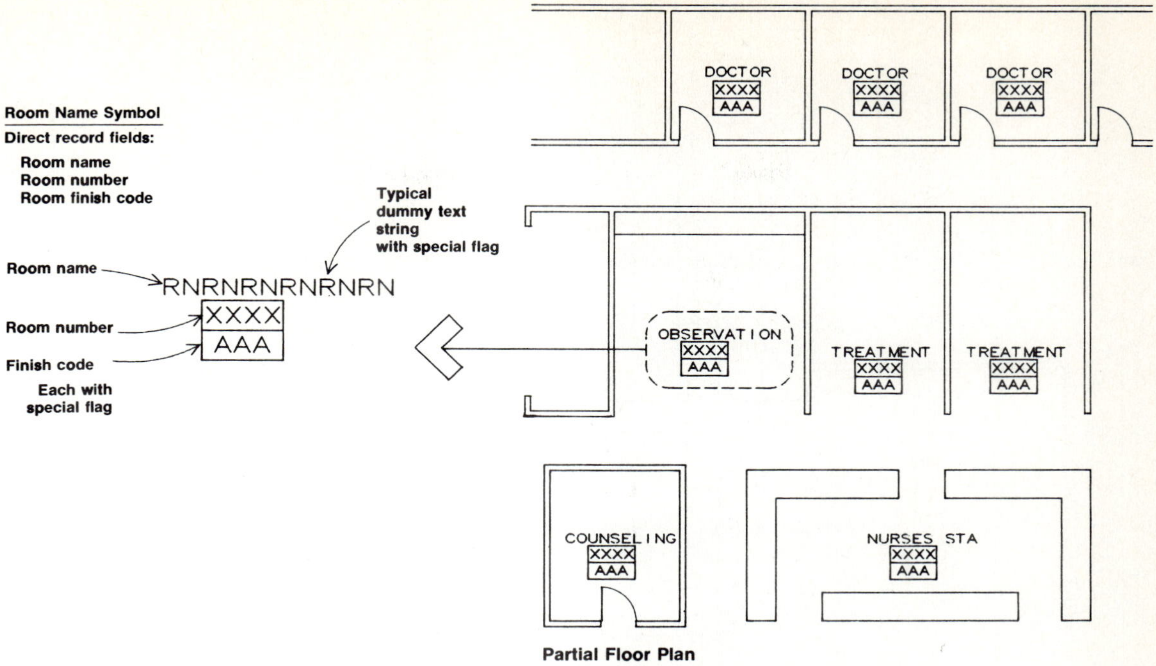

Figure 13-5 Room names are automatically displayed on a drawing from nongraphic records associated with a room name symbol which makes use of special flags.

the system will look for the remaining symbols and then number the entire set. It will also store each newly assigned room number in the direct file.

What if the room numbers have to change, not just one, say, but most or all of them? Fortunately, systems are particularly good at exchanging the contents of one field of text with another. Given a list of old numbers and a parallel list of new numbers, the system can automatically change one for the other. When the change is complete, the system displays it on the drawings with each room. The entire series can be renumbered in one procedure. In fact, other references to the rooms, such as the finish schedule, that also need to be renumbered can be done automatically by regenerating the report for the finish schedule (see Fig. 13-6).

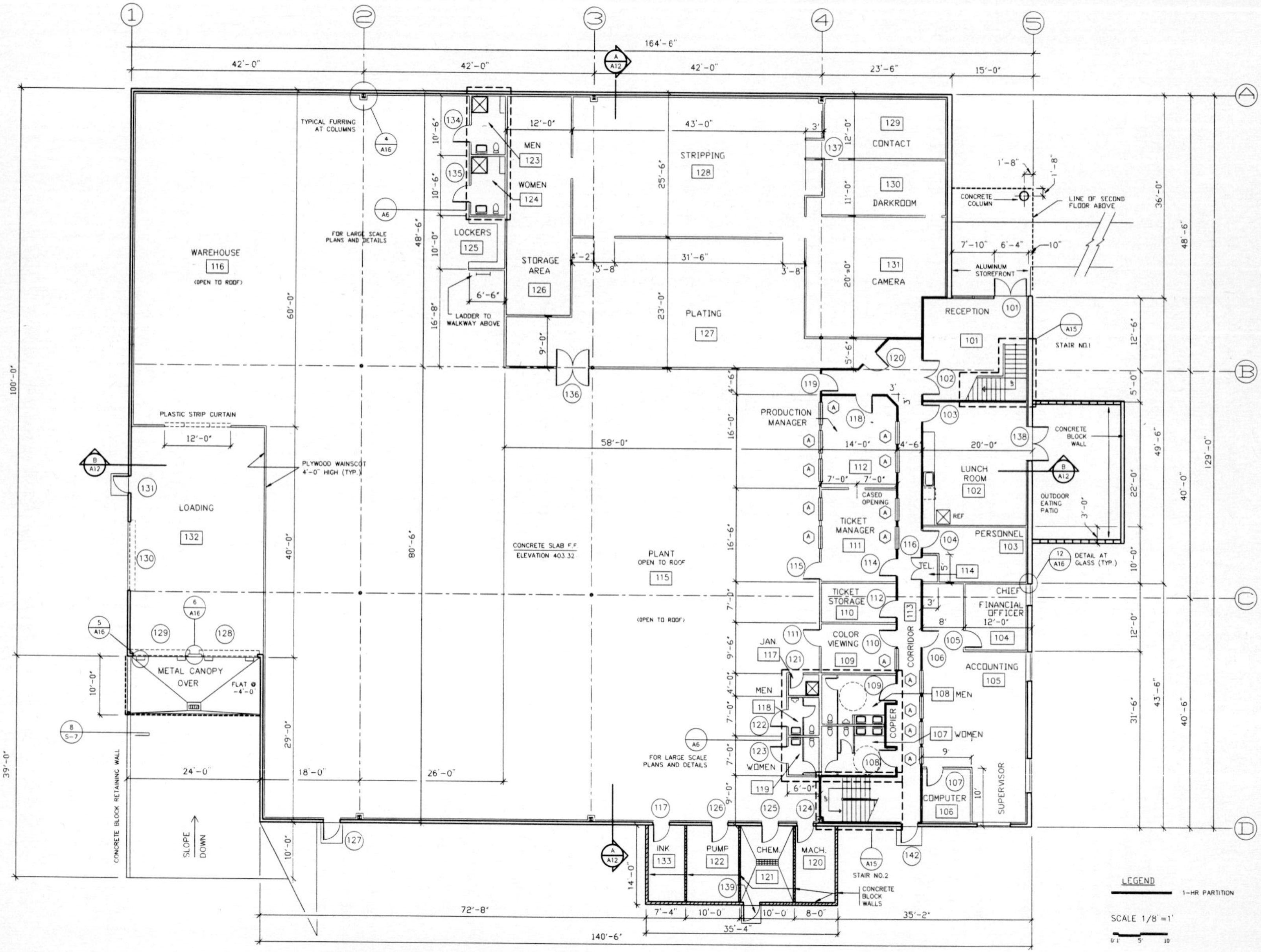

FIRST FLOOR PLAN

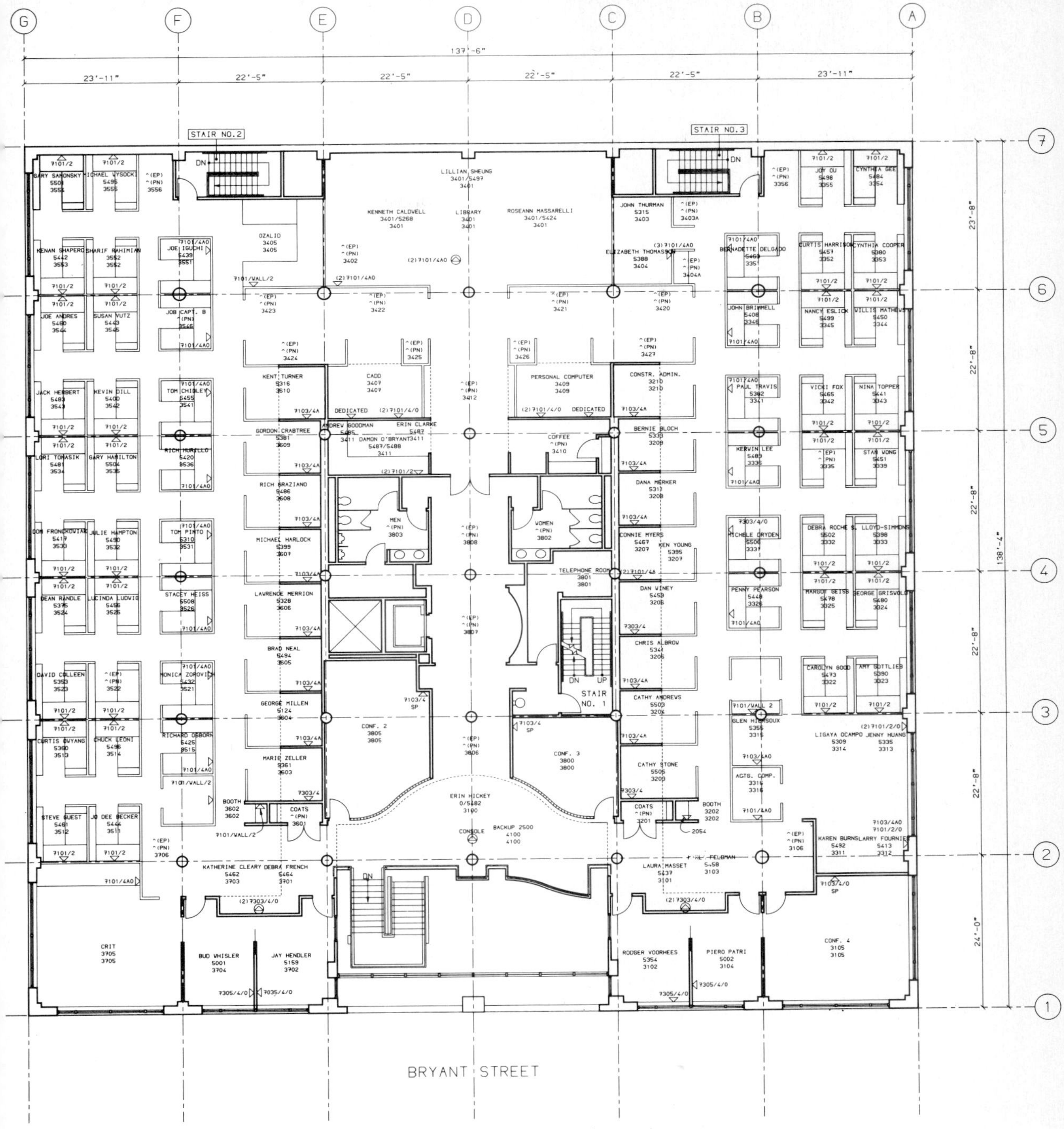

Figure 13-6 The opposite page shows a typical office and warehouse floor plan created on PC-based CAD system. (*Courtesy of Pyros Partnership, Costa Mesa, CA.*) This page shows a typical office floor plan serving as a space assignment plan for a facilities manager. The plan was created on a minicomputer-based CAD system. (*Courtesy of Whistler-Patri, Architects, San Francisco, CA.*)

Chapter 14

Indirect Files

"The traditional tools of the design professions are, most charitably, hopelessly archaic (grinding graphite on paper—instruments that are actually centuries old!). The habits of thought that go with old tools are equally archaic." [STIT84]

Unlike direct files, indirect files—although resident on a CAD system—are not part of the drawing. They are created and stored separately from the drawings. This separation has two key advantages. First, work on an indirect file can proceed at a separate pace from work on the drawings. Second, objects on the drawings can be changed as often as necessary without disturbing the information in the indirect file.

The separation, however, is not absolute. Although indirect files are separate from the drawings, they are linked by key fields to direct files that are themselves part of the drawings. As a result, when an indirect file is modified, a query to the direct file reflects the modification.

A graphic object on a drawing is connected to information in an indirect file, using a logical record that includes the fields from both direct and indirect files. The key fields with the direct record serve as a cross-reference to information in indirect files. Graphic objects in the same category, for example, furniture items, are connected to an indirect file by using copies of the same direct record. Each time an object is copied, the record refers to precisely the same area in the indirect file. Thus, information in the indirect file is connected to all copies of an object at once. This relationship is sometimes referred to as "global association." Objects can be distributed throughout the entire set of drawings, and still be connected to a central source of information.

Modifications to indirect files are done separately from the drawings. The drawings do not have to be active on the CAD system at the time information is added or changed. A one-time addition will affect many different objects on the drawings. In fact, indirect files can be created and edited with personal computers (PCs), word processing, or time-shared equipment and transferred onto the CAD system in a separate operation.

Since the information is stored in a central source (see Fig. 14-1), the indirect file, information must be entered only once and therefore must be checked only once. This centralized control of information is the main reason for working with indirect files and differentiating them from direct files that travel with the drawings. Here the benefits of a system of direct and indirect files are realized.

Indirect files have an advantage over direct files that makes them suitable for the progress of work on a design project. Their separation from the drawings yet connection to direct files makes them useful for coordinating the start-and-stop progress of work on drawings with nongraphic information, information which is derived from many different sources over the life of a project. Over time, information can be added to an indirect file without affecting the connection between the drawings and existing records in the file.

A design project requires the coordination of information that is developed at different rates and captured in the project documents at different times. As

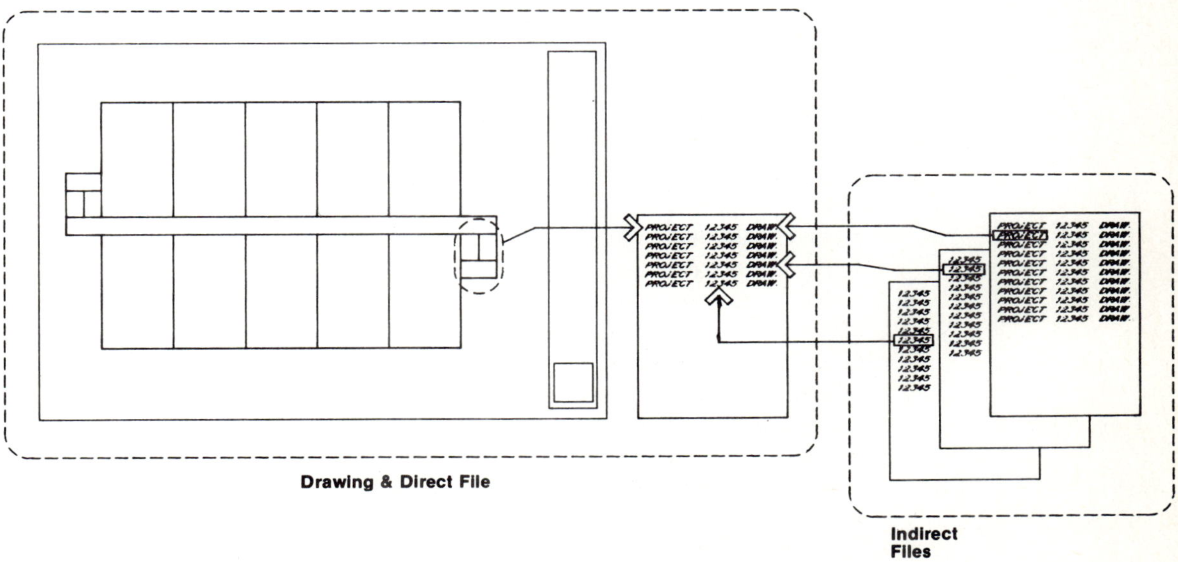

Figure 14-1 Relationship between drawing file, including nongraphic information, and series of indirect files stored separately from the drawing.

new information is added, information already in the file is likely to be relocated. This ongoing process is brought into sharp focus at the end of any major phase in the design process. At such points, we set aside a complete copy of the design documents for storage in an archive. A copy of any associated indirect files is also stored. After some time, however, work on the project proceeds, and the original documents are used again. If something is now added to the project documents, perhaps a paragraph is added to the specifications, indirect files can fall out of step with the direct files and with the objects on the drawings unless key fields connecting the two are in place.

Key fields in both the direct and indirect files minimize the problem of maintaining the connection to the drawings. For example, a paragraph of specifications is identified with a key field that includes a number for the division, section, and subsection. This number is also stored in a key field connected to an object on the drawing. With this numbering system, we do not need to indicate what page the paragraph falls on in the final or the archived version of specifications. The key field gives us a connection to the correct section of a master file of specifications. Consequently, objects on the drawings will always be connected to the right section. You can add information or move it around in the specifications without disrupting the connections between objects and specification sections. The key fields in both locations, the direct and the indirect files, ensure that the correct information will always be connected to the same graphic object no matter what we add or subtract to the indirect file. Door schedules, a fundamental design document, serve as an example of how design information is stored in both direct and indirect files in Fig. 14-2. Most of the information reported in the door schedule, such as width, material, finish, fire rating, and standard detail numbers, is not specific to one project. It can be derived from typical door configurations used on similar projects. Consequently, this information is stored in an indirect file that is part of the office standards data base. In fact, the only information needed to identify a specific door as part of the project is the project number, a serial number, and location, such as room number. As a result, the record that is stored in a direct file attached to each door symbol need only contain direct fields for these three items. It must also contain indirect reference fields, such as a door-type number which will correspond to the correct door in the office standards data base.

The indirect file for doors can also include references to files of specifications and cost-estimating information used to create other design documents. If door information is organized thus, we can easily change any set of 3'-0" steel doors into 3'-0" solid-core wooden doors. This is done with a single change to the record for material in the indirect file. For each door on the plans, the material indication is displayed in an indirect reference field. To change the type from steel to wood, the description of the record for material is revised in the indirect file rather than by revising each symbol one at a time. Once the indirect file is revised, the door schedule can be recreated as a report, and all the door materials will be updated.

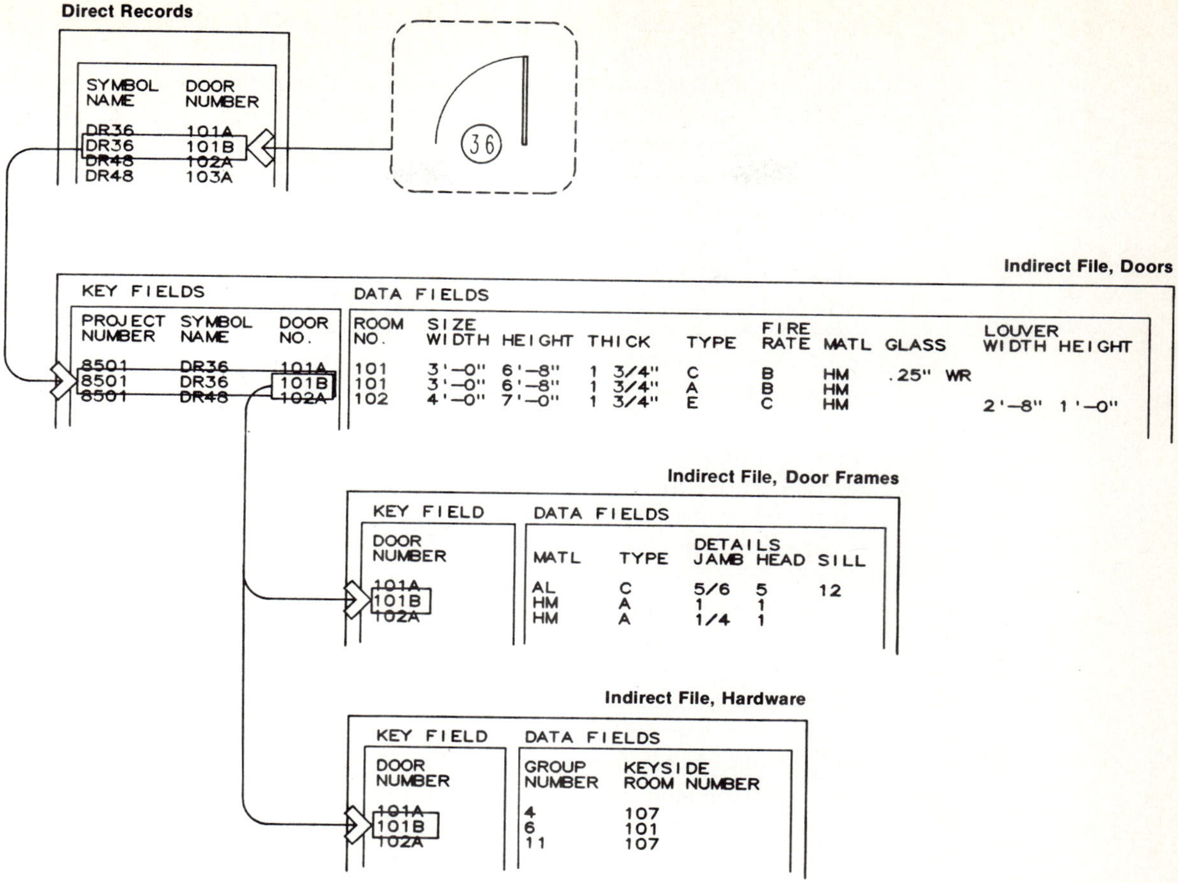

Figure 14-2 Information displayed in door schedules organized into separate indirect files. Information organized in this way is managed from an officewide data base, yet connected to symbols on different drawings, and reused for many different projects.

Data Entry for Indirect Files

Information is stored in direct and indirect files using different methods at different times. Some information is filled in ahead of time when an office data base for standard symbols and components is used. These standard objects remain the same from project to project. Any symbol copied from the office standards data base should already include the name of the graphic object and key fields to related indirect files, such as schedules, notes, cost estimating, and specifications. Typically, a record is attached to a symbol when it is first created, not when it is copied onto a drawing. Thus, the record will have several key fields that are already filled in when work starts on project drawings.

Later, when we need to distinguish one design element from another, serial number and location fields are filled in. This information can be supplied by the operator or by the system. If the system provides the serial number, it keeps a running total of objects that have been counted. The next object automatically gets the next available number. For a quick check, a schedule of only a few objects can be compiled by selecting the objects, filling in the required fields as lines of text, and creating a report.

Some software is written so that information can be stored in an indirect file during actual work on a drawing, using strategic data dependent on spatial or geometric relationships. For example, a calculation such as the capacity of a piece of heating and ventilating equipment is determined by analyzing diffusers on the drawing. The result of the calculation is related to other objects on the drawing such as the size of sections of duct work. The result of the initial calculation is stored in an indirect file by the operator or the system. From the indirect file, the results of the calculations are used to determine the size of each section of duct work that is connected to a typical piece of equipment. This is accomplished by attaching records that include a reference from the indirect file to each duct section. In turn, these references, or key fields, retrieve information that is based on the original calculation from the indirect file and use it to determine the size of each duct section.

The most dramatic techniques for storing information in nongraphic files use procedures that automatically capture design information. For example, the area of any closed polygon on the drawings can be automatically measured and stored. This area is later combined with a file of construction costs to create a construction cost estimate. In a second example, fields for locations of objects are automatically filled in by querying an indirect file to determine the name of the boundary which surrounds the object.

Procedures for storing information in an indirect file may not require the use of the drawing at all. This attribute is particularly useful when working with large quantities of design elements, such as furniture items for a major office complex. For each item, the name of the manufacturer, color, size, price, and order number must eventually be connected to furniture on a facilities plan. This information is first specified and stored as part of the architectural space program for the facility. It is entered as text information in a file remote to the CAD system. Later, selected fields from this file are transferred into an indirect file. Finally, the records attached to each furniture symbol on the drawings refer to the indirect file by the use of key fields.

Direct and Indirect Files—a Summary

A design element can be completely described in real world terms only with a combination of graphic and written information. These two very different kinds of design information must be tied together, ideally with a link based on actual project drawings so that written information always reflects the status of drawing work in progress. However, storing all project-related nongraphic information on CAD drawings is inefficient. Graphic objects that represent design elements are connected to written documents through direct files that are part of the drawings. These direct files include records that are associated with each graphic object. Direct files are the conduit, the index, to project-related written information. Recall that direct files are connected not only to the drawing but also to indirect files stored separately from the drawings. As explained in Chap. 16, with indirect files nongraphic information can be transferred both to and from a CAD system and other data processing systems.

Records in the direct file for names of objects and other key fields are like threaded couplings. They set up precise relations between different records in different files. Software which describes these relations combines a nongraphic record with a graphic object, providing the glue that holds the entire set of design documents together.

Chapter 15

Key Fields

"Computers appear to be purely verbal devices, even when they are working at pattern recognition, and their uses in design depend almost entirely on the description of design as a verbal process. To be sure, machines can be used to make pictures. But it is the eye that does the visual analysis. The machine usually enters in a relatively trivial way. . . . [T]here is normally no visual intelligence built into computer graphics." [PORT70]

Architecture involves identifying and locating objects in space. To an architect, identifying an object without spatial information is meaningless. "Where is the desk on the first floor?" is clearly an absurd question—there may be hundreds of desks. To answer this type of question, we need spatial identification such as a room number or department. The critical, if not determining, form of design information is contained in the spatial or geometric relationships between design elements. These spatial relationships are essentially defined graphically; CAD systems are particularly appropriate for resolving spatial questions. Once you have pointed to an object displayed on a CAD screen, the system determines not only what the object is but also where it is located. If the symbol for desk is on the system, the question can be answered unambiguously.

In traditional drafting, the symbol for the desk did not exist outside of a drawing. Putting the same furniture number on the drawing and in the furniture inventory was sufficient for identification, since we assumed that the number, shown in both locations, referred to the same design element, a specific desk. Now that data processing tools are doing drafting, the system must perform this association. Thus, a graphic object represents the desk, and this object has its own identification, records which point to a description of the object.

By picking the object on a CAD screen, we are selecting it with as much precision as if we had walked up and put our hands on it. This is intuitively obvious to designers but is not so obvious to a computer. Although the location on the drawing is unambiguous, the identification is not entirely complete. We have found the graphic object, but the system will require further instructions to find the complete description of the design element.

There may be hundreds of copies of the symbol for a typical desk on the drawings. How can we distinguish a particular symbol from all others when working backward from a report, for example? (How can we locate a specific desk—the one with the simulated wood-grain finish that belongs to the Manager of Poor Taste?) To precisely identify a design element, the system must be able to find the correct version of the symbol.

The Use of Key Fields

Once design information is distributed throughout the files of a data base system (on the drawings, in direct files that are part of the drawings, in indirect files on the CAD system, and, in some cases, in files on separate systems from the drawings) we must be able to find the information we need. Storing design information in files which have specified records and fields allows for the convenient management of information. The pivotal element in this multidimensional structure of files, records, and fields is the key field. Key fields indicate where data is stored in a file as well as how to retrieve it.

A key field is any field that contains a key. A *key* is "a group of characters usually forming a field, utilized in the identification or location of an item." [SIPP80] If the data in a key field in one file matches the data in a key field in a separate file, an identification is established. The records in both files refer to the same design element by definition. Symbol names, for example, are typically used as data in key fields. As a result, a graphic object on a drawing can be connected to any record of nongraphic information as long as the symbol name also appears in a key field in the nongraphic file.

Key fields define a logical structure for information. Regardless of what type of file, or how many files are involved, key fields make it possible to relate all the design information, both throughout a design office and within a particular project.

Architectural Keys

Architectural design information can be organized into a structure with the use of three fundamental keys:

1. The project number.

2. The room or space identification.
3. The name of the graphic object.

Most design information, and the graphic object that it relates to, is identified and retrieved with these three keys alone. The project number can be expanded to include the project phase and a revision number. Certain design problems, however, when combined with the characteristics of a particular data base system may require the use of alternate and/or supplemental keys. The keys must contain sufficient information to uniquely identify the record sought within a file of similar records.

Alternate keys for architectural design information include:

1. The serial number.
2. The drawing number.

Whether the serial number is a key or not, will depend on the particular design problem. Many specific graphic objects can be found by the use of serial numbers, such as a door or room number, as key fields.

Serial numbers are not always appropriate, however, as keys. Usually, a serial number indicates another copy of an identical object, such as the next 3'-0" door, within a class of similar objects. In a data file for a door schedule, the serial number does not provide any more information about the object beyond the existence of one more copy. The serial number will not help the system locate the correct text record within the nongraphic files for the door schedule, for instance. In this case, the serial number should not be used as a key.

In fact, serial numbers do not have to appear in all records. In architectural planning, for instance, the actual room number is not even known when space programming reports are completed. Another key to the room or space identification is the drawing name or number. Many design elements, such as floor systems, elevators, roofs, or exterior walls, are not related to a specific space or room. In such cases, the drawing number, or drawing identification, is a more appropriate key.

Even if a design element appears on more than one drawing, however, the drawing identification can be looked up as data in an indirect file. A drawing number file can include a complete list of design elements, based on a system of component numbers, paired with drawing numbers, along with a field for the view or particular version of the design element on the drawing. The drawing number usually does not signify that an object or a text record is unique. The drawing identification is not necessarily a key data field.

Under realistic production conditions, drawing identifications can be an expedient key. After all, designers tend to think in terms of drawings. If changes have to be coordinated throughout a set of drawings, every change can be stored in a decision file where each is identified by drawing number or numbers.

Another key that is sometimes required is the format name or structure of the record itself. The record format is a description of the types of fields contained in a record. The format name tells the system what kind of information to expect. For example, nongraphic information can be characters, such as a paragraph; an integer, such as a room number; or a floating point number, such as a dimension. Whether to use the format as a key depends on the characteristics of the particular system in use.

Different systems search for the format of a record in different places. With some systems, records with different formats can be combined within the same file. In this case, the format for each record must travel along with the record and its data fields. As a result, the format name must be cited as part of the key for any information in the record.

With other systems the format for each record is specified as part of the description of the entire file; it is not included within the record itself. With software of this type, such as dBASE II or III[1] and UNIFY,[2] all the records in a file or relation have the same format. You do not have to specify the format of each record as a key.

Multiple Keys and Families of Design Elements

Multiple keys provide a logical structure to design information. Every design element is a distinct entity yet also exists as a member of several different groups or families of similar elements. Each design element must be cross-referenced among these different groups. As a result, design elements usually require more than one identification, more than one key. For example, room 101 is a distinct element within project 8501. Yet room 101 is likely to reappear in project 8502. The project number must be included as an additional key with each object in the room so that the members of one project can be separated from members of other projects. If multiple keys are used, the graphic objects such as the furniture and equipment in room 101 can carry the same symbol names specified by the office standards data base in both projects. Multiple keys distinguish an item of data within more than one family of design elements; consequently, the same item can show up simultaneously in each of several different families. In fact, multiple keys enable us to reuse the same graphic objects and some of the same nongraphic information over and over.

A group or family of design elements is not the same as the collection of line work that is recognized as a group by the CAD system. Graphic objects are designated as members of a group on a CAD system by being included in a list that defines the group. Design elements, on the other hand, are recognized as members of a group or family because the same name, the key, is attached to each member.

Once it has sufficient keys, any record can be recognized and can travel by itself. This enables design information in the form of a graphic object or of one of its many nongraphic references to travel independently from other data. This data independence makes it possible for the members of different

[1] dBASE II and dBASE III are trademarks of Ashton-Tate.

[2] UNIFY is a trademark of UNIFY Corp.

families to be found and collected at any time. Like luggage being routed to an airplane, data arrives at different times and at different counters; it is tagged and then sorted through the baggage handling system. Later, the correct luggage pieces are collected, according to the tag each piece carries, onto a single cart for loading on a distinct flight. In the same way, multiple keys enable records to be assembled from separate files and collected into reports and schedules.

Valid Key Fields

Because key fields are so frequently used by the system, keep them as short as possible. When searching for a record, the system must perform a letter-by-letter comparison of each key, and no matter how fast the system is, this comparison takes time. Using the minimum number of possible characters makes the search process more efficient.

Although any field in a record can be a key field, it is more efficient to designate the first, or leading fields, as key fields. This makes it easier to compare the output between files. Software design is also simplified, and since many software utilities use the first field as a default when sorting a file, use of this convention minimizes instructions to the system.

Appropriate keys for use in an architectural office deserve some attention. In a way, they are a design problem. Valid keys form part of the office standards, such as allowable text sizes and line weights, in the office standards data base. A master list or data dictionary of pre-defined valid keys, including descriptions, should be part of the office data base. Valid, allowable entries for key fields are a guide for new keys, and can be defined before work starts on any specific project. In this way, a pattern can be set. At the beginning, the data dictionary does not have to include all possible keys. Gaps should be left in the list so that new keys can be added as needed.

The valid keys listed in the data dictionary are used to guide and correct system operators. Whenever a key is entered, the system double-checks if the key is on the list of valid keys. If the key is valid for the current design problem, work proceeds as usual. If the key is not found, the system can ask the operator if this is a new key or simply a typographical error. With this procedure, errors are reduced while the project documents are being created.

A list of valid keys would include the keys, along with their descriptions, for the following categories:

1. Project numbers.
2. Drawing numbers (or identifications).
3. Symbol or component names for these and other graphic objects: doors, windows, cabinets, plumbing fixtures, electrical and mechanical elements, furniture, equipment, hardware, walls, floors, roofs.
4. The names of direct and indirect files.
5. User identifications.
6. Key words for design-topic identification.

7. Construction-cost item identifications.
8. Master specification section numbers.
9. Office account numbers.

Build up your data dictionary gradually. As project work advances, expand the list as needed. When a project is completed, keys that were developed for the project and are applicable to other projects can be copied into the master file of valid keys. Valid keys are a resource; They not only define a structure for design information, they also guide future users and simplify training.

Key Fields and Other Data Base Systems

At least two different types of data base management systems are currently in general use. Different systems use different instructions to retrieve information. Fields that appear in separate files can be identified in one of two different ways.

In one type of data base system, the name of each field is unique to the file in which it is stored. As a result, only the name of the field has to be supplied to find a distinct item of information, the file need not be named as well. The system does not look in every available file. This type of data base management system uses what is referred to as a "centralized" data dictionary, which provides the system with its own internal directory of each file and its fields.

In the second type of data base system, the same field name can be used in different files. Since the system does not have its own internal directory, instructions to the system have to be more explicit. In this case, the name of the file must be provided along with the name of the field.

Both types of data base management system require that the name of one or more key fields be supplied to allow the system to find a precise record and field. On the drawing, one or more key fields must appear in the record attached to the object as well as in the indirect file. The keys point the system to the correct row and column in the indirect file: it is critical that the data in the key fields in both locations match. Fortunately, systems are very good at searching through long lists of fields to find matching records.

As mentioned, particular instructions about key fields depend on the type of data base system in use. A general data base management system, in which each field name is unique, requires the designation of key fields in each file. Since a field name can only be used once, key fields will have different names in different files. You must tell the system which fields are equivalent to each other and are to be used as key fields.

The second type of data base system, which allows you to use the same name for fields in different files, requires that you designate a specific field (or set of fields) as the key. With this type of data base, the system understands that key fields retain the same name in each file.

Both types of data base management systems have their strengths and weaknesses. The data base system that treats each field name as unique has the advantage of flexibility. You can identify any pair of fields as matching, as having a key field relationship. As a result, you can create new relationships between files long after a file has been created.

An additional advantage to this kind of system is that entire fields of information can be transferred conveniently from one file to another. Since each field name is unique, any existing references to the field are left unchanged after such a transfer. As noted, this capability is derived from data independence, which means that the contents of a file can be reorganized as the demands on a data base evolve. Consequently, both your office standards and your project data bases can mature and expand separately from the current software you happen to be using. Who knows what new data base system you will be using in the years to come?

The second type of data base management system has the advantage of simplicity. If the field name, where the data appears, is the same in each file, the relationship between the files has absolute identification, for both the person and the computer. The connection between the files can be recognized immediately. However, this type of system requires that relationships be planned before the file is created because it is not very flexible. When the time comes to generate a new report, for instance, any reorganization of fields, or new associations, must explicitly override the system's understanding of the file organization.

Direct Inspection of the Objects on a Drawing

To the casual observer of CAD, direct inspection, or querying of an object on the drawing, appears to be the simplest method for retrieving nongraphic information. Graphic software applications include functions that are designed to work with nongraphic files while the drawing is active on the CAD system. Indicate an object and name the direct file, referred to as a property or attribute file, and the system responds with a display of the record for the object, along with the fields in the record and the information they contain. Any information that has been stored is displayed. Even information in an indirect file is retrieved. Essentially, this is a spot check. You can see if the right information is in place by examining anything on the drawing that has a record attached.

In fact, this particular CAD capability has only recently been developed. As of this writing, it is still not available with every CAD system. The ability to pick an object on the drawing and ask for all the attached information is the result of a marriage between two different computer capabilities: the query capabilities of data base management systems and the graphic capabilities of CAD. Data processing techniques for manipulating nongraphic files emerged before the development of CAD. Although it may be taken for granted with some systems, reading a text file from a drawing is, in fact, a significant accomplishment.

Some CAD systems have carried this development to higher levels. The techniques described in this chapter can be performed only on systems that allow a fairly rich structure of direct and indirect files to be defined.

Although dramatic, this direct-query capability is in fact somewhat limited.

Selection of a graphic object from a currently active drawing instructs the system to search for information based solely on a specific pair of X and Y cartesian coordinates. The system finds the single graphic object along with its direct record. At this stage of CAD development, most systems are unable to search beyond the first logical record that is attached to the single graphic object selected.

Reports

The use of reports for retrieving information from nongraphic files is more versatile than the direct querying of each object. This is done by using software designed to extract information from the drawings and the files connected to them. Essentially, reporting software scans the drawings and files, and enables the CAD system to recognize any object, or set of objects, that has a record attached. Entire families of objects, or subsets within a family, can be specified, such as all the furniture items. The software copies the information that has been requested from nongraphic files and creates a separate file of extracted data (see Fig. 15-1).

The file of extracted data is not the same as the direct and indirect files that have been discussed so far. Unlike the direct or indirect files, a report is not a form for the storage of data. Once again, information, this time displayed in a report file of extracted data, is distinct from the files that store the information. The information is not permanently stored in this report. Reports glean information from direct files, indirect files, or both. A report, also called "output," is created when a display of the nongraphic design information is requested.

An additional software operation is required to convert the file of extracted information into a finished report. During the initial software operation, information is extracted while the drawing and its related files are scanned. In a second operation, this information is composed into a specific report format, including titles, column and page headers, and page footers. The report can be brought back to the CAD screen and displayed. It can also be made a part of the drawing. A door schedule, for example, can be plotted by combining a report with line work on a drawing. Finally, the report can be printed as a text document separate from the drawings.

As with symbols and direct files, several basic reports are supplied with most graphic software applications. For example, reports that can be used for door and finish schedules are usually available with graphic architectural software. However, reports that are supplied with the software are, of necessity, limited in scope, and they are for general use. To meet the needs of a particular office, the available reports may have to be expanded.

For many specific design problems, you will need to create your own reports. The first time a report is created, it must be designed. Basically, there are five steps involved in designing a report:

1. Name the report.
2. List the graphic objects, which will be inspected during the scanning process.

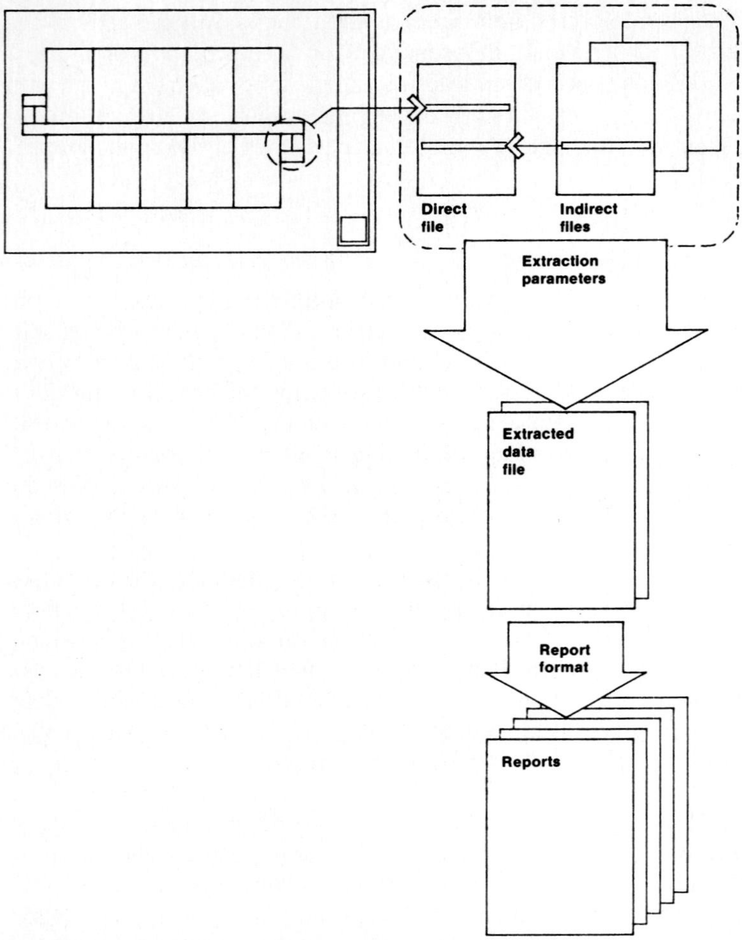

Figure 15-1 Relationship between reports (which do not actually store information) and direct and indirect files associated with a drawing. Creating a report requires both a separate extracted data file and a specific report format.

3. Name the direct and indirect files which contain the nongraphic information.
4. Designate key fields so that specific records can be identified within each file.
5. Establish the format of the report, stating the order in which the fields will be listed.

Once designed, a report can be used again and again, even on different projects, as a template. The actual description of the report is a document in itself. Standard report formats are a valuable part of an office standards data base.

Querying a Data Base

Reports, although satisfactory for a final document, do not satisfy all our needs for information retrieval. They must first be designed and then tested thoroughly before we can be confident that the appropriate records and fields have been assembled correctly. Reports take time. If many drawings must be inspected, as well as many objects on each drawing, reports can take a *long* time. Something between the spot check of a single graphic object and a report is often necessary.

The complete data base of files, with all its records and fields, should be available for inspection outside a drawing. A general data base query capability allows for interactive inspection of information by specifying selection criteria. A data base utility scans for information that matches the selection criteria, and lists the results. With such a utility, we can ask the computer to quickly retrieve any nongraphic information in the files. We can extract any possible logical record from the entire system of files and records.

Design information is rarely complete before the documents must be published. With a data base query capability, all the currently available information can be inspected. The relationships between records and the structure of the information itself can be tested. Without making a complete report, we can determine how much information is available as well as what must be added. Conflicts and inconsistencies can be eliminated when nongraphic information and drawings are compared.

At many points in the design process, such as during architectural space programming, we are unsure about exactly what information to include in a particular report. Reports are design documents and often must be modified or created for the first time according to the requirements of a particular project. Often, several reports are required and each report will reuse some of the same data. By querying the data base of files directly, we can explore different combinations of information. We thus have an opportunity to explore nongraphic design information, similar to that provided by sketching with graphic information.

Hospital planners, for example, must justify proposed expansions according to state-mandated "proof of need" requirements—the state must be satisfied that there is genuine need. A key factor in the justification is the gross square footage of the proposal in comparison with space in similar facilities within the region. The determinants of the size of a proposed hospital department include staffing, number of patient visits, number of medical procedures performed, and service population. Since each determinant includes different growth rates, different area projections will be generated by using different determinants. The problem is to discover which determinant has the highest correlation with the proposed expansion. An optimum projection can be realized only by assembling and reassembling the same information in several different combinations. This type of problem can be explored more conveniently with a data base query utility than with reports.

General data base management software is becoming available. In the past, this software was limited to use on systems with large storage capacities, but current versions are compatible with many different (both large and small) systems. Computer users at all levels are gaining a familarity with the convenience and power of data base management systems. As part of this trend, CAD manufacturers are currently expanding the data base management capabilities that are available along with their graphic software applications.

Chapter

16

Communicating Between Systems with Transfer Files

"We're the phone company. We don't care and we don't have to." LILY TOMLIN

Large sections of a project data base, such as architectural programming reports, records of decisions made by the designer and client, specifications, cost-estimating data, and building product catalogues, are appropriately developed and stored on systems other than the CAD system. Some of this information is used in project drawings, but manual filing techniques make the convenient transfer of information from these sources into the project drawings virtually impossible. With transfer files, the contents of such files are eventually connected to the drawings. CAD systems are, after all, merely another computer, and, with the appropriate procedure, transferring information between different computer systems is possible.

Much written design information originates on systems other than the CAD system and is stored in files on these separate systems. Often files in a project data base are located on several systems throughout a distributed officewide computer system. Such files are similar to indirect files stored on the CAD system and can include the same kind of nongraphic information in similar records and fields.

Transfer files are used to move information between such systems. It is important that selected fields of information stored in files on these systems can be transferred to and from the CAD system. Certain design information, such as room names, emerges from many different nongraphic software applications. Potential transfer files are created with systems such as personal computers, dedicated word processors, central multipurpose computers that also handle office accounting, for instance; or time-shared mainframe computers. The primary difference between transfer files and indirect files on the CAD system is the temporary life of a transfer file while information is moved from one system to another.

Specific fields of information are first transferred and then converted into indirect files, and from there, information is moved directly onto the drawings. Consequently, drawings can reflect information originally developed on other computer systems. This procedure can be reversed so that information that originates on the drawings, such as areas and item counts, is first stored in association with graphic objects and later transferred from the CAD system onto other systems.

The requirements that must be satisfied to transfer written information between systems are:

1. Organize files according to a specified format.
2. Include key fields in files.
3. Convert selected fields to a standard format and write them to a transfer file.
4. Make sure each system has a communication protocol which enables one system to receive files from or transmit files to another.

Since only requested information need be transferred, store the information in readily segregated fields. Excerpt only specific fields from the source file. The necessary fields can be temporarily copied into a separate transfer file and moved without copying all the information in the source file.

Once again, name each graphic object on the drawing which is to be associated with written information. The name of the object is stored in a direct file that is part of the drawing. With a name, the CAD system recognizes and can attach information to the correct graphic object. Remember, the name is one of the keys used by the system to match data with a key field in an indirect file.

As a final stage in the process, move the selected fields of text information with a transfer file onto the CAD system. When the same file format is used frequently on many different projects, you may wish to use a custom program to convert the file back and forth between internal binary formats that are recognized, on either side of the transaction, by both systems. This is known as a *conversion program.*

A simpler alternative for transferring information is to use utilities, which augment communication protocols, that are provided with both systems. The transfer file of selected data must first be normalized into a standard-format character file, an ASCII (American Standard Code for Information Interchange) file. The fields must be stripped of any special or embedded characters that are only recognized by a particular system. Within a normalized character file, the individual characters are coded using ASCII. ASCII is a standard data-transmission code that was introduced to achieve compatibility between data devices. For a further description of ASCII files refer to Chap. 8. Most systems include a utility that converts a proprietary file, which is specific to a system, into a flat character file. Such utilities also recognize a flat character file transferred from other systems. Finally, the CAD system must use a data base management system that will accept data from such a file.

The transfer file, now normalized, is transmitted over to the CAD system. Again, the most practical solution at this step is to use the communications utilities that are available with each system. Some CAD systems will accept data through communications networks such as Ethernet.[1] Some will accept data that is transmitted with communications software over a telephone line. Information can be transferred on a floppy disk, removable hard disk, or tape if the CAD system recognizes the format for the disk or tape. Communications can be treated like a black-box problem—the information is poured in at one end and shows up at the other. For our purposes, it is only important that the information arrive in an unaltered condition.

In reality, only a small percentage of written design information in a typical project data base has to be transferred to or from the drawings. Most of the large volume of information can remain on a separate system. Multipage reports, such as specifications, cost reports, and space projections, are assembled and modified after interacting with the drawings on the CAD system for strategic information such as a list of drawing components, material quantities, or item locations.

Certain information, however, is used frequently in many design transactions and should be transferred between the drawings and reused, on separate systems if necessary, as part of the project data base. Examples of nongraphic information that is transferred includes:

1. Lists of project drawings.
2. Accounting information such as operator time charged to specific projects.
3. Space planning criteria.
4. For staged construction projects, lists of subcontractor activity by area.
5. Room names and numbers.
6. Drawing notes.
7. Location information, such as zones, departments, floors, building numbers.
8. Areas.

---

[1] Ethernet is a trademark of Xerox Corporation.

9. Quantity takeoffs.
10. Furniture and equipment lists.
11. Information developed by consultants, perhaps working with separate analysis programs, such as load factors for electrical, mechanical, and ventilating systems.
12. Lists of changes to the drawings collected in a file of design decisions.

In the sections that follow, three examples of design information transferred onto drawings from separate systems are described. In the first case, room names are reused on the drawings from an original room and equipment inventory. Automatic transfer of symbols from the same file is described in the second case. Finally, the last section in this chapter describes the transfer of symbols and nongraphic information onto drawings using files developed for an architectural space program.

Names from Room Inventory to Drawings

An architectural space program is created when a design project is merely a glint in the architect's eye, long before the drawings are even begun. Part of the information in the space program is the identification of all the rooms that are included in the project. Standard rooms, such as office type B for a head nurse, and office type G for a doctor, are described and catalogued along with other program requirements. The same room name, however, must appear on the architectural plans. If the project includes hundreds, perhaps thousands of rooms, and if a CAD operator has to enter each room name one at a time, the name of any particular room on the plans could easily be incorrect. A more efficient use of design information would be to transfer the room names from their source document—in this case, a room and equipment inventory—directly onto the drawings.

The following example describes the transfer onto a drawing of information originally created for a furniture and equipment inventory report. Because hospital equipment is so expensive, extensive planning is done early in the design process to establish a realistic and detailed equipment program. The inventory is prepared for purposes of budgeting and is also used when the items are eventually procured. Much of the information is assembled during the programming phase and while the design drawings are still schematic. The objective is to take advantage of this early work by transferring some of the information to the design drawings. The original inventory being discussed was prepared on a time-sharing system remote from the CAD system where the drawings were taking shape. In this example, the room names were transferred onto the drawings.

The room names were stored in a simple text file shown as the Room Names File (see Fig. 16-1). They appear as headings on the equipment inventory reports.

Each record in the Room Names File had two key fields followed by a single data field. The first key field designated the zone or area of a floor where a

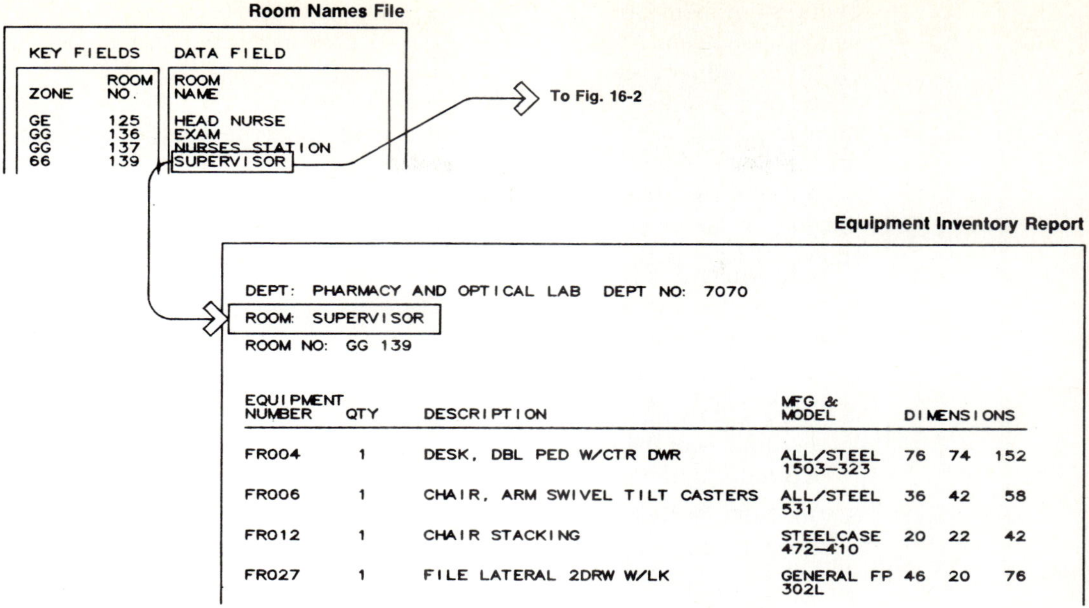

Figure 16-1 Title for an equipment-inventory report created from a file of room names; room-names file is also used to automatically transfer room names onto drawings (see Fig. 16-2).

specific hospital department was located. For example, GG indicated the ground floor laboratory area. The second key field, a room number, identified either a specific room or a type of room, such as a private office. Finally, the actual room name was the only field of data original to this file. All the records in this Room Names File used the same format.

The Room Names File was transferred in its entirety to the CAD system and used as an indirect file. Since it was created as a normalized character file, neither its format nor its contents were changed during the transfer.

To bring the room names from the indirect file onto the drawings, two types of graphic objects were used: boundaries and a room number symbol. First, a boundary was drawn around each department. Boundaries are a simple continuous line outlining each department assigned to a specific drawing level designated for boundaries. A nongraphic record was attached to each boundary. This record included an indirect reference field named ZONE. This identifies the record where the name of the boundary is stored. Notice that this field matched the first key field in the Room Names File. As a result, the designation for the zone in the indirect file is connected to the actual boundary on the drawing.

Next, a standard room number symbol was copied into each room on the floor plans. The symbol includes a text string with dummy text for the room number, e.g., "XXX," as well as the room name, e.g., "RNRNRNRNRNRN." Both dummy text strings are also designated with special flags recognized by the CAD system. The symbol has a nongraphic record attached with a direct field for the room number. Notice that the room number is the second key field in the Room Names File. The record attached to the symbol also includes an indirect reference field for the room name (see Fig. 16-2).

The room number in each of the symbols was entered to reflect the room-numbering system for the project. For the time being, the room name was left unchanged as dummy text on the drawing.

To make the final transfer from the Room Names File to text on the drawing, a minor enhancement to the existing software was written. The added software performs the following functions:

1. Scans a drawing to find all the zone boundaries and creates a "look-up" file that includes, for each zone, the object name of the boundary and its geometric extents (in *X* and *Y* coordinates).
2. Scans a drawing to find each room-number symbol; compares the *X* and *Y* coordinates of the symbol position to the *X* and *Y* extent of the zone, thus determining the zone where the symbol is located on the drawing.
3. Does an interference check to determine which of the zones encompasses the symbol if it is within the extent of more than one zone.

These first three steps can also be performed with location fields.

4. Reads the room number for each symbol from the attached direct record.

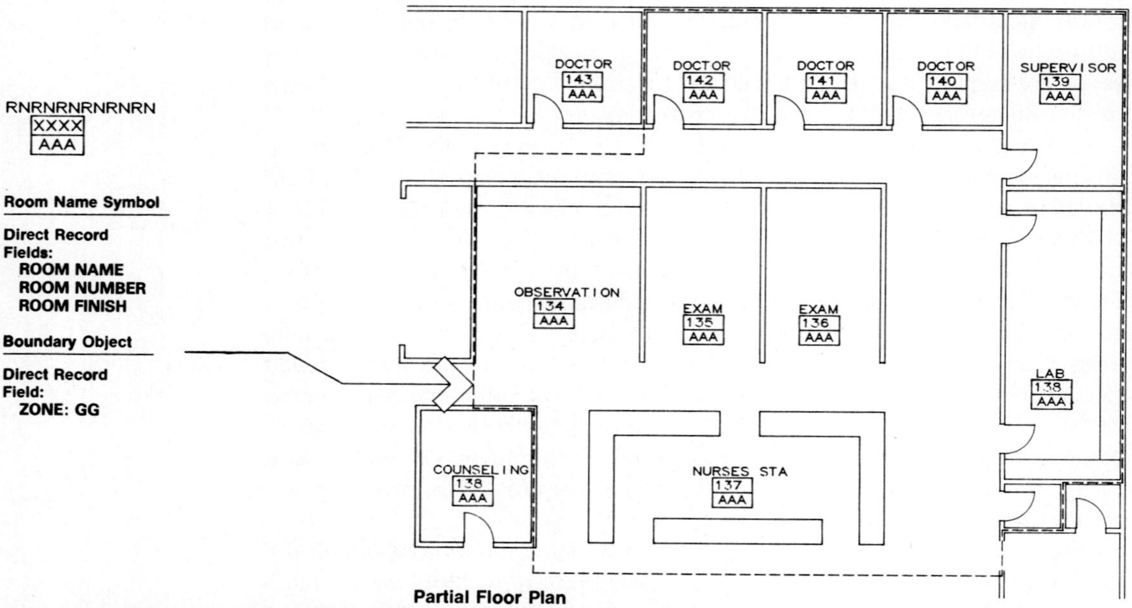

Figure 16-2 Room names automatically transferred onto a drawing from an indirect file—in this case, room numbers must first be in place on the drawing.

5. Looks up the corresponding record in the Room Names File using the room number and zone as key fields.
6. Exchanges the selected name from the indirect Room Name File for the dummy text "RNRNRNRNRNRN" on the drawing.
7. Repeats steps 1 through 6 for all the room symbols found by scanning the drawing.

Over 2000 room names were filled in on the drawings using this procedure. They were transferred from the file that was originally created for the equipment inventory: every room name transferred to the drawings was correct.

Automatic Placement of Symbols

With some modification, the procedure described in the previous section can be used to transfer graphic objects onto a drawing. For example, we can go further with information from the original equipment inventory file. Along with the room names, symbols for each piece of equipment are placed in the rooms. Unlike the room name example, where the room name symbol was initially placed in the room by the CAD operator, the system automatically placed the symbols for the equipment on the drawing.

Boundaries must exist for each room in this case. Also, the procedure described above requires an additional operation. An equipment list is extracted from the equipment inventory file and transferred into an indirect file on the CAD system. This equipment list file includes key fields for zone and room number. It would also include data fields for the appropriate symbol name and equipment number. After each room boundary is located, the equipment list for each room is retrieved from the indirect file. The system is then instructed to retrieve, from the project symbol library, the symbol named in the equipment list file.

The symbols are automatically placed within each named and bounded room. The system is instructed to locate the first symbol within the boundary for each room at a given distance from the upper left corner of the boundary. Additional symbols will appear in a row, one beside the other, if the system is instructed to increment the X-axis location of the next symbol by a multiple of the width of the last symbol.

In a last interactive step, the operator moves each symbol into the final position for the equipment within the room. With this semiautomatic procedure, much of the tedious and error-prone work is eliminated. The correct pieces of equipment, and correct number of pieces, are located in the right room without reentering the equipment list or double-checking. The time-consuming process of calling each item out of a symbol library is done automatically by the system. The only work that remains, the precise placement of equipment within each space and any necessary adjustment to surrounding conditions, makes the best use of the operator's human judgment and coordination.

Room Data Sheets—from Space Program to Drawing

The following example is derived from an architectural programming project where questionnaires and interviews were used in a participatory process along with CAD and data processing techniques to develop a space program for a proposed corporate headquarters facility. Along with planning for the initial design, the purpose of the architectural program was to define corporate and departmental space standards that could be used to plan and control changes within the facility after the initial move-in. Written material, which would ordinarily be presented as text information and tables in printed reports, was combined with drawings. By combining the written questionnaire summaries with graphic symbols, room data sheets were created that portrayed an image of each room configuration with integrated text.

For corporate planning, summary reports such as space projections were produced. However, from the same data it was possible to create a library of standard room configurations that were customized to reflect the individual requirements of each department. A CAD system was used to combine the text and graphic information into each of 400 individual room data sheets (see Fig. 16-3). A diagram was created that included the furniture configuration, a horizontal and vertical scale, along with walls and doors (if any). The name of the department and subunit and the title of the occupant were displayed as a title on each sheet. A descriptive paragraph along with a list of the furniture and requirements for each space, such as for security, communication, and amenities, were included on each room data sheet. Since it was on a CAD system, the final results were documents that combined text and graphics and that could be edited like a word processing document.

All the elements on the room data sheets, both graphic and nongraphic, were assembled automatically in a background process. Once the border of an empty drawing was indicated, the CAD operator had no more work to perform. Each room data sheet was created in approximately 30 seconds.

The facility was planned to house approximately 35 departments. In turn, each department included an average of four or five subunits, such as administration and planning, engineering, customer information, etc. At the level of individual spaces within each subunit, there were from 3 to 12 different types of rooms for director, secretary, file storage, supervisor, engineer, etc. Some of these spaces might be repeated several times within a subunit. With minor variations, approximately 400 space configurations needed to be programmed.

As might be expected, responses to the questionnaires revealed considerable variation in the expressed requirements and preferences of each department. The room data sheets actually combined in a single document a summary of the questionnaire responses with a picture of the corporate space standard. Together, this combination enabled us to define space configurations that both conformed to the corporate standard and reflected the unique requirements of each subunit within a department.

Because these documents were developed during the schematic design phase, many items, such as telephones, copying machines, and chalk boards,

OCCUPANCY:	5 or less
PROXIMITY:	extrance/reception
PROXIMITY:	conference space
CEILING HT:	9 feet
DOOR:	lockable
DOOR:	glass door
DOOR:	36 inch minimum
FINISH, FLOOR:	carpet
FINISH, WALL:	vinyl fabric
POWER:	normal power
POWER:	4 outlest per desk
SECURITY:	Stnd. Bldg., fire alarm, hand pull
SECURITY:	CCTV camera
SECURITY:	receptionist
SECURITY:	all but those screened earlier
AMENITY:	natural light
AMENITY:	noise abatement
AMENITY:	planting
AMENITY:	3 art pieces
COMMUNICATION:	bullentin board
COMMUNICATION:	magazine rack/dispaly
COMMUNICATION:	photo organization chart
COMMUNICATION:	telephone
COMMUNICATION:	intercom
COMMUNICATION:	paging
COMMUNICATION:	music
EQUIPMENT:	20 linear Ft. of sectional couch
EQUIPMENT:	side & coffee tables

Holding area for invited guests, vendor people awaiting meetings, (including some VIP's). Informal meetings too brief to use conference room. If shared with personnel, serves as waiting area for job applicants, interviewees, and new employees.

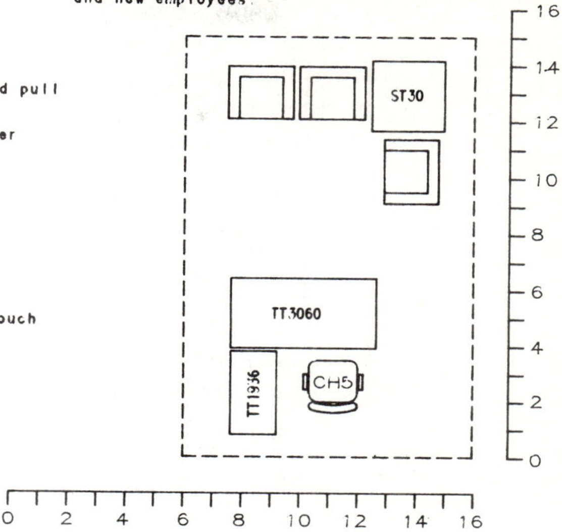

STND. EQUIP.:	TT3060	DESK
STND. EQUIP.:	TT1936	DESK RETURN
STND. EQUIP.:	C5	CHAIR
STND. EQUIP.:	CH10	GUEST CHAIRS
STND. EQUIP.:	ST30	TABLE

NAME:	RECEPTION	TOTAL AREA:	150	SF EACH:	150
DEPT/CLUSTER:	12 ADMIN. & PLANNING	TYPE:	K-2	STAFF:	0

Figure 16-3 Room data sheet from an architectural space program for a typical reception area showing a furniture configuration and including a description, list of conditions, and equipment; text and graphics automatically combined onto each sheet in a single operation. (*Courtesy of Design Logic, Inc., San Francisco, CA.*)

do not appear as symbols along with the furniture. Their final location within the space had not been determined. They are, however, included in the list of requirements for each space. The room data sheet was the first document in the design process to join these relatively fine-grained requirements with a space configuration. Consequently, it is the list of space requirements that distinguishes one space from the next.

Four hundred configurations is a considerable number for either a single individual or a central committee to evaluate. However, because a large variety of unique room data sheets could be created so easily, each department manager could be presented with space configurations for their department alone. As a result, each of the 35 department heads only had a dozen or so room data sheets to review. At this number, the minor variations that allow a space to conform to the functions of a specific department were easy to recognize and were meaningful to the department staff.

Forty corporate space standards had already been established by the client. Although schematic, they included a basic area allowance for a typical position along with a furniture configuration. The corporate space standards were used as a guide during the information-gathering stages of the project. At the end of the programming phase, the original corporate space standards were replaced by the room data sheets.

During the initial information-gathering stage, different questionnaires were used for different types of spaces. This reduced the amount of information that an individual manager had to supply. Questionnaires were divided into eight categories based on how a space was generally used. With this system, each individual had to respond only to questions that were specific to their area of specialization. The eight space utilization categories included:

1. Department level traffic.
2. Conference and class rooms.
3. Special equipment spaces.
4. Lobby and reception areas.
5. Library or resource center.
6. Storage, files, and vaults.
7. Office or workstations.
8. Computer rooms.

Schematic versions of three file layouts along with the room data sheet are shown in Fig. 16-4.

The three files were used during the process of transferring information from the survey and space program to the room data sheets on the CAD system. A copy of a room data sheet is shown in Fig. 16-3. A brief segment of listings from an actual interview file is also shown in Table 16-1. Other files, which are not shown, were used to create and process the questionnaires and to log and control changes to the room data sheets.

The Space Projection File is the main source file of information. In the procedure for transferring information onto a room data sheet, it sets the primary relations. The other two files served as reference files where information was looked up as needed.

The Space Projection File was created on a business data processing system using a program similar to a spreadsheet program. The spreadsheet program projected, allocated, and balanced the space requirements among the different departments within the project. A nominal square footage was assigned to each department and its subunits by applying the existing corporate space standards.

In a separate operation, responses to the questionnaires were recorded and summarized with the use of a survey analysis system. Each questionnaire was identified with a four-digit code; the first two digits identified the department; and, the second two digits identified one of the eight possible space utilization categories. In Fig. 16-4, the department is 12 and the category is 04, which corresponds to a lobby and reception area in Department 12.

Each available choice on the questionnaires, such as required floor finish or degree of privacy, has a preassigned code. When a questionnaire was

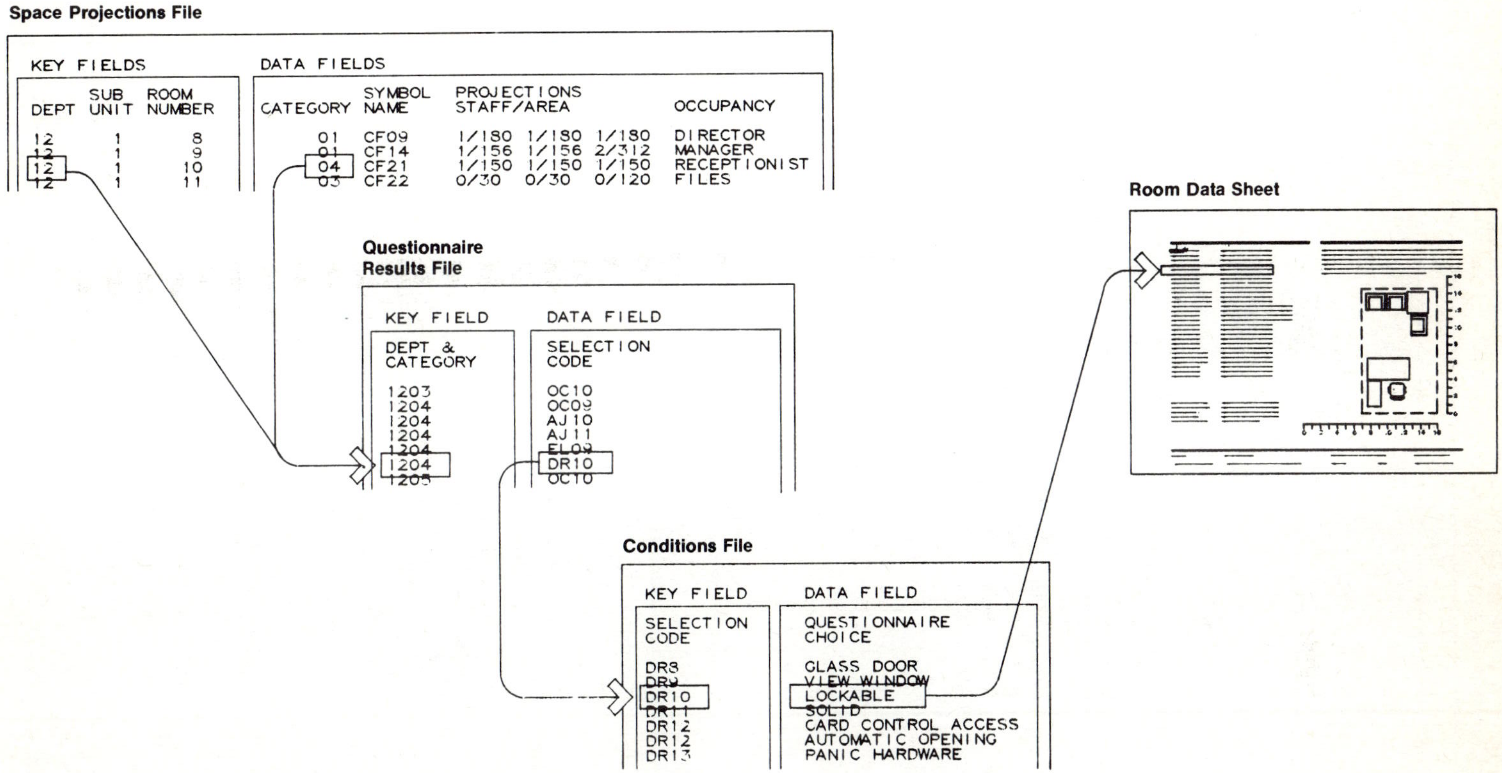

Figure 16-4 Organization of three files used to automatically create the list of conditions for the room data sheet shown in Fig. 16-3. (*Courtesy of Design Logic, Inc., San Francisco, CA.*)

TABLE 16-1 File Listing from Questionnaire Results and Conditions Files Displayed as List of Conditions on Room Data Sheet[a]

Department	Requirement		Response	
7400	512	Access hours	Off-hour access required	
7400	2311	Adequacy	Reception	Inadequate
7400	2312	Adequacy	Small conference room	Inadequate
7400	2322	Adequacy	Large conference room	Adequate
7400	2333	Adequacy	Reproduction room	Inadequate
7400	2342	Adequacy	Lounge	Need but don't have
7400	2346	Adequacy	Service vehicle access	Inadequate
7400	312	Architectural	Daylight required	
7400	313	Architectural	Acoustic privacy	
7400	314	Architectural	Acoustic control, voices	
7400	315	Architectural	Acoustic control, machines	
7400	317	Architectural	Special fire protection	
7400	318	Architectural	Increased floor load	
7400	321	Architectural	Work space with storage for computer output	
7400	322	Architectural	Secure storage for 6000 computer tapes	
7400	414	Equipment	Will affect space layout	
7400	415	Equipment	Unusual-size files	
7400	416	Equipment	Computer equipment	
7400	417	Equipment	Word processor	
7400	432	Equipment	Printers	
7400	342	Security	Special requirements	
7400	343	Security	Required computer security	
7400	344	Security	Required limited access area	
7400	345	Security	Required locked files	
7400	346	Security	Required storage areas	
7400	121	Work styles	Internal, frequent face-to-face with staff	

[a] Table reprinted courtesy of Design Logic, Inc., San Francisco, CA.

returned, the four-digit identification code was recorded along with the code for each choice that was made on the questionnaire. Together, this information was stored in the Questionnaire Results File.

Notice that the description for each choice is not included in the Questionnaire Results File. The descriptions, along with the questionnaires, were originally created on a separate word processing system. There were over 550 unique questionnaire choices—each with a separate description. They are repeated over and over on hundreds of questionnaires. The original descriptions were transferred into a separate indirect file on the CAD system, the Conditions File. As a result, the description for each choice is stored only once in a look-up file.

Each of the 40 corporate space standards was recorded on the CAD system as a room-layout or footprint symbol. Each symbol was given a name. The symbol name was stored as a direct record attached to the symbol and was cited in a data field in the Space Projections File.

In addition to the footprint symbols for each corporate space standard, one additional symbol was created. This symbol served as a combination of sheet border and template. It was designed so that the written information as well as the footprint symbol could be automatically composed onto an $8\frac{1}{2}$- by 11-in sheet (see Fig. 16-5). The visible graphics on the template were a border, a graphic scale, and layout lines for the text information and sheet title.

Along with the visible elements of the template, five invisible location points were added. These were tic marks that were not plotted. The location points served to position the title, descriptive paragraph, and list of furniture and requirements on the sheet. Each location point had a special flag or kind number assigned. The system recognizes these kind numbers and thus uses the specific location of the tic mark to place each object on the sheet.

Finally, a record was attached to the template symbol and stored in a direct file along with the drawing. A string of dummy text was added in the upper left corner of each sheet. The nongraphic record for the symbol included a field that would replace the dummy text on the sheet with a drawing number. This drawing number identified each room data sheet as a unique document.

All of the information necessary to generate a room data sheet was now assembled on the CAD system. The graphic information had been created as

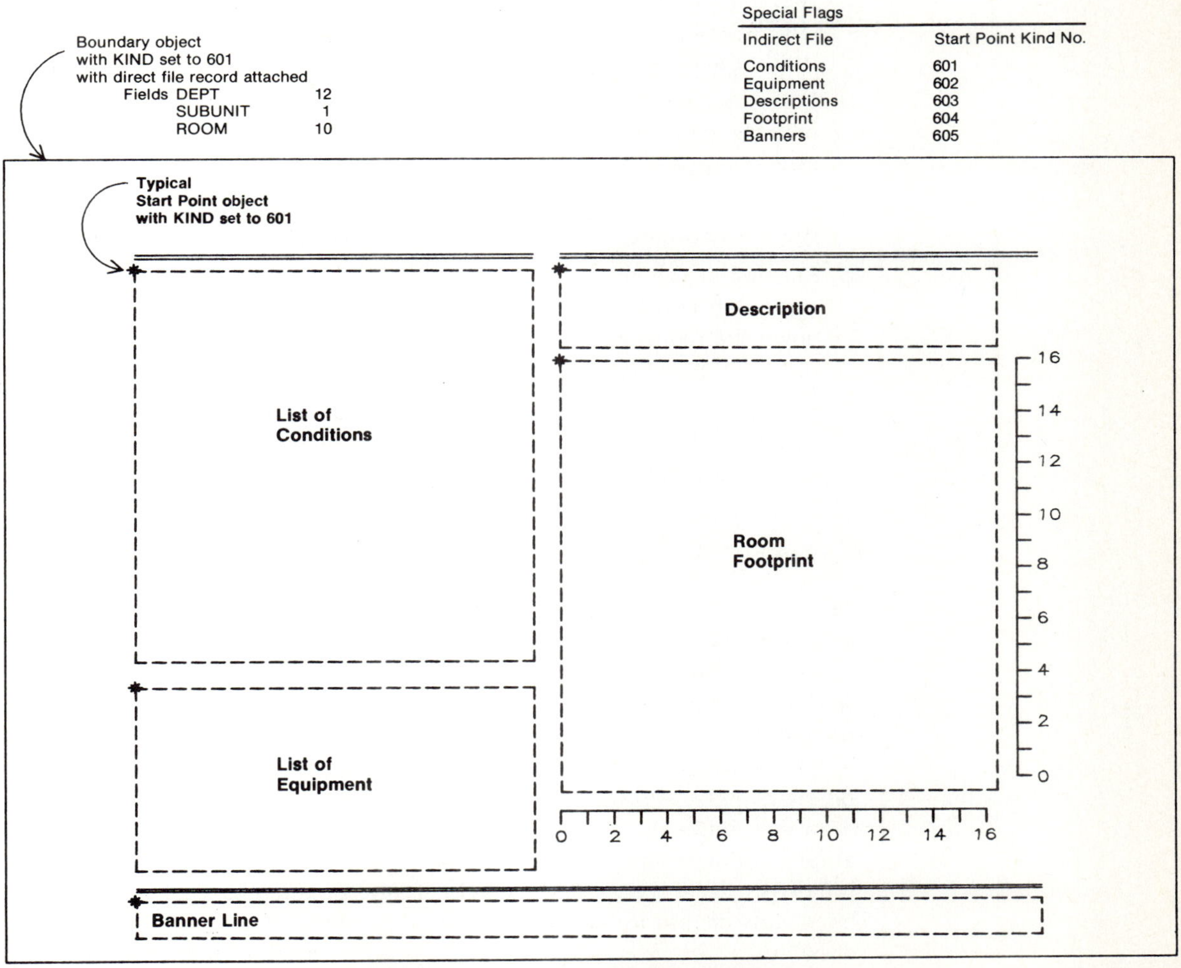

Figure 16-5 Template (created as a symbol) for the room data sheet showing the location of points with special flags which automatically position information on the sheet. (*Courtesy of Design Logic, Inc., San Francisco, CA.*)

symbols, and the written information was transferred from business and word processing systems into three indirect files: the Space Projection File, the Questionnaire Results File, and the Conditions File.

Special purpose software was written to pull both graphic and nongraphic information together quickly and generate the 400 room data sheets in an automatic operation. Following is an outline of the functions performed by the special purpose software:

1. For each line in the Space Projection File, retrieve a copy of the template symbol from the symbol library. Copy the title of each space from the field labeled "Occupancy" in the Space Projection File onto the banner line at the bottom of the sheet. (A point with kind #605 marks the starting point of the banner line.)
2. Again using the Space Projection File, combine the department identification number with the space-category number into a single identifying key. (In Fig. 16-4, 12 is combined with category 04 to become 1204.) This is used to look up data in the Questionnaire Results File.
3. For each item in the Questionnaire Results File, with a key that matches both the department and space category number, read the corresponding selection codes.
4. Use each selection code to look up and retrieve the phrase that describes the questionnaire choice in the Conditions File.
5. Starting at the point designated with kind #611 in the template (in the upper left corner), write the phrase onto the room data sheet. Continue down the room data sheet listing conditions (repeating steps 2, 3, and 4) until the questionnaire results that match the current key are exhausted.
6. Using the same record in the Space Projection File, retrieve the symbol name for the footprint. Next, place the symbol using two of the location points designated with kind #604.
7. Look up and place the descriptive paragraph for the room.
8. Repeat 1 through 6 for each line in the Space Projection File.

The procedure used in this case is an example of what we refer to as "generative graphics." In most cases, graphics such as architectural drawings are generated solely with interactive procedures carried out by a CAD operator. In this case the drawings are created directly by operating on text files from a program. Except for initiation and control of the procedure, the CAD operator is not required. The system performs all the work required for the assembly of nearly complete drawings. Minimal editing was required to reach the final drawings; however, the system assembled the bulk of the graphic and nongraphic information in a fully automated procedure. This procedure is a prototype. It can be used with architectural production drawings to assemble details or interior elevations from a data base of preassembled standard drawings.

Section

4

Three-Dimensional and Solid Modeling

This final section provides an overview of the basic concepts used in computer-resident three-dimensional or solid modeling, reviewing methods used to create components in a three-dimensional model. Included is a discussion from a system operator's perspective of the assembly of a model and the organization of geometric data to store and represent three-dimensional objects within the system. As in previous sections, the concepts apply to existing CAD systems of all sizes. The final chapter, Chap. 22, explores certain development issues, including working drawings derived from a three-dimensional model and spatial subdivision, a methodology for creating three-dimensional models developed in the field of medical science.

Chapter

17

Introduction to Three-Dimensional Modeling

"The world is two dimensional, or it is 'n' dimensional, but it is not particularly three dimensional."

ROBERT STULTS, SYSTEMS DEVELOPER

Three-dimensional modeling refers to the comprehensive graphic description of an architectural design for purposes of visualization as well as analysis. For convenience, references to three-dimensional modeling also include what is known as *solid modeling*. In practice, these two terms are used interchangeably. (The assumptions of solid modeling that distinguish it from three-dimensional modeling, which is used solely for visualizing a design, are explained in Chap. 18.)

Current architectural design practice uses drawings and physical models which attempt to represent, as realistically as possible, the design as it will appear when completed. Computer-based three-dimensional modeling is similar. Physical models created at small scale from such materials as wood, plastic, and even clay replicate an architectural design in three dimensions. Occasionally, full scale models, such as for hotel rooms, are constructed. Assembling or altering these predecessors of computer modeling reveals the inflexibility and the expense of physical models and the opportunities afforded by a three-dimensional computer model.

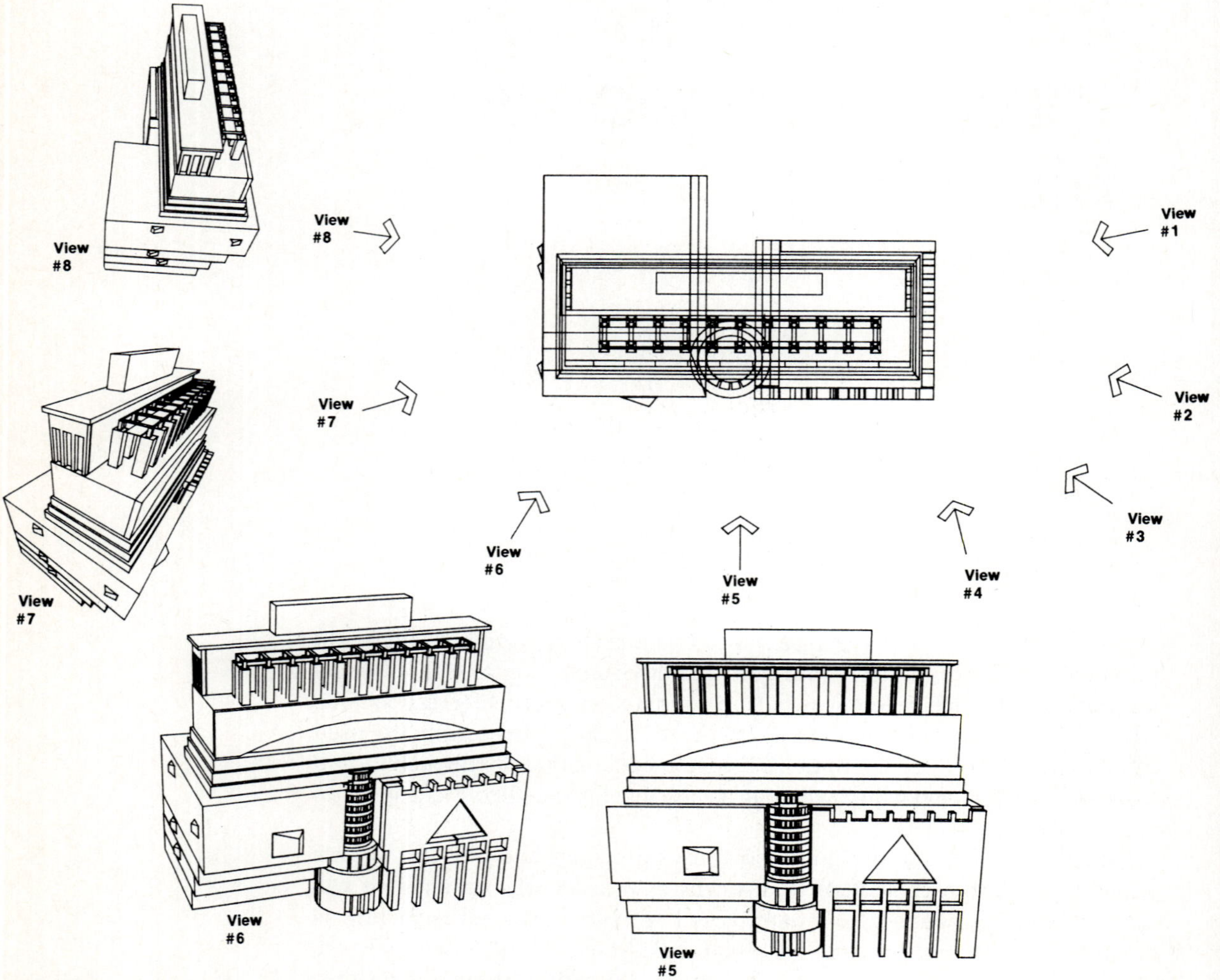

Figure 17-1 Shown on pages 184 and 185 are alternative external views of a proposed multistory urban building derived from a three-dimensional model.

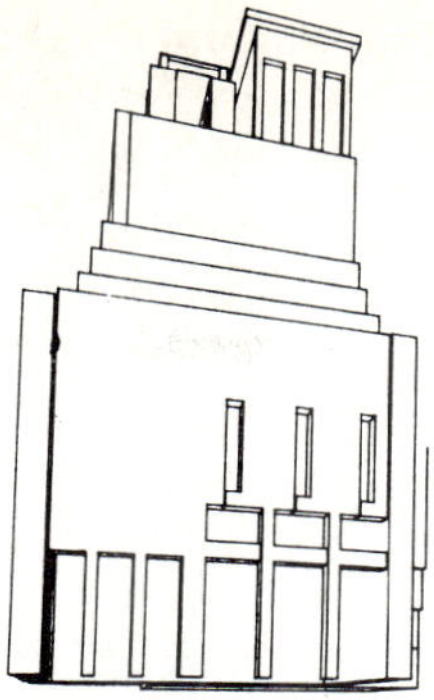

View
#1

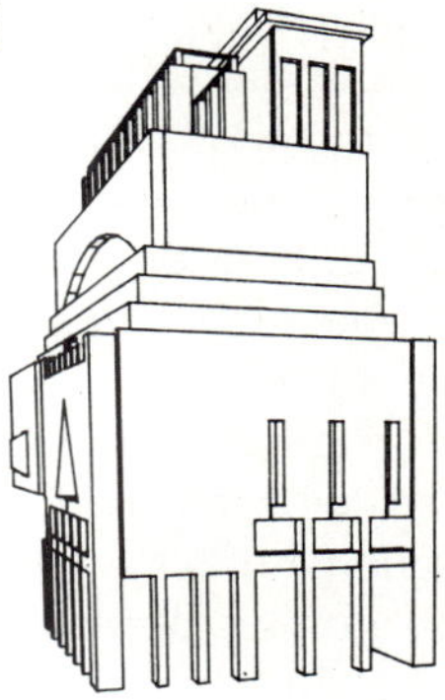

View
#2

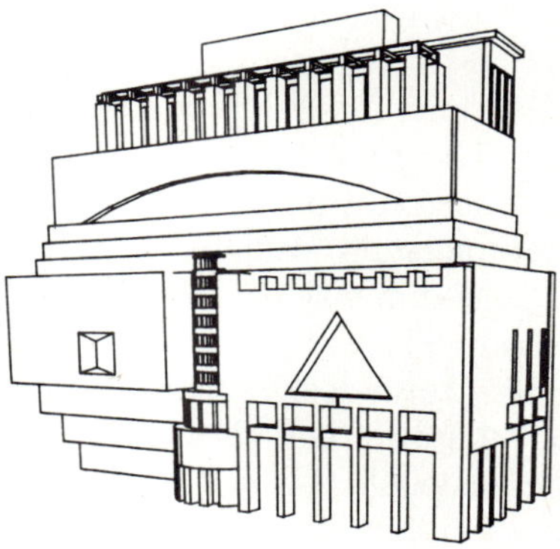

View
#3

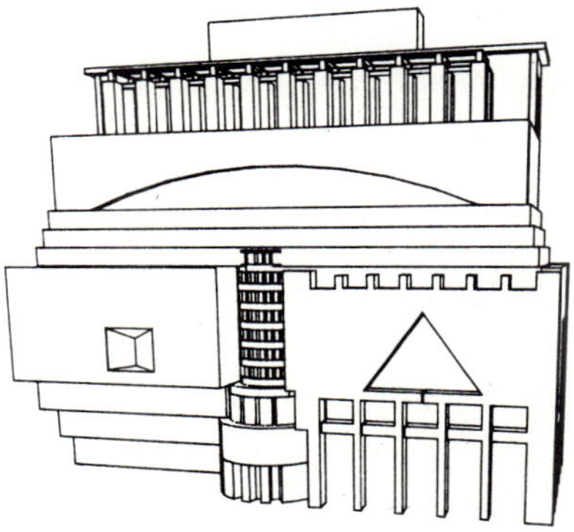

View
#4

Computer-based three-dimensional modeling amplifies traditional renderings, or representations of a building, executed as perspective or axonometric projections for the purposes of presentation. Here also the traditional medium, although convincing, is inflexible. Once a rendering is done, it is frozen in time. The design may change, but it is usually too expensive to redo the rendering and so it quickly becomes obsolete.

Three-dimensional modeling systems hold out the promise of providing unlimited views of a design (see Fig. 17-1). The model is easily revised so that renderings are up to date and display the most current state of the design.

The following chapters refer to plans, sections, and elevations for a project as two-dimensional orthogonal drawings, or simply two-dimensional drawings. This convention distinguishes such drawings, whether or not they were created as views of a three-dimensional model, from other drawings derived from a three-dimensional model such as perspectives or axonometric projections. The equivalent three-dimensional-model views are referred to as "hidden-line views."

Another promise of computerized three-dimensional modeling is the direct relationship between hidden-line views and two-dimensional drawings. A strong relationship allows the least possible amount of redundant operator entry, both graphic and written. Thus, in practical terms, this means the three-dimensional model is created directly from the two-dimensional drawings or the drawings are created from the model. Drawings created directly from a three-dimensional model use what we refer to as a "model-based system."

At this time, for architectural drawings, these promises are only partially fulfilled. The methodologies, procedures, and software utilities described here are derived from a cross section of three-dimension software applications commercially available in both architecture and other fields. Computer-based three-dimensional modeling is only now emerging from development in fields outside of architecture as well as from universities, as a practical tool for architectural design. Three-dimensional modeling on CAD systems has not had the brief period of commercial development and proliferation that two-dimensional CAD has enjoyed. It is still quite new.

The operations for creating a three-dimensional model on a computer differ substantially from those used to create the physical models or renderings referred to previously. The medium of a CAD system is less tactile, but, in many important ways it is more direct.

Three-dimensional modeling, especially solid modeling, was originally developed for applications in the fields of aerospace and industrial design where it is used to represent models of vehicles, machines, and their parts. As part of computer-assisted design and manufacturing (CAD/CAM) applications, it is used to represent entire manufacturing processes, including milling and casting for machined parts. Application of three-dimensional modeling in the fields of physics, medical science, and graphic art has recently produced dramatic advances. As a tool for composing and analyzing physical information about objects with complex shapes, the strengths of three-dimensional applications are apparent. It is important to realize, however, that three-dimensional modeling applications have developed outside the fields of architecture and environmental design. As a result, converting these applications into practical design tools for architects presents certain challenges to development.

Unfortunately, the origins of three-dimensional and solid-modeling applications impose some burdensome constraints. A model of an architectural project has characteristics that are significantly different from models used in other fields such as industrial design or medicine. The term "solid model" applies only partially to models in the environmental design field. Solid objects represent perhaps only 25 to 40 percent of the graphic objects shown on drawings in an architectural project, for instance. During the design process many architectural forms are not sufficiently defined to enclose complete solid objects. In this case, surfaces are used to define shapes rather than solid objects. More important, in two-dimensional construction drawings that typically comprise a complete model for an architectural project, much information—in the form of abstractions and symbols—is either diagrammatic or cross-references to other information. Currently lettering is not shown on three-dimensional drawings. Nonetheless, the data processing technology developed for solid modeling provides critical analytical mechanisms, such as interference checking, that are useful in architectural design. New visualization tools provided by three-dimensional modeling also offer tremendous opportunities for enriching the design process. Whether the name *solid modeling* applies, it has been transferred along with the software technology.

Similar to two-dimensional CAD, operations on a computer-based three-dimensional model use interactive graphic procedures. As we know, the spatial relationships between elements in a design can only be observed and judged by eye. Hand-and-eye coordination when placing objects is therefore critical. As with physical models, computer-based interactive graphic procedures combine hand motion with visual feedback about relations between objects located in space. Consequently, creating a comprehensive three-dimensional model for an architectural design on a computer is only feasible with such procedures.

The significant difference between two-dimensional drawing systems, which are now the predominant design methodology, and computer-based three-dimensional modeling is the shift in the focus of design documentation from a collection of drawings to a single-source model for the drawings. In current practice, the model of an architectural design as a whole, although recorded on a series of drawings, actually resides in the mind of the designer,or the collective mind of the design team. A three-dimensional modeling system records the model for the design project as a single unified entity in a computer-processable medium.

Three-dimensional models become a comprehensive single source model for an architectural design. Drawings are generated from the model and reflect the three-dimensional model at a point in time. From this point of view, drawings are distinct from the model, are somewhat temporary, and are therefore dispensable—the drawings merely report on the current state of the model. Rather than the drawings, the model as a single source would be archived when the project is finished.

For now, however, two-dimensional drawings remain the primary vehicle not only for documenting the design for approval and construction but also for updating the model. Regardless of how the design documents are stored, a three-dimensional model is created or modified while looking through two-dimensional views of the design. Consequently, two-dimensional drawings are likely to remain, in the foreseeable future, our primary windows into a three-dimensional model. As interactive graphic procedures are used, however, the distinction between the diagrammatic nature of two-dimensional drawings and the solid objects in a three-dimensional model must be kept constantly in mind.

Applications of Three-Dimensional Modeling in Design

Developments in flight simulation, animation, and medical imaging show how objects and whole environments are recreated with sophisticated realism by three-dimensional modeling systems when viewed from any angle. Similarly, in architectural practice, the predominant application of three-dimensional modeling systems is visualization of a design project. Clearly, such a visualization tool helps a client or a community understand a proposed design. Nondesign professionals usually are not trained to read traditional two-dimensional design documents. Three-dimensional modeling not only expands a client's grasp of a project but consequently expedites decision making. At this stage, applications of three-dimensional modeling in architecture are justified largely for the projected views of a design they generate.

Three-dimensional views, treated like traditional renderings, are used in presentation meetings to clients, lenders, consultants, and public institutions such as government review agencies, city planning departments, or neighborhood associations. Such three-dimensional renderings are photographed directly from the CRT screen, plotted, or filmed by video-tape camera. External views of a project, typical internal spaces such as lobbies, hotel rooms, or offices, and special-purpose rooms such as conference rooms, operating rooms, or kitchens are completely depicted. Such projected views are used not only for client presentations but also to expand marketing opportunities for design services.

In the design process, the importance of visualization tools can hardly be overestimated. To a large degree, owners and occupants of building, as well as the entire community depend on architectural designers for the appearance and character of their building environments. Any tool which increases people's ability to visualize a project as it is being designed is enormously valuable (see Fig. 17-2). If future occupants or users can conveniently preview the outcome of a design with projected views from a three-dimensional model, the design process is enriched.

Inside the design office as well, three-dimensional models enhance perception. For the design team, three-dimensional models help determine the

Figure 17-2 Shading (and coloring) superimposed on a three-dimensional model creating a completely rendered exterior facade: Note the subtle change in shading from the bottom of the model to the top. (*Courtesy of Skidmore, Owings, and Merrill, Houston, TX.*)

overall appearance of a project and consequently aid aesthetic decisions. After all, aesthetics is one of the charters of architecture.

Architectural practice applies computer-based three-dimensional modeling to visualization in the following areas:

1. Massing studies.
2. Line-of-sight and visibility studies.
3. Renderings based on projected views with hidden lines removed, sometimes including studies of color and lighting.
4. Design studies and detail views of elements within a building or its components.

In each of these areas, the power of three-dimensional modeling derives from the unlimited number of views generated from the same model. In this sense, a computer-based model is similar to an actual physical model: it can be looked at from any angle. Unlike hand renderings, where the angle of view is limited to the number of views selected, any view of a computer-based three-dimensional model is available. Views are taken from both outside as well as inside the model. With additional film or video equipment, multiple views are recorded one after the other and combined into animated films. This technique creates moving views of a project as it is seen while flying, driving, or walking either around or through the model.

Early in the design process, massing studies, with or without hidden lines removed, illustrate the visual prominence of both the composition as a whole as well as elements within the proposed design. Such studies show a limited amount of detail or line work. In many cases, wire-frame representations are sufficient. Entire urban environments, including major sections of cities, are currently modeled in this way with three-dimensional systems. Computer-generated massing studies have emerged as a powerful city planning and urban design tool. Valuable massing studies are performed with three-dimensional modeling systems of limited capacity available on personal computers.

Three-dimensional modeling allows lines of sight, both around and through a design, to be studied. Within a project, line-of-sight studies are important for aspects of site planning; design of surveillance systems; theatre design; location of signs; design of emergency exiting paths; and visibility in museums, exhibits, hospitals, and retail sales displays (see Fig. 17-3A and B).

Similar to the study of lines of sight, the visibility of a proposed project within an existing environment is studied with three-dimensional modeling. Since the model is projected from any specified angle, how a project is seen in the distance, along approach routes, or within existing panoramas, is portrayed convincingly. Projections of a model are even superimposed on video images of an existing landscape, providing a new level of realism.

Creating studies of visibility and line-of-sight is extremely time-consuming with hand-drafting techniques. Even with two-dimensional CAD, such studies are usually not thorough.

In the broadest area of application for visualization, projected views from models are developed into renderings of a design. The difference between an unmodified view from a three-dimensional model for purposes of study and a rendering is only a matter of degree. Although in the early stages of commercial development, software utilities for modeling architectural spaces with lighting, shading, color, and even surface textures are available and becoming less expensive (see Fig. 17-4A and B). Presentations from three-dimensional models can be enhanced with software utilities for sketching and coloring. For example, the utility Paint Box applies color and line work interactively on top of projected three-dimensional views. With such utilities, images from three-dimensional modeling systems are gradually becoming less cartoonlike and more recognizable as realistic renderings.

Finally, a time-honored hand-drafting design procedure is extended for use with three-dimensional modeling applications. When developing ideas, designers typically create perspective views of elements within a project. With or without the aid of mechanical projection tools such as grids, these design sketches include detailed views of project parts as well as overall views showing the composition and character of the design. For example, a designer may develop several sketches of the exterior window system. Some sketches focus on one aspect of the windows, such as the sill or head, and others explore the entire exterior elevation. In a separate operation, including, if necessary, dimensioning and redrawing, such design sketches are developed into preliminary construction drawings sometimes referred to as "design development drawings."

Similarly, designers use computer-resident three-dimensional modeling

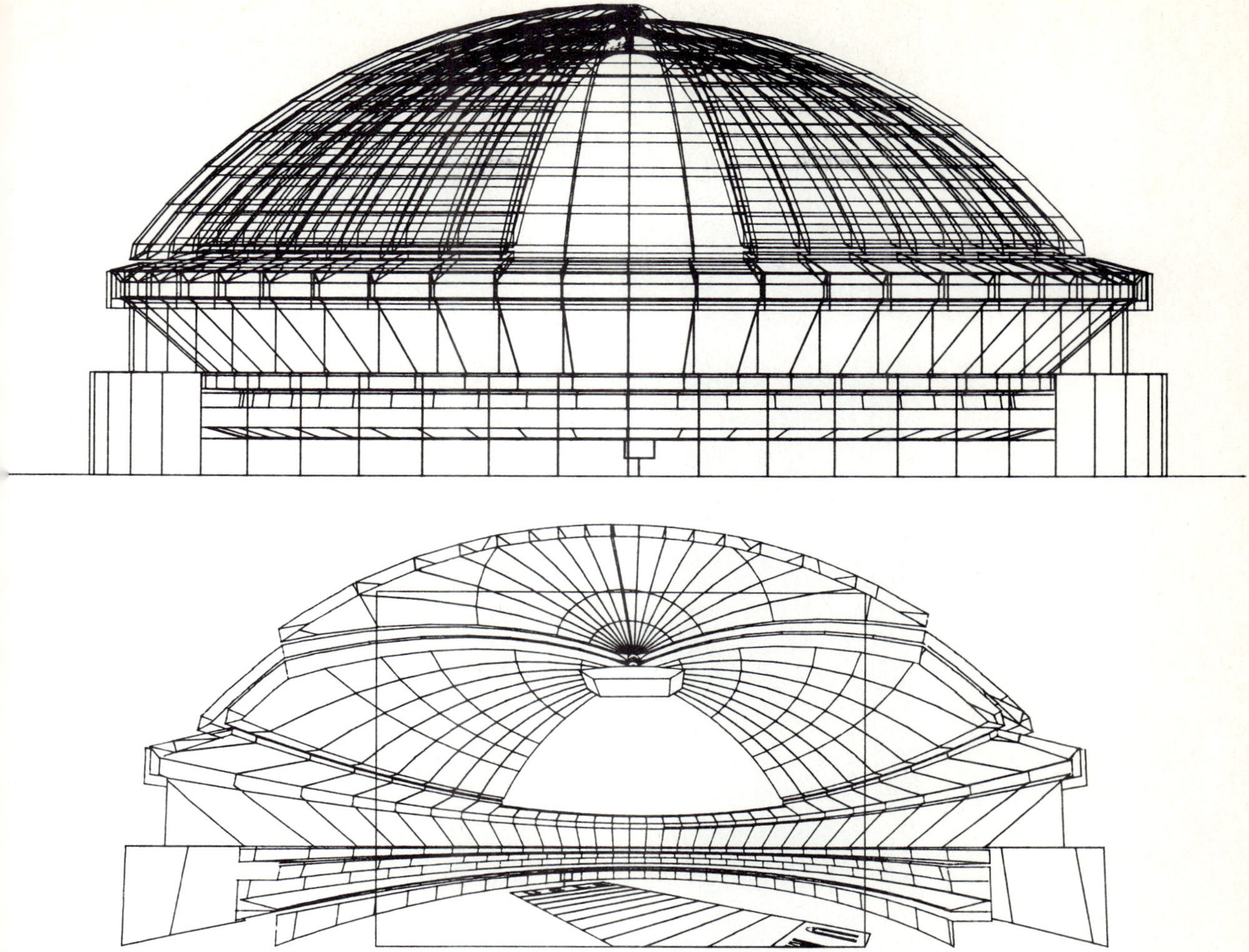

Figure 17-3 Parts A and B show a wire-frame view of a stadium created with a three-dimensional modeling system and an interior section from the model used to analyze lines of sight onto the playing field. (*Courtesy of CalComp, Anaheim, CA.*)

systems in this same design development procedure. The advantage modeling systems provide over the manual approach to sketching is the ability to view design elements from more views than that provided in a hand sketch. Also, designers can record nongraphic design information, such as the proposed area, density, or site utilization, as direct records with objects in the model.

Building Design Analysis

A second area in architectural practice where three-dimensional modeling systems are applied is broadly defined here as building design analysis, which involves a variety of quantitative design problems. For many design

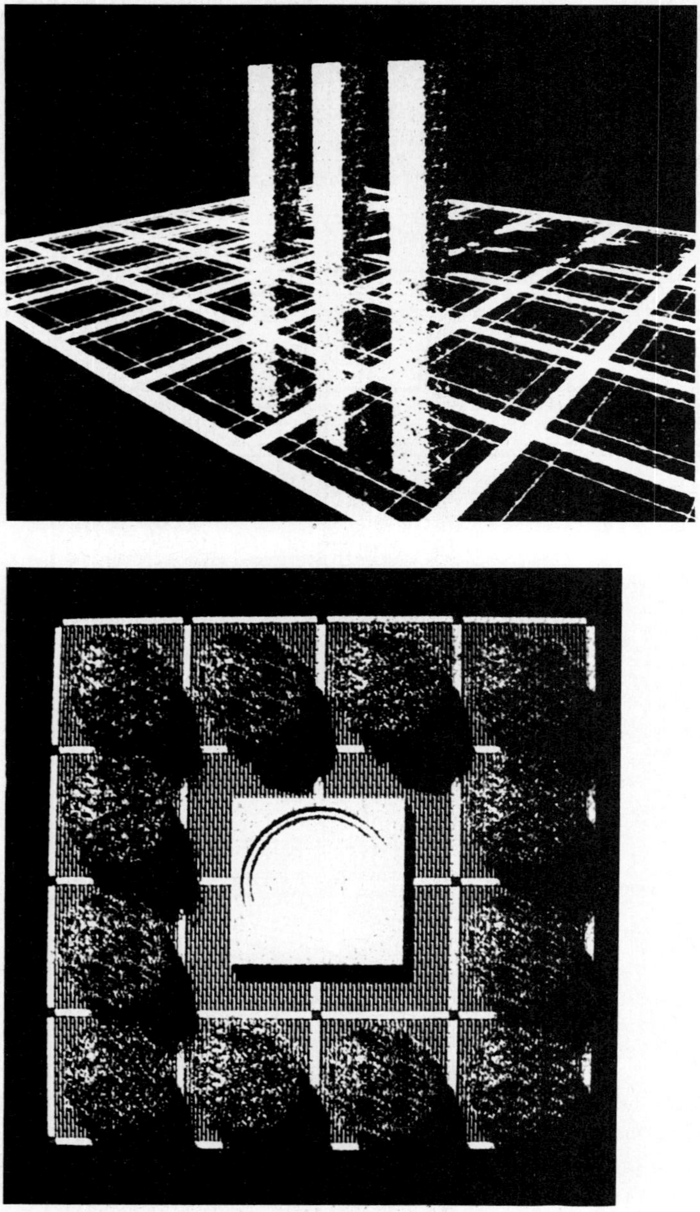

Figure 17-4 Parts A and B show computer-generated surface textures and reflection applied to three-dimensional models of sample spaces creating realistic renderings of materials. (*Courtesy of Skidmore, Owings, and Merrill, Houston, TX.*)

problems, the project as a whole must be analyzed. Structural design, interference checking between building systems, acoustical design, thermal design, circulation modeling, quantity takeoffs, even building code conformance all require the designer to analyze the entire project, including how the various elements in the project interact. Solutions to drawing management problems, such as cross-referencing documents and coordinating consulting disciplines, also require a complete project overview.

The internal data structure of a solid or three-dimensional model lends itself to analysis that requires a coherent view of the entire design. In contrast, information about a project stored on typical two-dimensional drawings, even when assembled on a CAD system, is distributed throughout a large set of drawings and files. Since objects on different drawings are easily overlooked, performing analyses on a project stored in this typical multiple-drawing form is time-consuming, cumbersome, and error-prone. A three-dimensional model, on the other hand, constitutes a single document for the project as a whole. The possibility of either overlooking or including an object more than once in an analysis is eliminated. Practical results from analyzing a three-dimensional model for structural design has been demonstrated by pioneering work in the office of S.O.M. in Chicago, for example. For the types of building design analyses outlined above, three-dimensional modeling holds out the promise of significant efficiency.

Area takeoffs from two-dimensional drawings are currently the source of information for material quantity surveys, heating and cooling load analysis, lighting system design, and even daylighting analysis. Even if area takeoffs are done automatically, volumes are determined by an additional interpretation of the elevation drawings combined with hand calculations. Yet information about the volumes within a building is essential to calculations for heating and ventilating loads. By using the full three-dimensional properties of a space stored in a three-dimensional model, the system calculates volumes automatically.

The automatic use of three-dimensional volumes in design analysis is demonstrated by studies of shading in the field of urban design. Simple three-dimensional volumes of a proposed high-rise building along with its neighbors are created in a three-dimensional model. Shadows cast by the proposed building over streets and neighboring buildings are generated from the model and examined (see Fig. 17-5). Thus, the amount and the duration of sunlight blocked out is determined.

A computer also can evaluate the objects in a solid model to determine if in fact they are realizable or valid shapes. (Refer to Chap. 18.)

Since by its nature a three-dimensional model is a single representation of an object, problems associated with drawing coordination are minimized. With two-dimensional architectural documents, multiple views of a space are drawn. Objects that should appear in more than one drawing are not always included in each view of the space. Because it always refers to a single, nonredundant source, two-dimensional drawings from a three-dimensional model will not generate conflicting representations nor omit an element that

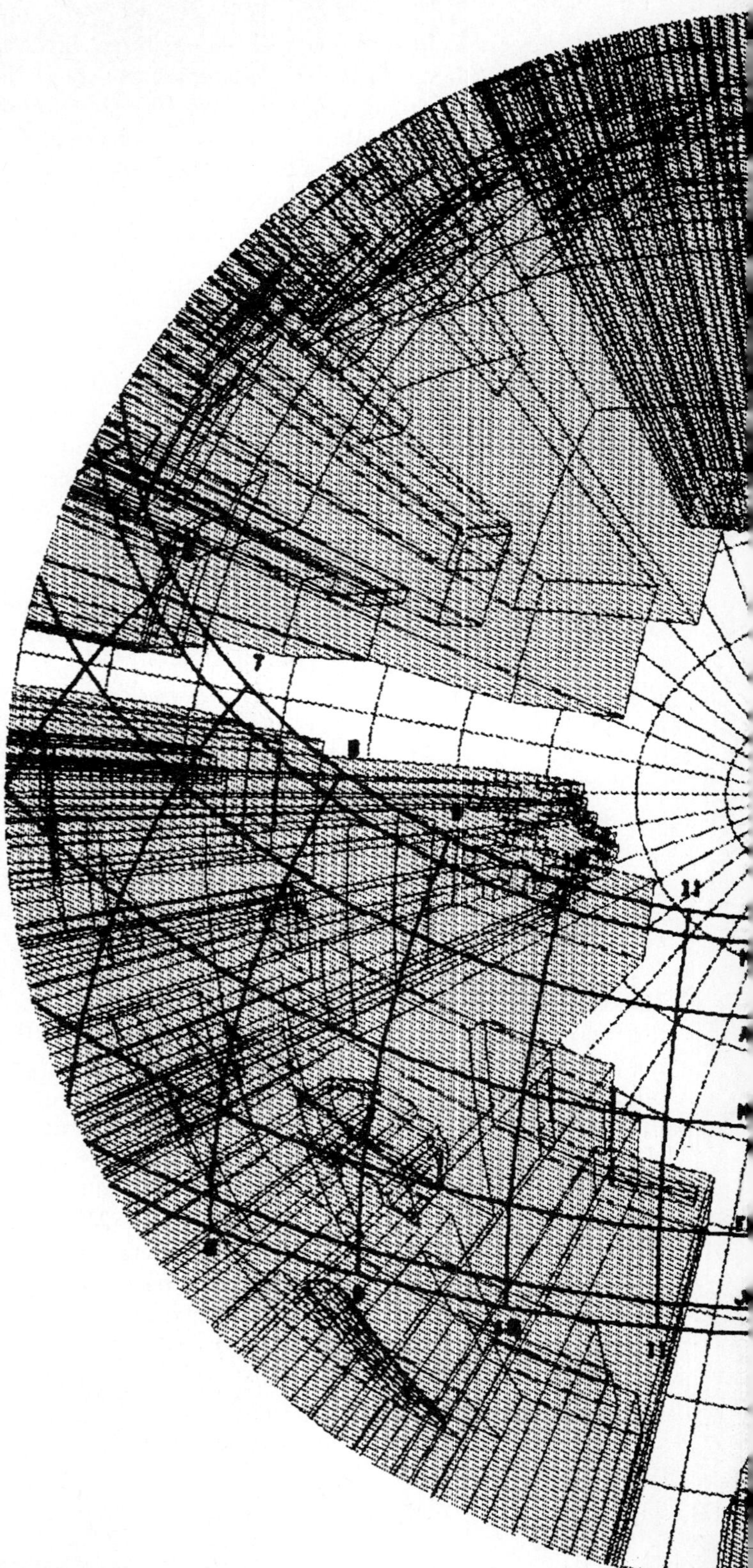

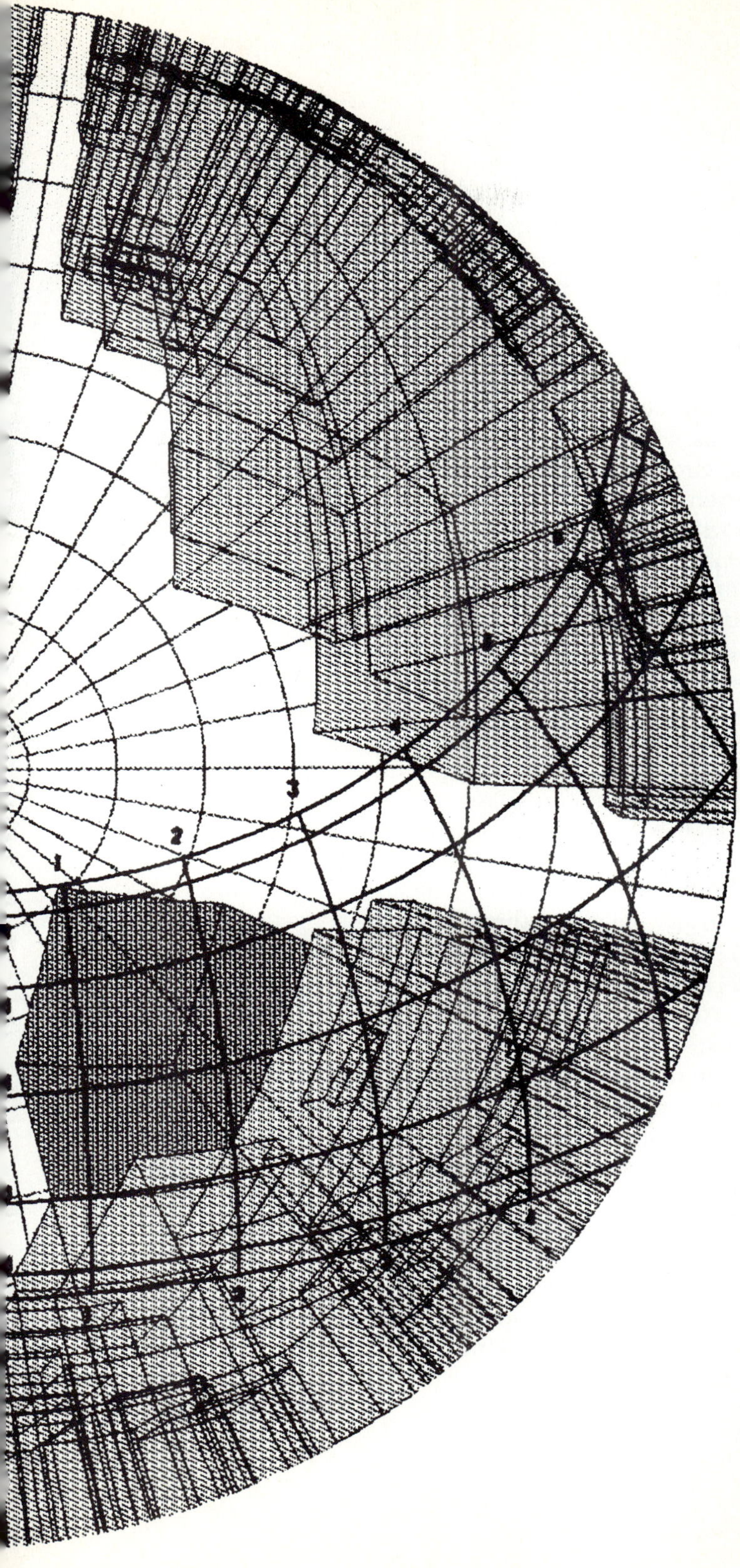

Figure 17-5 Building design analysis based on three-dimensional modeling: Effect on available solar light at street levels from a proposed addition to a skyline is revealed by using a fish-eye view and superimposing the design on both the existing buildings and the path of the sun. (*Courtesy of Ken Sanders, Santa Ana, CA.*)

should appear. Also, the failure to remove all references to a deleted element is precluded.

Architects carry a liability for omitting from drawings items that are required for the design. A considerable amount of time is required to cross-check documents for such omissions, but if drawings are extracted from a three-dimensional, or single-source model of a project, such omissions are minimized. When a three-dimensional model is the source for two-dimensional drawings, a new degree of control over documentation is thus possible.

Some building design problems require quantifiable design analysis of spaces that are difficult to represent conventionally. For example, spaces that appear bounded in plan are sometimes included in volumes that flow from one area to another, moving in some places vertically and in others horizontally. Such spaces are currently widely included in modern urban malls, arcades, and atriums within high-rise buildings. Here, conditions such as privacy, acoustics, circulation of people or equipment, lighting, air movement, heat gain, even human safety are difficult to analyze. Such analysis is greatly simplified with a three-dimensional model of a space.

Three-dimensional modeling is not applied as widely to building design analysis as it is to visualization tasks. Although the emphasis is likely to remain on visualization, the authors anticipate that as software utilities for design analysis become more available, building design analysis will be included with visualization in cost justifications for three-dimensional modeling software.

Such analytical tools enable architects to provide new services. In turn, three-dimensional model-based analysis reassures clients and communities that the results of economic resources assigned to construction projects will be buildings with higher levels of utility.

Background vs. Interactive Processing

Most CAD operations for building a three-dimensional model are carried out while working in an interactive mode. The operator enters or locates an object in the model space and it is displayed immediately, in at least one two-dimensional view. However, data processing operations such as visualization or design analysis are carried out on a three-dimensional model as a whole and are performed in the background rather than interactively. Such operations are set up in advance, a software procedure is initialized, and then there is a delay while results are generated internally. The results are displayed only after the internal processing, which sometimes requires several minutes or more, is completed.

Except for confirming those operations used to build the model, such as locating an object, results of interactive changes are not observed immediately. For instance, the effect of lighting and shading, or removal of hidden lines when an object is first added to the model is not observed until the entire model is reanalyzed by the system and redisplayed. Such operations are performed on the complete model and every object within it. As a result, a considerable number of internal calculations are required, and redisplay of a model takes time.

TABLE 17-1 Processing Times for Operations on Various Three-Dimensional Models

Time (minutes)	Process	Quantity of shapes	Description/Comment
<1	Update 3-D model from 2-D drawing scan	>100	Seven types of 2-D symbols placed in model as cubes. On a mini-based CAD system.
1	Hidden-line view	100 surfaces	Using Encarnacao priorty method on medium-size, single-processor, time-share system. [GIL078]
3	Refresh wire-frame views	75	Five basic views of building model, including plan and elevations. On a mini-based CAD system. See Fig. 20-4.
3	Hidden-line view	105	Set of cubes. On a mini-based CAD system.
10	Hidden-line view	75	One view of building model, see Fig. 17-1.
90	Light-source-shaded image	3	Ray-traced rendering of a sphere, a cylinder, and a shiny surface. On an IBM 4341. [SABE83]
>5	Light-source-shaded image	3	Same as entry above, using scan-line algorithm, but shadows and reflections are not handled.
varies	Color-shaded raster image	114	Requires 1/10 the time required to do hidden-line view of the same image. [SABE83]
2	Color-shaded raster image	11,692 surfaces	For 1024 X 1024 resolution. On an IBM 4341. [SABE83]
30	Color-shaded raster image	32,000 triangles	Landscape image generated using frame-buffer algorithm. On frame buffer and Vax 11/780. Requires only 2.5 minutes on specialized experimental equipment. [FOUR85]
12	Color-shaded raster image	131	Locomotive with one light source and no shadows using vectorized ray-tracing method on a constructive solid geometry model. On a CDC Cyber 205. [PLUN85]
480	Light-source-shaded image	<25	Complex image of a gallery with mirrowed walls, using ray-tracing method. [GREE83]
<0.5	Color-shaded raster image	>1,000,000 voxels	Skull and tissue, in an octree model. Refer to Chap. 21. On IBM 4341. [FARR85]
2–5	Color-shaded raster image	>100,000 voxels	Skull and spine, in an octree model. Refer to Chap. 21. On DG Eclipse S/200. [CHEN85]
7.2	Gradient-shaded raster image	>3,000,000 voxels	Details of spinal column, in an octree model. On mini, DG Eclipse S/140. [FRIE85]

Certainly, more operations on a three-dimensional model should be handled interactively. Analytical operations such as interference checking could be performed on a region at a time within the model. Realistically, however, interactive analysis and visualization of a three-dimensional model would require a considerable investment in computer power for raw number crunching (Table 17-1 compares processing times for operations performed on various three-dimensional models—note the magnitude and range of operating time and processing resources required.) For the near term at least, background processing is a reasonable compromise between the costs of a larger system on the one hand and any delays for background processing on the other.

The contrast between the immediate response generated by interactive processing and the delay that accompanies background processing underlines the fundamental difference between two-dimensional documentation as it is currently assembled on CAD and the nature of a computer-resident three-dimensional model. A three-dimensional model is distinct from the documentation and, more than a set of drawings, is a unified version of the complete design project.

Chapter 18

Three-Dimensional Methodologies

"Initially a tool to discover truth, perspective was condemned when it became incapable of serving anything but beauty." [DESC82]

With three-dimensional modeling systems, several different methodologies have developed. They form separate, but sometimes intertwined, branches. The data structure for the models and the types of primitives used in each methodology distinguish the branches. Current three-dimensional modeling systems use three primary methodologies:

1. Boundary representation (Brep).
2. Constructive solid geometry (CSG).
3. Spatial subdivision.

Hybrid methodologies are emerging that change the representation of three-dimensional primitives to meet the needs of a specific application. Specifically, most implementations of CSG also include some provision for boundary representation. Thus the branches are intertwined. Most systems, however, work primarily with one of these three methodologies.

The first methodology, Brep, predominates in three-dimensional modeling systems that are currently available on CAD for architectural design; CSG is applied extensively in the field of CAD/CAM; and the last, spatial subdivision, is new. As of this writing, it is applied most notably in medical science. However, spatial subdivision's data structure, and the efficiency it offers, seems particularly well-suited to architectural models. In fact, a precursor of this methodology was used experimentally in the late 1960s in the field of urban design. Since spatial subdivision is as yet unavailable in architecture, a complete discussion is saved for later (see Chap. 21).

Boundary Representation

Because of their similarity to wire-frame projections, designers find boundary representations easy to understand. In this case, the term *boundary* refers to the outline, or polygon, which defines the surfaces of a three-dimensional object. As a result, the transition from two-dimensional design drawings to Brep three-dimensional modeling is conceptually relatively easy.

The fact that a volume is surrounded by a connected set of surfaces along any of its sections underlies this methodology. Accordingly, a record of the faces fully represents a solid three-dimensional object. To describe each object, the faces and edges are linked together in a hierarchical data structure. At the lowest level in the data structure of a Brep model, objects are stored as a list of the edges around each face on the object. The edges may be stored internally as either lines or as vertices. This linked set of edges forms a closed polygon making up the face (Fig. 18-1). Faces in turn enclose a volume, or a solid. At the top of the hierarchy, volumes are combined into a complete model.

Brep methodologies are applied extensively in architectural applications because of the relative efficiency with which they generate hidden-line views. If a three-dimensional model is projected as a wire frame, for example, the lines displayed are the actual polygons which define each three-dimensional primitive. Another reason for their widespread use is the fact that Brep methodologies are consistent with the way sections are currently used in architectural drawings.

Constructive Solid Geometry

Constructive solid geometry methodologies are based on the use of simple generic shapes to create three-dimensional objects. The minimum set of shapes consists of blocks, cylinders, tubes, cones, spheres, and tori (doughnuts). These are referred to as "primitives" for CSG models. Each CSG primitive has a terse representation based on a template. The template consists of an identifying code, an algorithm, and a set of parameters describing the proportions of the object. For example, the template for a cylinder contains spaces for two numbers—the radius and the length of the cylinder. In terms of computer memory, CSG is thought to be an efficient form of representation, especially when curved forms are represented. It takes less computer memory to store a formula than to store a list of vertices for a curve.

In CSG, generic shapes are combined with each other to form more elaborate shapes. Like boundary representations, a CSG model uses a hierarchical,

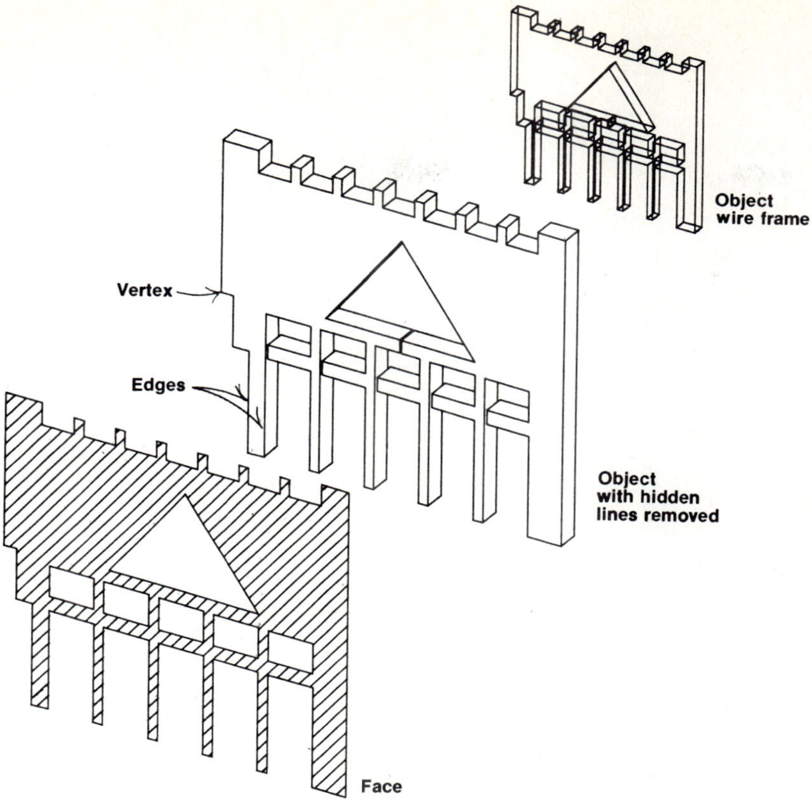

Figure 18-1 Three-dimensional object represented as a collection of edges and faces.

or treelike data structure. In this case, the simplest elements in the data structure are generic shapes rather than edges (see Fig. 18-2). Each branch in the hierarchy represents some intermediate object, and the entire tree represents the model of a design as a whole.

Constructive solid geometry requires a different form of mental abstraction on the part of the designer. Architectural shapes must be abstracted into permutations of their simplest geometric forms. To aide this process, some systems allow the operator to extend the vocabulary of primitives to include shapes frequently used by an application.

Although CSG offers efficiencies when storing three-dimensional objects or calculating volumes, it is inefficient for purposes of display or projection. Therefore, it has seen widest use in fields where analysis of mass properties, volume, and center of gravity, for example, are important.

Wire-Frame vs. Hidden-Line Views

The lines or surfaces in a three-dimensional model are projected either as axonometric or perspective views of the model from any angle onto a two-

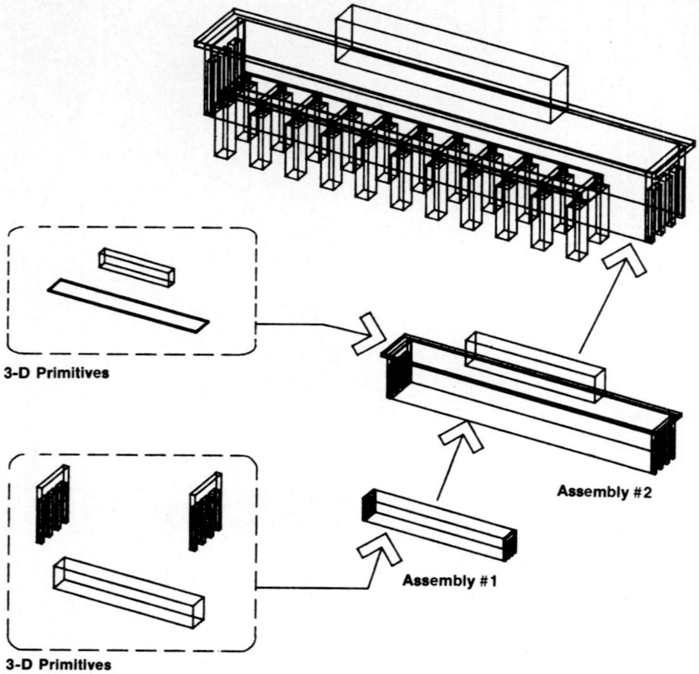

Figure 18-2 Hierarchical organization of primitive three-dimensional objects which defines a complete three-dimensional model based on constructive solid geometry.

dimensional viewing plane (see Fig. 18-3). In each case, a transformation matrix, which is based on the viewing angle, is applied to every vertex in the model. Each vertex is transformed into a simple X and Y coordinate that corresponds to where the vertex is seen on the two-dimensional viewing plane (or picture plane). Since the calculation is applied to every vertex in the model, generating such projected views requires a considerable amount of processing time.

If every line in a Brep model, or every line used to approximate a CSG model, is projected and displayed for a view, the result is a wire-frame projection (Fig. 18-4). A design shown entirely as a wire frame is sometimes difficult to interpret. Since lines for objects in the foreground overlap lines for objects in the background, the picture is confusing. Still, for certain design studies, such as judging the effect on a composition when an object is moved or removed, a complete wire-frame view is useful. If lines in the background are differentiated by displaying them as dashed or at a lower intensity, wire-frame views are a valuable preliminary design analysis tool. For a realistic final image of the design, a view that doesn't show the lines that are obscured by objects in the foreground is preferred. Here, the result is referred to as a "hidden-line view."

For hidden-line views, it is important that three-dimensional primitives be interpreted and displayed as surfaces rather than independent lines. Two or more lines, unless connected to define a surface, cannot obscure other lines. For this reason, even objects that are based on CSG methodologies are translated into surfaces for purposes of display. Surfaces are subdivided into planar polygons where the simplest planar polygon is a triangle. Although not used exclusively, most images from solid models, like those used for machine parts, are approximated with triangularized surfaces for purposes of display.

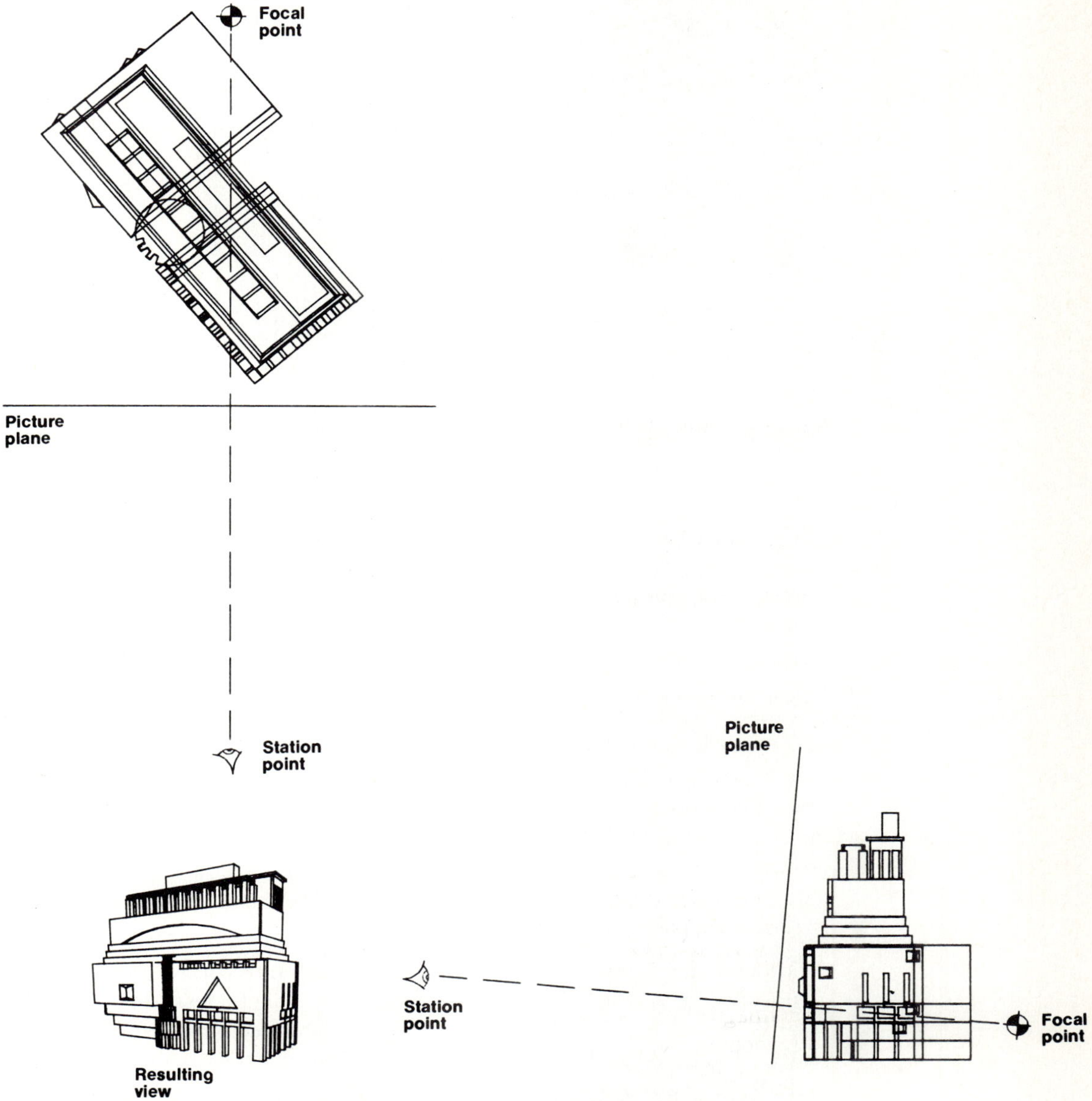

Figure 18-3 Establishing a projected view from a three-dimensional model using a viewing plane (picture plane), station point, and focal point, in both plan and side view.

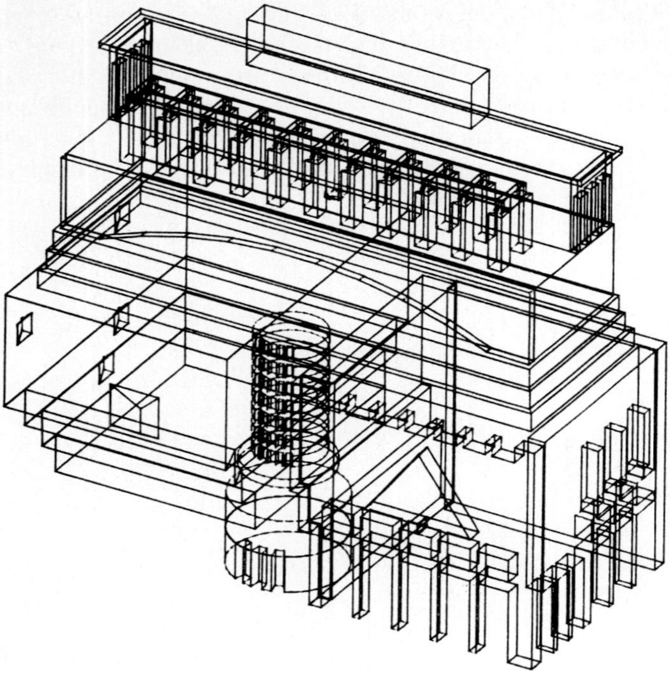

Figure 18-4 Wire-frame view of a three-dimensional model.

If primitives are constructed such that their lines or points define surfaces, those surfaces that overlap or obscure other surfaces are determined by the system. Thus, edges of an obscured surface are recognized and suppressed without being displayed, producing the desired hidden line view (see Fig. 18-5).

Solid-Modeling Assumptions

We must look outside architectural design for definitions of solid modeling. As defined in the field of industrial design, the underlying assumption of solid modeling is:

> "While wire frame and surface models define a part's edges or sections of its surface, a solid model completely defines its enclosure. A solid model guarantees a physically realizable shape and may be unambiguously interpreted by CAD/CAM applications programs." [JOHN84]

Although enclosure is an important concept in architectural design, architectural space is not strictly defined by enclosure. Nonetheless, this is the central issue in a solid-modeling system. As an architectural design is formulated, designers work with shapes that are not completely defined. This is antithetic to strict solid-modeling operations. Shapes in architectural design hover between shapes which are solid and ones which, because they are incomplete, can only be depicted as wire frames. Moreover, architectural design includes graphic information such as reference symbols, dimensions, and drawing guidelines which exist only as lines and are not themselves defined shapes. In practice, architectural applications of three-dimensional modeling use a mixture of wire frames, surfaces, and the primitives defined by solid modeling.

For the purpose of visualizing an architectural design, a solid model is not absolutely essential. However, two aspects of the definition above do apply to architectural design. First, an object in a solid model represents a realizable or valid shape. Second, the model can be interpreted unambiguously by related application programs.

The process of creating primitives in a solid model ensures that they are valid, precluding the generation of objects that cannot be constructed in reality or nonsense objects. The classic nonsense object is a Klein bottle, a surface that folds back onto itself. A valid solid primitive defines a volume that is complete and unambiguous. If described only in two-dimensional orthogonal views, an incomplete definition of a three-dimensional object is possible. An object that looks correct in plan and elevation may not actually define a volume. In two dimensions such a mistake is easily overlooked. A solid modeling application serves to guide the designer through the creation of three-dimensional primitives that represent volumes which are by definition valid.

Solid-modeling systems determine analytically whether two volumes overlap, coincide, or occupy the same space. Two or more solid primitives that do not occupy the same volume are considered a valid solid model. Thus the combination of all objects in the model is analyzed to determine if the primitives make up a valid model as a whole.

Validating a three-dimensional model in this way is instrumental to the design process. Any exceptions, where two or more primitives occupy the same space, are flagged as locations where the design requires further resolution. This analysis is the key to interference checking, which is particularly pertinent to the layout of interstitial spaces—where structural and mechanical building elements are installed.

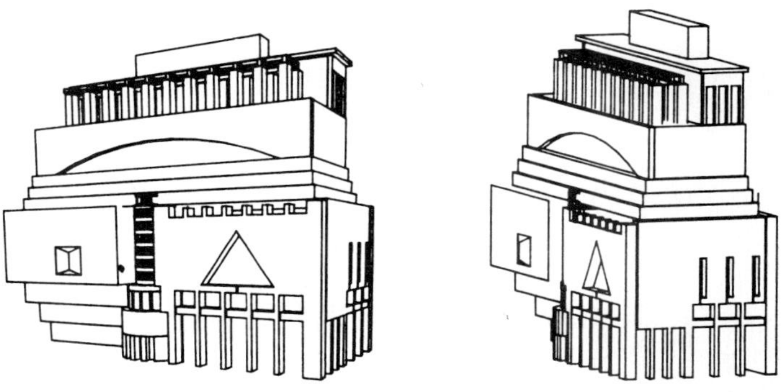

Perspective View **Orthographic View**

Figure 18-5 Two separate hidden-line views of the same model.

In certain circumstances, the intersection of three-dimensional primitives is desirable. Such an intersection becomes a third object, or an intersecting shape.

Once the basic conditions are met, if the primitives are valid solid objects and if the model itself is valid, then operations can be performed on the model as a whole. Such operations include:

1. Extraction of two-dimensional drawings as plan or elevation views.
2. Cutting sections.
3. Hidden-line removal and display.
4. Rendering of light source, shading, and surface textures.
5. Interference checking.
6. Calculations of mass and volume.

Chapter

19

Three-Dimensional Primitives

"Harmony of form consists of the proper balancing and contrast of the straight, the inclined and the curved."

Owen Jones, Proposition 10,
Grammar of Ornament, 1890

As with two-dimensional drawings, creating a three-dimensional model starts with the use of basic building blocks—primitive objects, or, simply, primitives. On two-dimensional drawings, primitive objects include points, lines, arcs, and text. Similarly, in a three-dimensional model primitives are graphically the lowest common denominator. A *primitive* in a three-dimensional model is defined as: a set of points, lines or edges, curves, or surfaces that defines a single complete and unambiguous volume.

Three-dimensional primitives appear as shapes approximated by straight lines. Where the primitive is a list of points or vertices, the lines merely connect the points. Curves may be stored in one of several ways: as a set of vertices, a set of parameters such as radius and included angle, or as a pair of points and a pitch or tangent angle associated with each point. The surfaces that constitute a Brep primitive are stored as either a set of connected lines or a set of points. In general, three-dimensional primitives, in either Brep or CSG form, can only be further reduced to points.

It is interesting to note that within this geometry a line is seen as a special case of the curve. This reflects the origins of three-dimensional modeling in such fields as aerospace, where complex curves are the norm. A straight line is mathematically the simplest case of a curve.

Once created, primitives are positioned directly in the modeling space or stored in a library and retrieved for use later, much like two-dimensional graphic symbols. Primitives can also be transformed, as can two-dimensional objects, with operations such as scaling, rotation, and mirroring. For example, a three-dimensional primitive for a 12- by 12-in column can be rescaled to represent a 14- by 14-in column.

The initial primitive is displayed in a working view for verification. If correct, the primitive is named and stored in a library or file, or it is added directly to the model. Adding directly to the model when primitives are first created is appropriate for one-of-a-kind shapes, such as an entry handrail, that are not used repeatedly throughout the model. After all additions, the resulting combination of three-dimensional primitives makes up a complete three-dimensional model.

If stored separately from the model, primitives can be called out at any time and can be combined into larger assemblies or objects. For example, the combination of a rectangular volume sitting on a cylinder defines a pedestal. Once a primitive is combined with other primitives, the combination itself can similarly be stored for reuse or added directly to the model. What we call objects are the general class of both three-dimensional primitives and combinations of primitives.

Three-Dimensional Primitives and Their Utilities

The types of real-world objects that can be modeled, the accuracy of the model, and the potential for future enhancements all depend on two characteristics of the modeling system. The first characteristic is the internal data structure of the model. The structure determines how primitives are combined into a model as a whole. Data structures for three-dimensional models tend to be hierarchial. Some incorporate operations performed with boolean algebra. The structure can be carried either in a generalized data base management system or in a specialized file structure to optimize performance for a specific application. Since a discussion of data structure is included in the material on Brep and CSG methods, it is not included at any length here. The second characteristic of a three-dimensional modeling system is the type of primitive objects the model contains. A single modeling system can recognize more than one type of primitive.

Just as a set of graphic utilities is used to create and store two-dimensional objects, a variety of utilities are used by three-dimensional modeling to create and manipulate primitive objects. In some instances, the same utilities are used in both two-dimensional and three-dimensional applications. However, three-dimensional modeling uses additional unique utilities. Along with shared utilities—such as those for drawing lines and arcs or rotating, copying, and mirroring objects—three-dimensional primitives are created by:

1. Modifying generic primitive objects and their parameters.
2. Extruding sections or generating swept objects.
3. Connecting polygons or surfaces.
4. Placing points in three-dimensional space.
5. Cutting objects.

Each utility relies on interactive graphic procedures while working in one or more two-dimensional views of the model.

Modifying Generic Primitive Objects

The first utility uses a vocabulary of generic shapes or volumes. Although the ability to modify primitive objects is aligned with the constructive solid geometry (CSG) methodology, it can also be used with Brep methodologies. Remember that generic shapes include spheres, cylinders, tubes, cones, blocks, pyramids, and tori (doughnuts). One of these generic shapes is used to define each primitive.

A software program generates a primitive according to parameters that describe the generic shape. When the generic shape is selected, the program responds with a display of dimensions and characteristics of the shape including default values. These can be modified. For example, to create a handrail from a cylinder, the diameter and length of the original cylinder are reentered. Once the shape parameters are modified, the revised primitive is stored as a three-dimensional object and can become part of a model (see Fig. 19-1). It is stored in the form of a record. Different methodologies store the shape and its parameters in different ways. Some systems work with an audit trail or a monitor file; here, the parameters are recorded during the initial construction. Such audit trails can be reused like a macro. With boundary representation methodology, the form derived from modifying the generic shape is translated into a list of lines or points. The record for the primitive is simply the list. In this latter case, how the primitive is constructed is not actually recorded. In either case, the primitive can be modified by regenerating and revising the original generic shape.

Extrusions

The second utility for creating three-dimensional primitives uses extrusions or sweep operations. With this utility, a section is first drawn in two dimensions. The section is any combination of lines and arcs. Although the section as a whole is a closed shape, the lines or arcs along the section must not intersect themselves. The section is then moved along a path or rotated about an axis, thus "sweeping" out a shape (see Fig. 19-2). The shape is described by lines that connect the edges of the section from one position to the next. This utility is appropriate for many architectural elements.

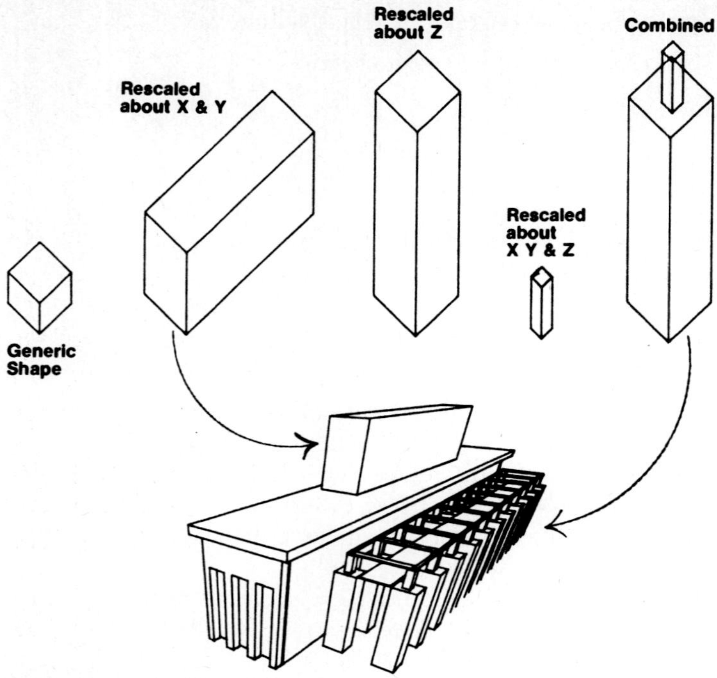

Figure 19-1 Generic three-dimensional primitive object, in this case a cube, which is modified creating several different three-dimensional primitives which, in turn, are combined into part of a complete model.

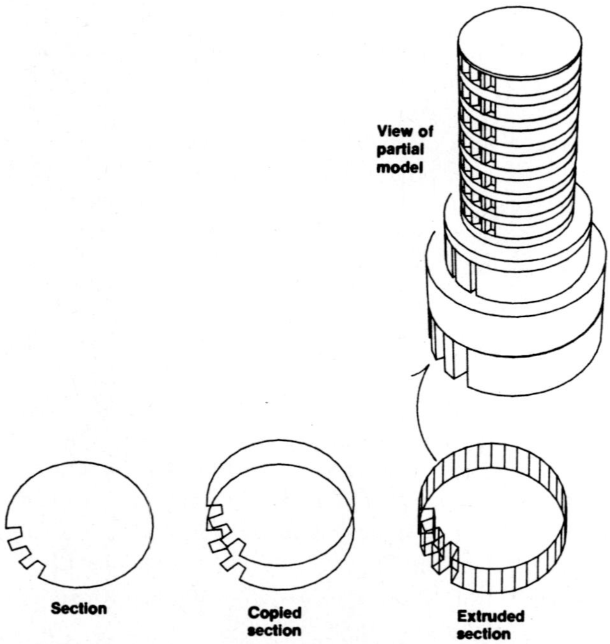

Figure 19-2 Section moved vertically, or extruded, defining a three-dimensional primitive.

The path is often simply described by a floor elevation and a ceiling elevation. Or, the path can shift and rotate as it ascends, such as the handrail of a spiral stair. The path itself is a sequence of points located in three-dimensional space. Potentially, at each position along the path, a degree of rotation and tilt is specified for the plane of the section.

In architectural design, the majority of paths include simply a start and end elevation, with no tilt or rotation. Consequently, the typical command for swept objects is to pick a section and copy it at a given distance, whereas for vaults and domes (and the occasional finial) the sweep is defined by an axis of rotation.

Objects with very complex shapes can be composed with this utility. Shapes that do not lie on a simply defined plane, such as a section of a modified cone, can be extruded. Such forms are found in certain machined parts, such as impellers. Although these shapes are not used frequently in architecture, the potential for including them in architectural design is intriguing.

Connected Polygons

The third utility, connected polygons, is similar in effect to extrusions. With extrusions, at every point along the path each section is identical. With connected polygons, each section can differ from the next. Again, sections are a set of lines or arcs created in two dimensions. Each is oriented in space by either translating, tilting, or rotating. Once sections are in position, points along the edge of one section are connected by the system to points along the edge of the next section (see Fig. 19-3).

To ensure an unambiguous volume, some constraints must be accepted. Fundamentally, sections cannot intersect. With three or more sections, each must be arranged so that the connecting lines do not intersect. If the surface

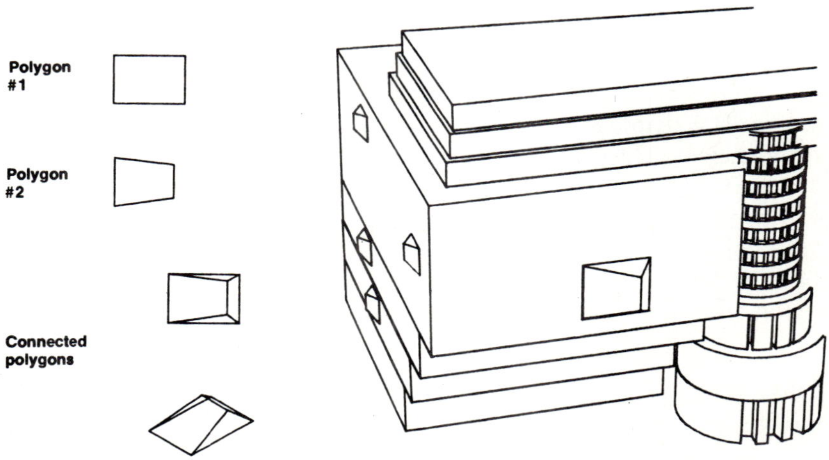

Figure 19-3 Two sections, or polygons, combined; with vertices connected, they define a three-dimensional primitive.

folds back on itself, such as a hollow shaft, the sections must be aligned to avoid line intersections along the edge of each section.

If two sections have the same number of vertices, it is assumed that corresponding vertices are connected to define the surface of the object. The ability to indicate the starting point, along with the direction for the series of vertices around each section, is critical to the use of this utility. The first point on the first section is connected to the first point on the second section and so on.

If the number of vertices differs from one section to the next, additional interaction is required. The connecting lines are entered either on a point-by-point basis, or by a start and endpoint of a series. In the latter case, a heuristic is also used, such as connecting two points on one section to each point on the next section.

Points Placed in Three-Dimensional Space

This utility for creating three-dimensional primitives places individual points or vertices in three-dimensional space. The operator selects a point directly on the surface of the model. Points are selected either in two-dimensional views, or on an isometric projection. As the operator selects them, the points are connected into lines. When the points and lines complete a volume, the three-dimensional primitive is complete.

Although this sounds like the most straightforward technique, it is inappropriate for most three-dimensional primitives. Remember, operations are performed on a three-dimensional object while working with essentially two-dimensional views. Unlike a physical three-dimensional object, understanding where points are located in relation to each other in all three dimensions is difficult in two-dimensional views. Thus it is hard to define a complete volume merely with points, even when the points are shown connected with lines. As a result, this technique is slow. It is easier and quicker to draw a two-dimensional shape and project, extrude, or fold it into the third dimension. Nonetheless, working with points is useful for operations such as editing the shape or surface of an existing object.

One currently available modeling system is specialized for work directly on the surface of a shape. It includes the use of an interactive reference grid in three dimensions. The grid is arranged like two of the sides and the bottom of a box (see Fig. 19-4). An object is projected within this volume and onto the three gridded surfaces of the box at the same time. This technique is appropriate for objects that are understood largely as a surface, such as an automobile body. It is intriguing to consider where such a modeling system can be applied in architectural design.

Cutting Objects

The utility for cutting objects creates three-dimensional primitives using boolean algebra to modify one three-dimensional object with another three-dimensional object. Operations such as union, intersection, and difference,

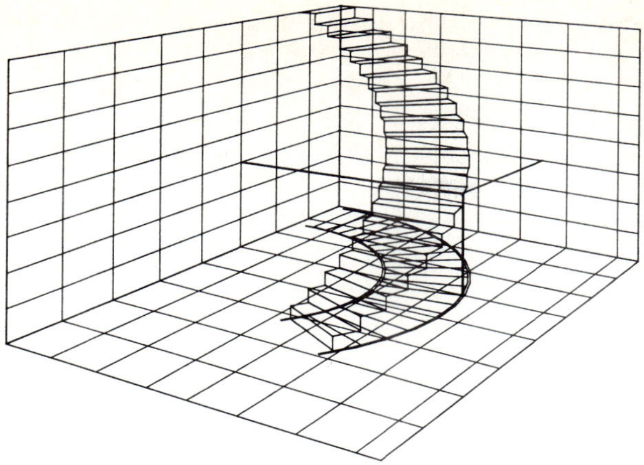

Figure 19-4 Representation of a three-dimensional modeling space where points are projected onto the surface of an object (a stair) from surrounding two-dimensional views.

which are similar to addition and subtraction, are performed on two or more three-dimensional primitives. The original primitives are created with either Brep or CSG methodologies. During such operations, the result of one object overlapping or abutting another is analyzed and a resultant shape is created (see Fig. 19-5). For example, one object may cut a volume out of another.

As a utility, cutting objects is appropriate for such basic architectural design elements as windows and doors in walls. A window, for example, should merely remove the section of the wall where it is located like a cookie cutter.

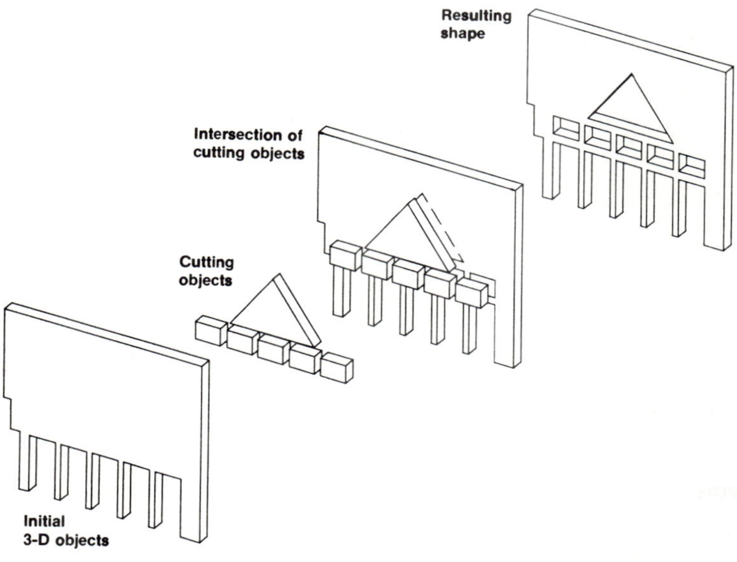

Figure 19-5 Representation of an operation using boolean algebra where one three-dimensional object is cut with another, thus creating openings.

Cut-object utilities are comparable to those that insert symbols in two-dimensional CAD by gapping the wall lines in plan. Without these utilities, however, the three-dimensional object for the wall must be segmented and wrapped around the opening. Usually, this results in at least one line connecting the outline of the wall, as seen in elevation, with the outline of the opening.

This utility was developed primarily to illustrate machined parts in three dimensions. Without it, CSG-based modeling systems would be restricted to a very limited vocabulary of shapes. Unfortunately, as of this writing, a cut-object utility is not included in most of the commercially available three-dimensional modeling applications for architectural design.

Chapter

20

Three-Dimensional Model Building

"The heart of the matter was determining the degree of reality one could achieve. Indeed, the [17th century] battle was fought in the name of reality to find out which technique—rigorous geometry or perspective tempered by the painter's eye—came the closest to it." [DESC82]

Once three-dimensional primitives are defined, regardless of the methodology used, a variety of operations are available for building complete three-dimensional models. Such operations overlap those used to create three-dimensional primitives but are also distinct from them. Operations for building three-dimensional models include the following:

1. Extruded two-dimensional plans.
2. Scanning two-dimensional orthogonal drawings.
3. Three-dimensional placement.

Other operations, such as direct model building, exist outside the building design field. With direct model building, a system scans an existing object and creates a three-dimensional model within the computer. This is in contrast to building up the model out of separate primitives with a series of interactive operations.

The choice of operation is largely a function of the type of design element and how it is represented. The first two operations take advantage of graphics already created on two-dimensional drawings such as design or design development documents. The last operation is applied directly to a three-dimensional model without the necessity of preexisting two-dimensional drawings.

Extruded Plans

Using extruded plans, as an operation, creates a three-dimensional version of objects, such as walls and columns from existing two-dimensional plans. Volumes as well as surfaces are created. It is a specific case of the extrusion technique used for three-dimensional primitives. If walls have been drawn with this process in mind, extrusions are a very efficient operation.

The operator extrudes the wall by indicating the wall lines on the floor plan and entering a height, usually the ceiling height (see Fig. 20-1). A surface is created by projecting a wall line upward. The system assumes that each point on the line is connected to a corresponding point at the ceiling or at the top of the wall. The connecting lines form edges or corners for the wall.

Usually, wall lines shown in typical two-dimensional plan drawings do not lend themselves completely to extrusions as three-dimensional volumes without some further line work. Only wall lines that describe a closed section in the two-dimensional plan can be extruded into a volume. Since symbols for windows or doors interrupt wall lines, or they abut other objects like columns, wall lines do not usually enclose sections. In these common cases, the jamb lines for an opening in the wall are usually connected to the symbol and not the wall.

Here, the walls are treated as surfaces. Rather than a volume, two planes are extruded. Although surfaces do not define a volume, they are recognized

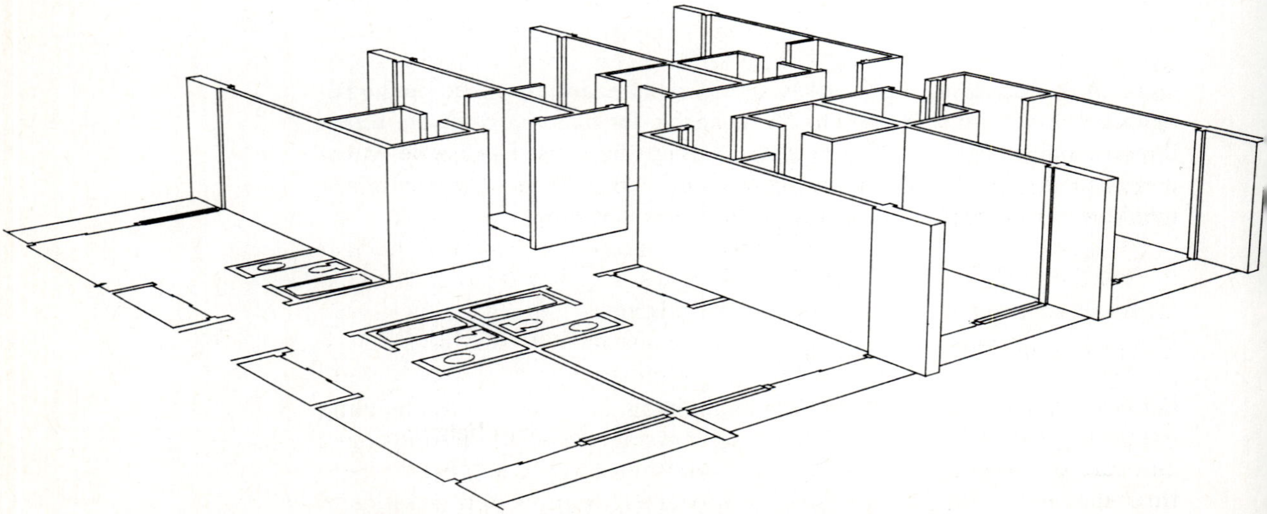

Figure 20-1 Extruded walls create a partial three-dimensional model.

by three-dimensional modeling systems for purposes of hidden-line views. Realize that when the system checks for the interference between two objects, surfaces are an ambiguous case—specifically, objects can be located within two or more surfaces without intersecting them.

Some graphic functions which draw walls in two dimensions also record a height for the wall in a nongraphic record as the walls are drawn in plan. In this case, a three-dimensional version of the wall can be created automatically by merely indicating the wall and initiating the extrusion. Since this operation only applies to walls, the three-dimensional model is completed by combining this operation with others.

Scanning Two-Dimensional Drawings

With the scanning operation, symbols located on two-dimensional orthogonal drawings are used to direct the location of comparable objects within a three-dimensional model. Essentially, the system replaces each two-dimensional symbol located on a plan with a three-dimensional object. Once two-dimensional symbols are located on a drawing, the replacement operation is performed with an automatic procedure; symbols do not have to be indicated one at a time. Rather, the entire plan, or an area within a plan, is indicated and the system scans the area for symbols. Another method indicates specific two-dimensional symbols and thus adds or excludes them from the scanning process. In either case, where the system finds a two-dimensional symbol, it substitutes a predefined three-dimensional object in the same relative location within the three-dimensional model (see Fig. 20-2).

Like two-dimensional symbols, this operation requires that the three-dimensional objects have been created, named, and stored ahead of time in libraries or files. In the two-dimensional plan view, two-dimensional symbols become place holders for the three-dimensional objects.

The system looks for any objects within the specified area which have nongraphic records attached. When such an object is found, it examines the record for fields with a name recognized by the software such as Elev, Height, and 3-D. For example, in the field called "3-D" the system expects to find the name of the comparable three-dimensional object. The name of the three-dimensional object may either be the same as the two-dimensional symbol or it may be different. It is only important that the name is stored in a field which is recognized by the scanning operation.

The location of the three-dimensional object is inferred from the location of the two-dimensional symbol. The *X* and *Y* cartesian coordinates for the origin of the symbol indicate the location of the origin for the three-dimensional object. The degree to which a symbol is transformed, rotated, mirrored, or rescaled is then read from the geometry information stored in the control block for the two-dimensional symbol.

Transformations in elevation, even those as elementary as height above a base, are the most common form of additional information needed to locate three-dimensional objects. As we know, the height of an object above the floor, the Z coordinate, is not usually shown in plan view. This information is

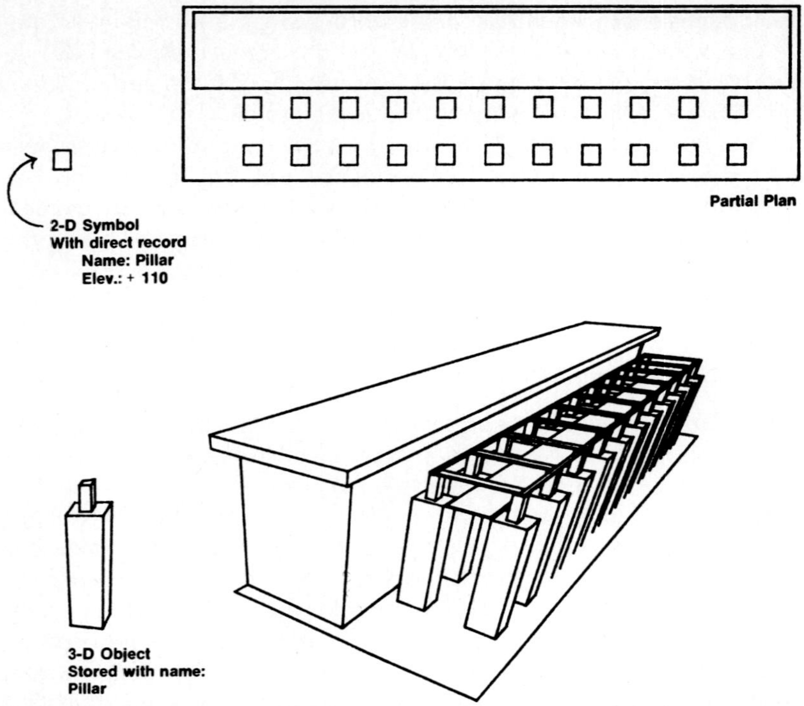

Figure 20-2 Representation of replacing two-dimensional symbols with three-dimensional objects using a two-dimensional drawing-scan operation.

transferred to the three-dimensional model in one of several ways. The height, like the name of the three-dimensional object, can be stored in a nongraphic record attached to the two-dimensional symbol. Or, if the height is not stored with the symbol, it is assumed to be the elevation of the floor or grade. As the drawing scan progresses, the system prompts the operator to enter heights for those objects shown without one. Height can also be extracted from an elevation view of the symbol. This is appropriate for symbols that are transformed or rotated about the Z axis, such as a sloping element. The height of design elements that are repeated vertically, such as horizontal window mullions, are also transferred to the three-dimensional model in this way.

Drawing-scanning operations are useful for three-dimensional objects that are more completely defined according to an elevation view. In many cases, the outline of an object on a two-dimensional plan is quite different from the object's outline when seen in elevation. On two-dimensional plans, most design elements are rendered as abstractions. For example, a window shown in plan is a single line. In reality, this line may represent an entire window wall with both horizontal and vertical mullions. In cases such as this, replacing a two-dimensional symbol with a completely different three-dimensional object is quite appropriate.

For convenience, three-dimensional objects can sometimes be used to create two-dimensional symbols. In some cases, such as a column, the outline on a two-dimensional plan is literally a horizontal section of a three-dimensional object. Most modeling systems will draw a two-dimensional version of a three-dimensional object in any specified view. This is appropriate for design elements whose outlines in either plan or elevation are directly related to their shape when projected in three dimensions.

During the scanning of a drawing, the group structure of a two-dimensional symbol is not transferred to the three-dimensional object. The way group structure is used in two-dimensional drawings does not necessarily apply to a three-dimensional model: three-dimensional objects have a different structure based on the data structure of the model and the nature of the three-dimensional primitives included.

A drawing-scan procedure easily generates the first pass or initial assembly of a three-dimensional model. The procedure is also useful for updating or revising the model after changes or additions, such as added furniture, are made on the two-dimensional drawings.

This procedure has the advantage of speed. By eliminating much time-consuming interaction, objects in the three-dimensional model are located automatically by the system rather than by an operator. The operator does most of the work locating objects while creating standard two-dimensional drawings, before three-dimensional operations are begun. On most systems, two-dimensional graphic operations have a quicker response time than three-dimensional operations. To further expedite the process, two-dimensional CAD applications have a richer vocabulary of graphic operations than is yet available in three-dimensional applications. After all, two-dimensional applications are more mature.

Placement in Three Dimensions

Three-dimensional placement is a utility for working directly on the model. Here, the designer locates an object by entering a point in space relative to other objects already displayed from the model. This is done by picking a point in one of several two-dimensional views of the model (see Fig. 20-3). Next, an object is named and retrieved from storage. Initially, the object is shown in two dimensions where the point is entered in one view only. The origin of the three-dimensional object is located at this point. The designer then moves and rotates the object into final position by subsequently entering points in other views.

Since only two dimensions are defined by any one view, manipulating objects along each of the three *X*, *Y*, and *Z* axes requires at least two views. *X* and *Y* appear in plan, while the *Z* axis, along with either the *X* or *Y*, appears in an elevation view. Consequently, the designer enters at least two points to establish all three coordinates. Additional views, particularly an isometric view, help to clarify the position of a point in space and thus speed up the operation.

To maintain reasonable response time, the results of operations such as moves, rotation, or rescaling are displayed in one working view at a time.

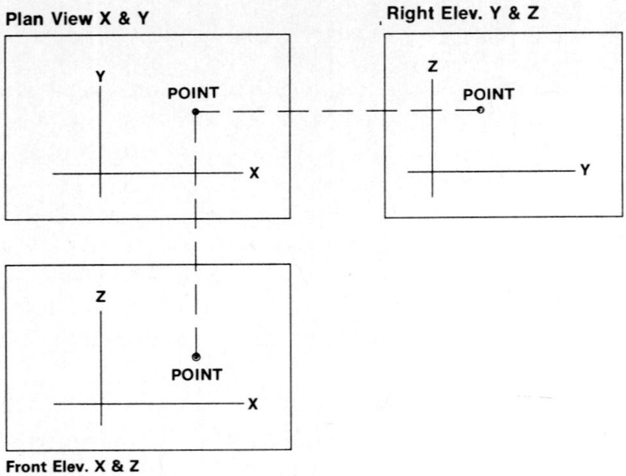

Figure 20-3 Placing points in three-dimensional space requires that work is first done in one two-dimensional view, such as plan. When this operation is complete, a point is then located in another two-dimensional view, such as side elevation. Thus all three *X*, *Y*, and *Z* coordinates are established accurately in a two-step operation.

Consequently, the three-dimensional object initially appears in only one view—simultaneously moving an object in multiple views requires a considerable number of internal computations.

When the placement operation is complete, the object is projected into the remaining views (see Fig. 20-4). The designer can then shift to another view and continue adjusting the position of the object. In this case, the object remains unchanged or is suppressed in other views until the adjustment is complete.

Placing objects while moving from view to view in this manner is effective for one-of-a-kind design elements (see Fig. 20-5). This operation takes advantage of the operator's hand-and-eye coordination for objects or locations that require judgment or fine tuning. However, because it is also relatively slow, it is not as appropriate for repetitive design elements.

Lettering and Dimensions in Three Dimensions

Some design information, such as lettering on drawings and scaled dimensions, is not inherently two or three dimensional. Although they help define physical elements, lettering and dimensions (both referred to as text in this section) do not represent physical design elements in themselves. In a three-dimensional model, lettering and dimensions have somewhat unique characteristics not shared by objects that represent actual design elements.

Although commonly used on two-dimensional drawings, as of this writing, functions for including text are not commonly available with three-dimensional modeling systems. As three-dimensional modeling develops, these will probably become available. At the very least, dimensioning is needed to assist operations that create three-dimensional primitives as well as operations that place objects directly in three-dimensional space.

Ideally, two-dimensional design documents and working drawings are also generated from the three-dimensional model. If the three-dimensional model is the source for a drawing, the drawing itself is dispensable. Consequently, any information necessary for a complete working document must be redisplayed from the model. In this circumstance, information such as lettering and dimensions must be stored with, maintained, and retrieved from the actual three-dimensional model.

Managing text in a three-dimensional model is currently an area of software development. A key question is whether text should be oriented to the surface within a projected image of the model, or restricted to two-dimensional orthogonal views of the model. Ideally, text is displayed in either orthogonal or three-dimensional projected views from the model. However, the characteristics of each type of view, and the readability of any results, must be carefully considered.

Text must be displayed in working views, such as two-dimensional plans and elevations. However, it usually is not displayed for projected views, such as perspectives and hidden-line views. If an object designation such as "transparent" or "symbolic" is available, it can be applied to text. Thus lettering and dimensions could be excluded from hidden-line operations, if desired, and otherwise be displayed.

If text is included in hidden-line views, at certain distances and angles of view, it becomes unreadable. Some method is required to filter out unreadable text. A straightforward solution is to allow the operator to delete text from the current view, based on observation and judgment, without removing it from the model altogether. Also important to readability, text must be mirrored as needed so that it is right reading when viewed from different angles.

The plane on which text lies must be designated in some manner. This is distinct from the view plane on which the model is projected. In a projected view, text can appear to fall on the same plane as the floor, for instance, or alternately, it can appear somewhere above the floor in midspace.

For two-dimensional orthogonal drawings, the characteristics of different drawing views must be considered. The system must recognize the specific drawing view. Some text appears with only certain views, such as room names that are shown on the plan but not on the elevations. Other text appears in more than one view, such as a note indicating material which appears in plan as well as elevation. One attribute of text must record the drawing view or views where the text appears.

Some text only appears in an orthogonal view if it is drawn at a certain scale. For example, at $\frac{1}{16}$-in equal to 1 ft, some rooms are shown in outline without room names. At larger scales, the room names are shown. As with two-dimensional views, text must be associated with some scales and not others.

In certain cases text is oriented to an object rather than the drawing or view. The name of an item of furniture, for example, is related to the symbol for the item. If such an object is located at an angle relative to the rest of the

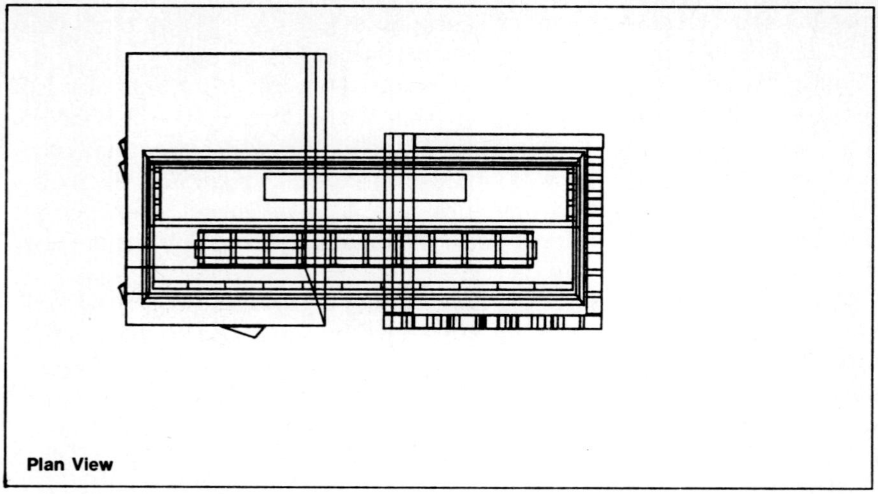

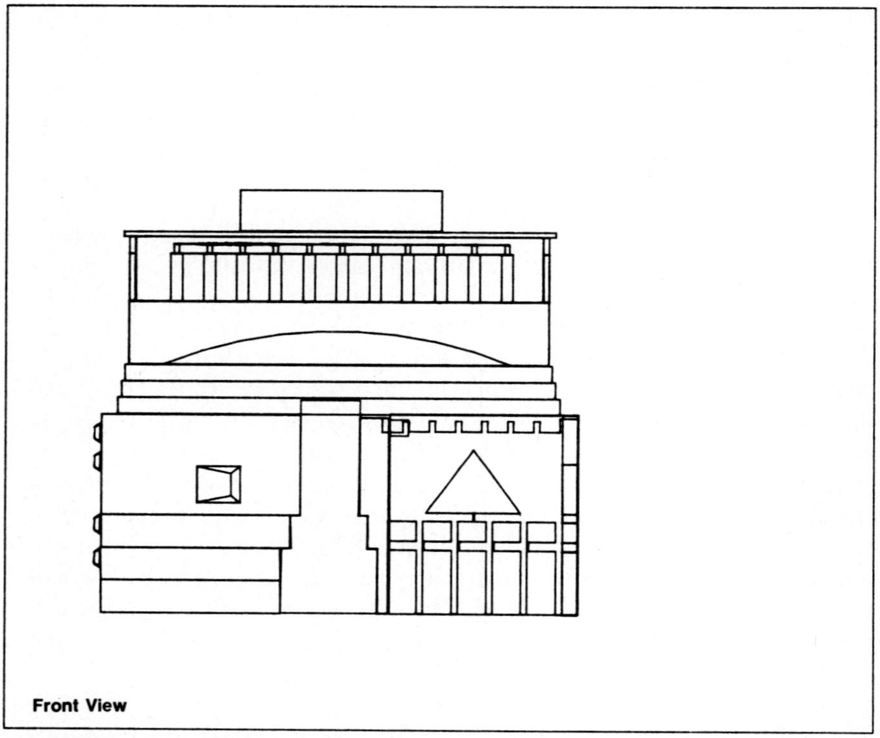

Figure 20-4 Five working views of the same model: This arrangement within one drawing is used for placing objects in three-dimensional space.

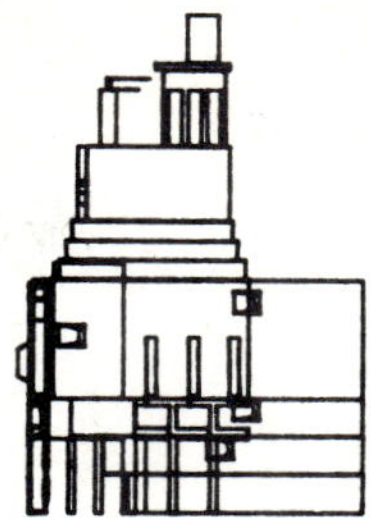

Left View

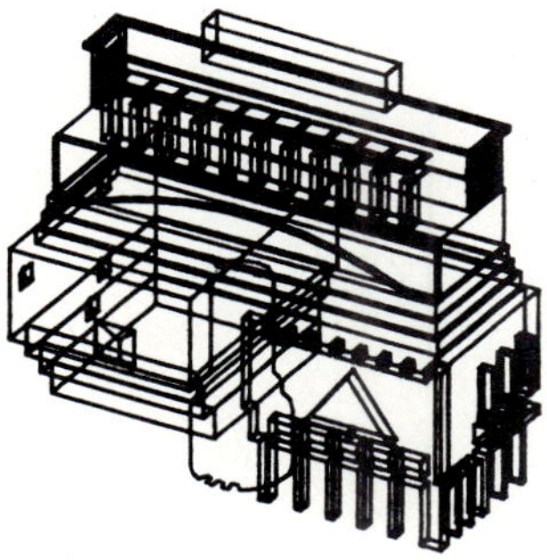

Nonorthogonal View

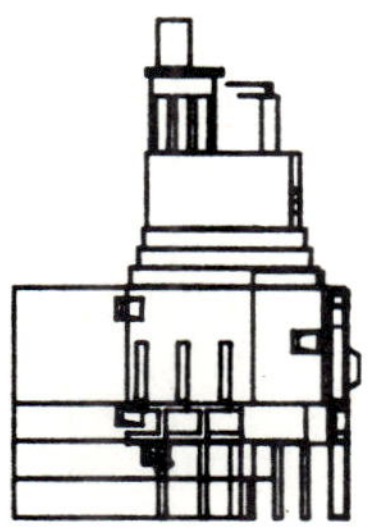

Right View

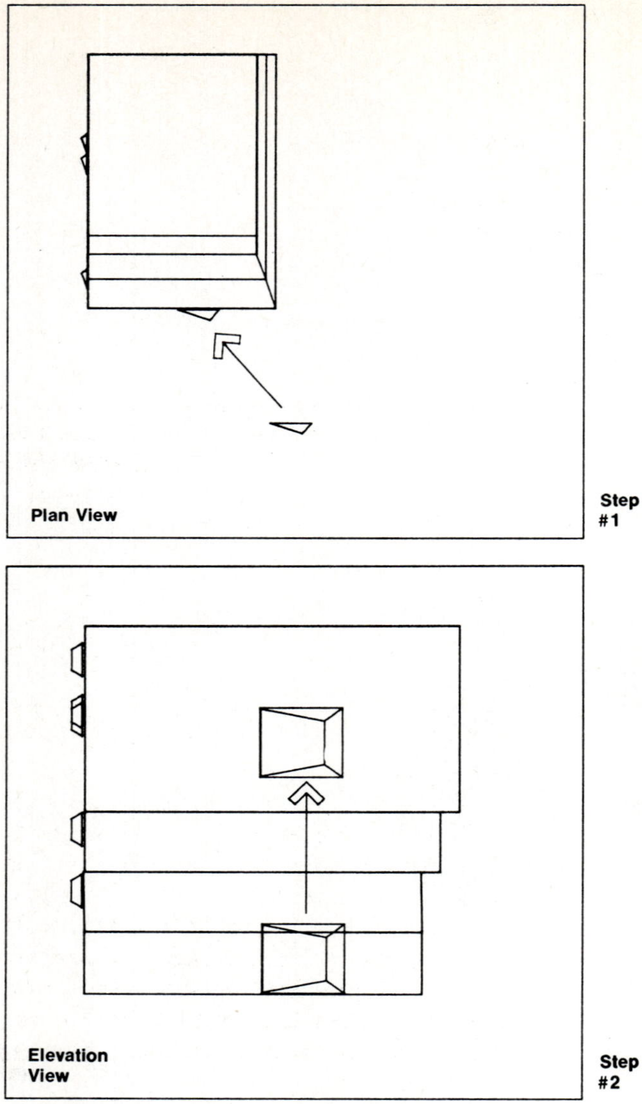

Figure 20-5 Moving a three-dimensional object into place in a two-step operation, first in plan view, then in elevation.

design, any dimensioning or lettering that accompanies it is similarly oriented. Text that is object-oriented requires an angle of orientation specific to the object and separate from the drawing view. Similarly, some notes are oriented to dimension lines. These would be managed with a stored angle of rotation that is specific to the dimension line.

Text is oriented in one of several different ways. In the simplest case, text is oriented to the drawing and is always right reading either horizontally or vertically. But the number of variations is great. As we can see, text requires a system of attributes that enable the three-dimensional modeling system to control the display of text depending on the particular drawing, view, scale, or orientation of an object.

It should be possible to associate text with three-dimensional objects as a special form of primitive. To become part of the model, text does not require the use of three-dimensional graphic operations per se. It would be associated by either naming the three-dimensional object or picking the object in a view. Lettering, for example, would be entered with the usual utilities, with direct keyboard entry, or by transfer from an existing text file.

It should also be possible to associate dimensions with three-dimensional objects (see Fig. 20-6). Dimensioning would share most attributes developed for lettering and require additional ones as well.

For dimensioning on two-dimensional drawings, the operator indicates two points, two lines, or a combination of lines and points. Working directly on a three-dimensional model, the operator would enter dimensions by selecting a vertex, an edge, a surface, or a combination of any two of these. Thus dimensions could span any two points in space.

Dimensions are sometimes drawn to a construction or reference line. In a three-dimensional model, such reference lines are positioned in three-dimensional space. Reference lines could best be treated as a special-purpose form of three-dimensional primitive similar to dimension lines and could travel with the model like other three-dimensional objects.

Admittedly, the number of parameters outlined here for text is extensive. For the foreseeable future, lettering and dimensions will probably be limited

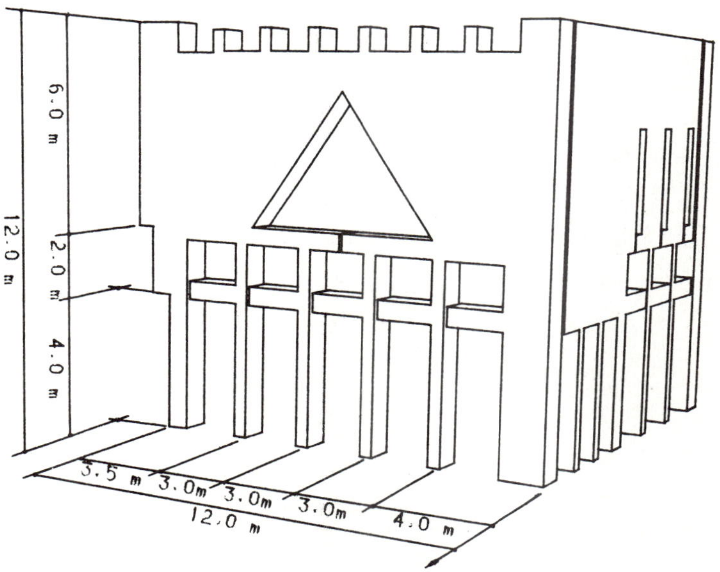

Figure 20-6 Architectural dimensions shown in conjunction with a three-dimensional model: Note possible correlation of horizontal and vertical elements in a single drawing.

to the two-dimensional picture plane where an orthogonal view of a three-dimensional model is displayed. In an ideal situation, the current level of utility available with text for two-dimensional CAD drawings would be extended to three-dimensional models themselves and the projections derived from these models. Dimensioning and lettering directly in a three-dimensional space holds out new possibilities. A new type of design and construction document could be generated. If text were combined with the clarity of three-dimensional projections, for instance, the potential ambiguity and well-known redundancy found in orthogonal drawings could be reduced.

Chapter

21

Spatial Subdivision

"Determining what structural and behavioral information needs to be encoded typically involves many compromises between the simplicity and intellectual tractability of the model on the one hand, and its accuracy or degree of 'realism' on the other." [FOLE82]

New methodology for creating three-dimensional models has recently been published in the field of medical science. Referred to as "spatial subdivision" [CARL85], its underlying data structure and geometry depart from both Brep and CSG methodologies. Rather than organizing three-dimensional objects into a complete model according to their X, Y, and Z coordinates, this methodology looks at the space as a whole and subdivides it until sufficient detail is realized (see Fig. 21-1). As is discussed later, this approach has a precedent in the early development of computers for architectural design.

Spatial subdivision offers significant advantages in terms of computer processing efficiency. Each of the primitives in the modeling system is identical. Consequently, the system does not have to store a geometry record for each primitive; it merely records the address of the primitive. Thus, with octree encoding, the data that makes up the entire model is compressed:

> The octree is a regular cellular decomposition of the object space (universe). The universe is subdivided into eight cells of equal size. If any one of the resulting cells is homogeneous, meaning that it lies entirely inside or outside the object, the subdivision stops. On the other hand, if the cell is heterogeneous, that is intersected by one or more of the object's bounding surfaces, the cell is subdi-

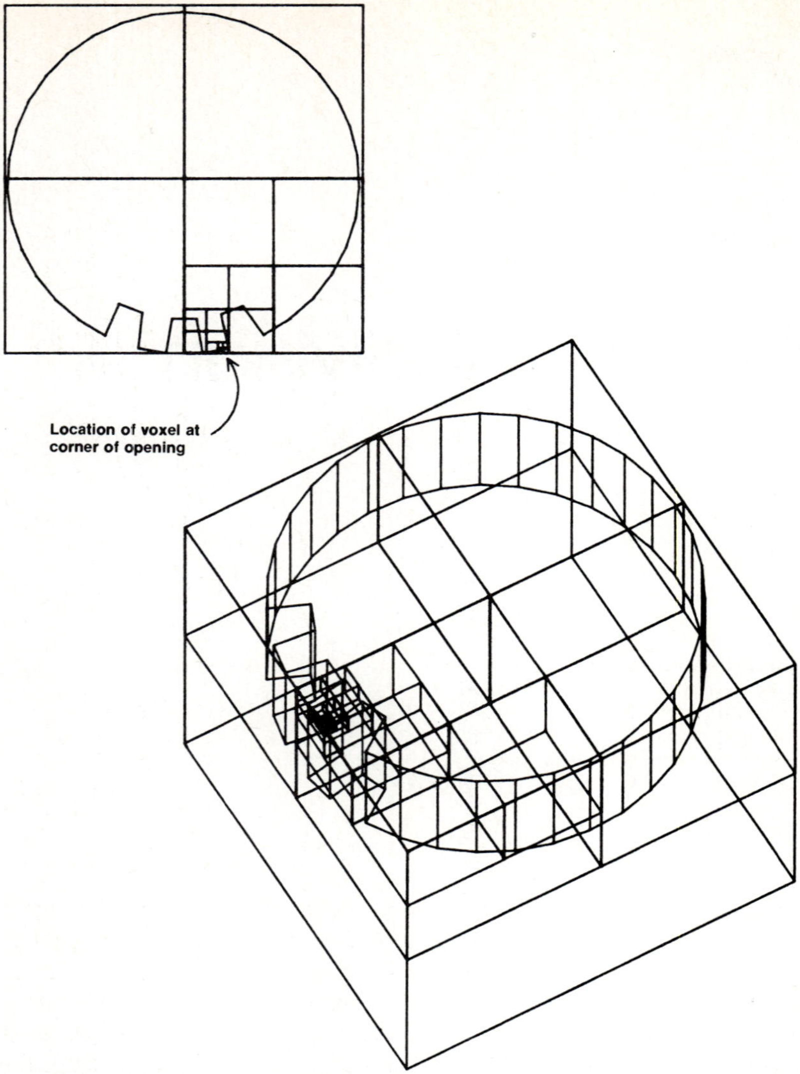

Figure 21-1 Representation of an octree modeling system showing the cellular decomposition of an object into voxels. In a real three-dimensional model, the cubes would reduce to a very small size, thus achieving a detailed rendering of the surface.

vided further into eight subcells. The subdivision process stops when all the leaf cells are homogeneous to some degree of precision. [CARL85]

Boundary representation and CSG modeling systems, as well as two-dimensional graphics systems, use the origin of an object defined by cartesian *X*, *Y*, and *Z* coordinates to locate the object. Octrees do not use coordinates to locate physical objects in space. Rather, the system creates the entire model by subdividing a volume into subcells, and these into further subcells, until no further detail is required. Each cell or cube is bisected by a horizontal and a vertical plane, thus creating eight subcells.

An octree uses a single bit, within an 8-bit word, to indicate whether each of the eight subcells in a cube is full(on) or empty(off). The byte, or complete word, in turn is used to form the address of the cube (see Fig. 21-2).

With spatial subdivision, primitives are referred to as "voxels," which are either cubes or rectangular parallelepipeds. A strict octree structure produces a set of square facets between the empty and full cells. It therefore approximates the modeled surface with squares which are parallel to the sides of the original starting cube. Precise detail, surface curvature, is simplified. A very large number of cells are required to represent a complex object accurately.

The advantage of an octree data structure is that, for many operations, only simple arithmetic calculations such as integer additions, shifts, and compari-

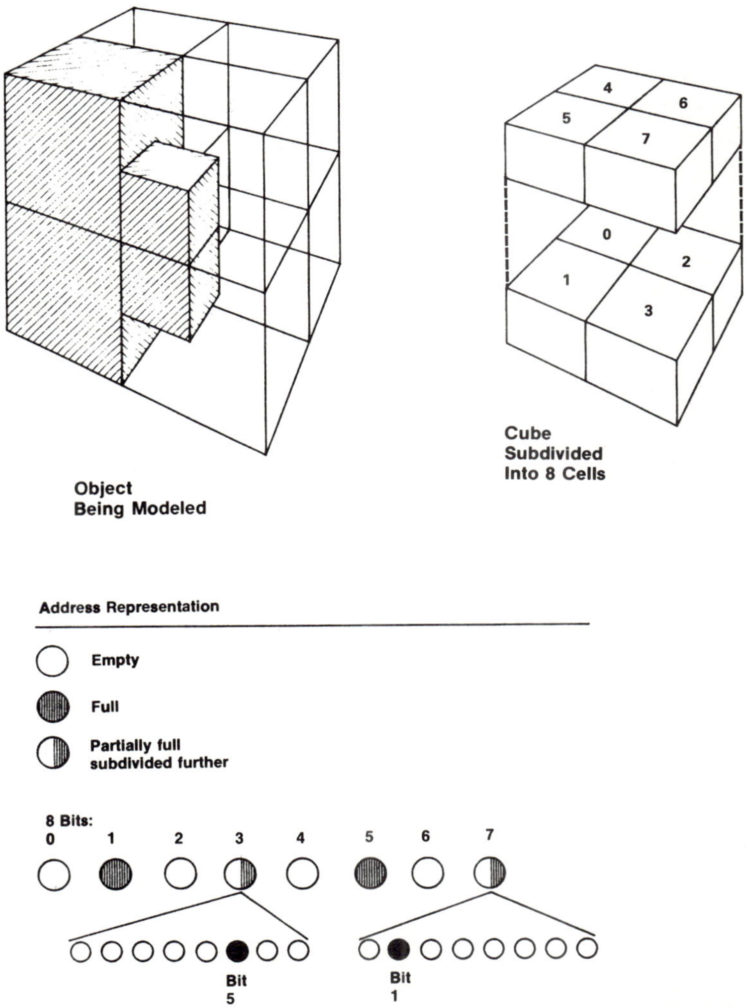

Figure 21-2 A representation of space subdivided into an octree. The data structure of an octree model indicates whether each cell is empty, partially full, or completely full.

sons, are required. Operations such as combining, cutting, translation, rotation, scaling, even interference checking and hidden-surface removal are performed very quickly. For example, interference checking is as simple as comparing the addresses of two objects—if the addresses are the same they occupy the same subcell.

A more significant advantage of an octree-based modeling system is its ability to exchange computation time for precision. In the field of medical science, where octrees are currently applied to three-dimensional modeling, a coarse image of an object such as the human skull is generated very quickly. Later, details derived from high-frequency imaging emerge as more processing is carried out. A similar situation exists in architectural design: finer resolution emerges as design work progresses. Another similarity can be seen when we view an architectural model; finer and finer details appear as we approach it.

The following hypothetical case illustrates how an octree modeling system might be applied to an architectural project. If a single cube encloses a 1-ft volume, and the model includes 3,000,000 cubes, the model would define a space of perhaps 100 by 150 by 200 ft. This is comparable to a 16-story design project of 250,000 total square feet with a floor-to-floor height of 12 ft. Even at this scale, the response time for a complete three-dimensional hidden-line display of the model should be only a few minutes. This estimate is based on response times achieved in medical science using models containing at least many cells as our hypothetical model [FRIE85]. Compare this hypothetical response to those achieved with currently available architectural modeling systems.

Realistically, a 1-ft cube is still too coarse for the smallest unit in an architectural model. Current practitioners work to $\frac{1}{4}$- or $\frac{1}{16}$-in tolerances, or, in metric, centimeters and even millimeters. Fortunately, higher resolution has already been achieved by combining spatial subdivision with other three-dimensional methodologies.

Polytrees

Recently, a hybrid spatial-subdivision methodology for CAD/CAM applications, referred to as a "polytree" has been developed [CARL85]. This three-dimensional modeling system takes advantage of the efficiency offered by octrees and includes the finer resolution achieved with a Brep methodology. The skeleton of a polytree data structure is essentially an octree. However, alternate processing is applied at a certain level of detail. The model is subdivided until the lowest level within the hierarchy is sufficiently simple. Each cell is reduced to one of the following conditions (see Fig. 21-3):

1. The cell lies entirely inside the object and is full.
2. The cell lies entirely outside and is empty.
3. The cell contains one vertex or one point from the object and only the lines connected to that point.

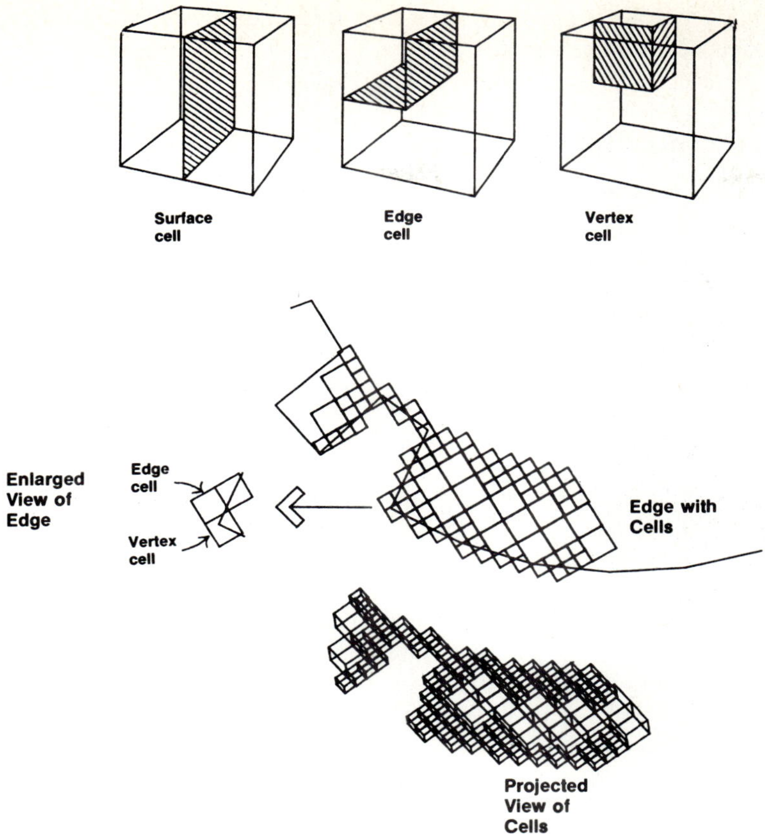

Figure 21-3 Subdividing an architectural element into cells in a representation of a three-dimensional modeling operation based on a polytree data structure.

4. The cell contains a portion of an edge of the object with one or two connecting surfaces.
5. The cell contains one planar surface which intersects the cell.

Additional processing is only required for cells that contain a vertex, edge, or surface. At this level, a Brep data representation is applied to the contents of the cell. Since polytrees retain the *X*, *Y*, and *Z* coordinate data of the original object, they can be used in conjunction with these other three-dimensional modeling systems and their algorithms. By shifting to a Brep methodology here, a polytree should be sufficiently fine-grained for details such as window mullions and railings.

For functions such as interference checking, the cells require no further analysis, and polytrees are processed like octrees with simple arithmetic. As of this writing, a polytree methodology has not been implemented as an architectural three-dimensional modeling application. However, as a branch of solid modeling technology already implemented in other fields, polytrees might be applied to architecture where a similar need exists for three-dimensional models of complex objects.

Architectural Tomography

Spatial subdivision has developed in conjunction with scanning technologies referred to as "tomography" in medical science. Scanning reads an existing object such as a human organ and provides input to a spatial subdivision modeling system. In closing, it is interesting to speculate on the possible application of scanning technology to the construction design field. Equipment for scanning buildings, similar to that used in the medical field, is not currently available. However, a building-scanning system might take the form of a broadcasting device placed within a building and moved from floor to floor combined with a receiver that is carried around the outside of the building, or moved from place to place within the building. A series of "pictures" would be taken at prescribed points within each room, along perimeters, as well as along the corridors. Or a series of broadcasting and receiving devices could surround the building. The pictures result from either an ultrasonic or electromagnetic wave transmitted intermittently from the broadcasting device to the receiver. The wave medium is expected to travel through lightweight building materials such as suspended acoustical ceilings or non-load-bearing partitions. The broadcast wave would bounce off structural members, air-handling equipment, pipes and valves, light fixtures, convenience outlets, and so on. The broadcasting device would then receive an echo from the signal. The echoes would create a sequence of pictures, oriented to the configuration of the building and coordinated with a surveyed control point, that in turn create a complete image of the building in computer memory. Based on this form of architectural tomography, a CAD system would be programmed to convert the image automatically into as-built or facilities drawings, in either two or three dimensions. The broadcast wave, carefully timed, would also recover distances, and therefore dimensions would be created on the drawings automatically. All that would remain to complete such drawings would be lettering, notes, and titles, which would be added interactively.

Urban5 Graphic System, a Forerunner

Looking backward along the path of computer development in architecture, a polytree data structure echoes the original intent of an early design model using cubes to define and analyze space. In the late 1960s, an application of the spatial subdivision concept was attempted in the field of urban design. Developed at MIT, the URBAN5 graphic system is an example of the abstraction used in octrees. Here, the geometry selected was a collection of 10-ft cubes (see Fig. 21-4). Hypothetically, a composition using such cubes provided a graphic abstraction of urban design environments. It also enabled a range of basic design interrelationships to be analyzed:

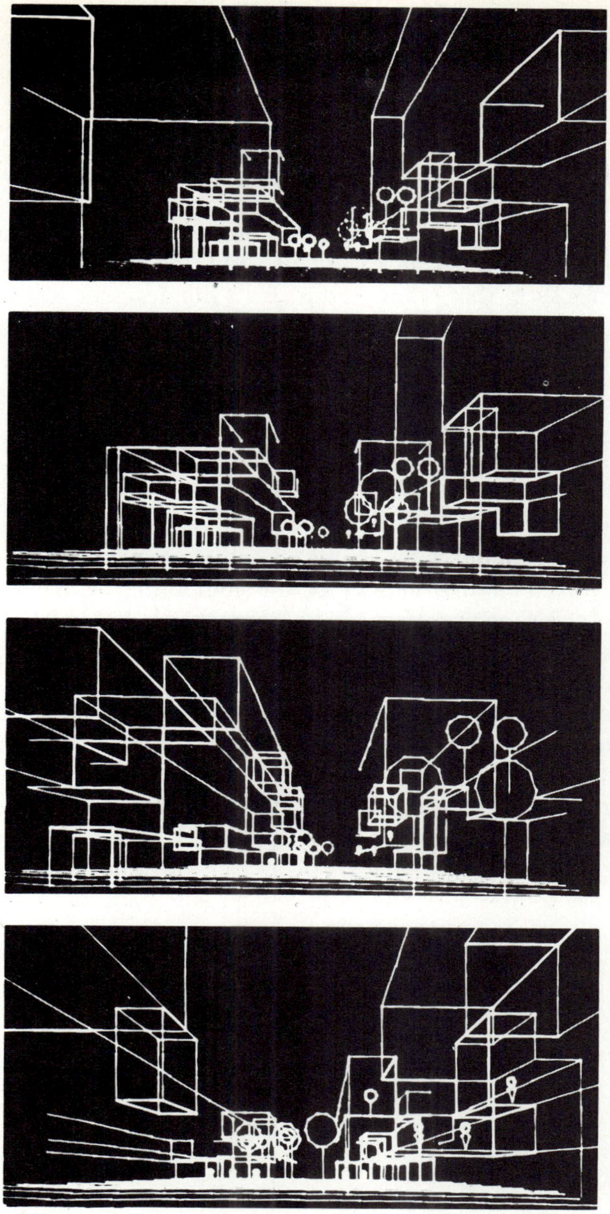

Figure 21-4 Early computer design model (1960s) using cubes to define space: a precursor of the abstraction of space into cubes used in octrees. [NEGR70]

> Design manipulations invariably wield locational data expressed in terms of position, distance, area, or volume. This natural geometrical referencing suggests a data structure where each physical location (solid or void, building or open space), to as small a grain as possible, would describe itself in an autonomous fashion (even the voids!)." [NEGR70]

Rather than attempt to furnish a comprehensive graphic language between architect and machine, the experimenters tried a language of nouns (the cubes) and verbs. Although the original abstraction distorted some parameters, the simplification permitted advances. In this vernacular, the designer assembled blocks in three dimensions. Both the designer and the machine could assign nongraphic attributes to each cube. Each cube, and the model as a whole, could be queried and searched:

> Information search, by either designer or machine, would occur for the most part in a localized fashion, investigating by proximity (by neighborhood, by street, or by immediate adjacency). The thrust of this sort of data structure argument is that information is retrieved by geometric (topical) search rather than by intersecting generalities. [NEGR70]

Realistically, a 10-ft cube is too coarse for actual design practice. At the time, however, it taxed the capabilities of the computing technology available. Since then, software development has brought spatial subdivision to the point where programs are capable of generating views of complex objects in just a few minutes. Medical imaging devices combined with ultrasound scanners now capture the object attributes, such as shape, density, and temperature, of human organs and translate them into three-dimensional images using spatial subdivision. The preprocessing of 3,000,000 cubes and their assembly into a three-dimensional model file can require as little as one-quarter of an hour [FRIE85].

Chapter

22

Construction Documents Based on Three Dimensions

"By and large, the design of commercially available products has been motivated primarily by a bottom-up concern with cost-effective hardware technology that meets performance constraints and not by a more general top-down, 'software-first' strategy based on user requirements." [FOLE82]

Any object currently recorded on two-dimensional CAD drawings can be recorded in a three-dimensional modeling system. However, for construction documentation that is derived from a three-dimensional model, many problems involving standards and conventions, such as the display of lettering and dimensions or connections to nongraphic design information, still must be resolved. Solutions will emerge from practice and these technical problems will be solved.

In the long run, three-dimensional or solid modeling in architecture is expected to merge with conventional two-dimensional design and construction documentation. However, this does not necessarily mean that documentation based on a three-dimensional model will completely replace two-dimensional drawings. Realistically, two-dimensional drawings will probably remain indefinitely as the dominant form of design documentation both for building approval and at the construction site, where they should be displayed on a CRT screen in the job shack.

Design work on a three-dimensional model is not likely to replace the current methodology of creating individual two-dimensional drawings of a project. Instead, a combination of both individual two-dimensional drawings and projected views from a three-dimensional model seems more likely. Ideally, two-dimensional plans, elevations, sections, and even details are generated from a single unified model of a design project. Practically, it is easier to create a three-dimensional model from two-dimensional drawings than the reverse.

In spite of expressions by architects that they would prefer to work in three dimensions, it may be some time before this approach is widely used for documentation. Although designers are familiar with sketching in perspective, creating a three-dimensional architectural model which is resident on a computer system presents conceptual hurdles more formidable than those recently overcome while transforming existing two-dimensional drafting methodologies into CAD operations. Users of two-dimensional CAD applications have shown that standard drafting techniques can be reapplied successfully in a computer medium. However, three-dimensional modeling applications have yet to cross this bridge. Using three-dimensional operations, one is no longer creating a drawing or sketch while working with lines, dimensions, and lettering. The objects handled in three-dimensional space differ from the abstractions and symbols that designers are familiar with on standard design drawings. With three-dimensional modeling systems one constructs volumes in three-dimensional space. These operations require a very different frame of mind from that used for two-dimensional drafting or even while sketching perspectives for purposes of design.

Eventually, architectural drawings created from three-dimensional modeling systems may expand beyond the limitations of two-dimensional documentation. The effect of dimensions and lettering included in projected views of a model is highlighted in Chap. 20. With three-dimensional modeling, the assembly of building components can be illustrated graphically by simply editing the position of objects in the model to create exploded views of parts of a design. Where exploded views are used currently in construction, they are generally perceived as more useful than the standard form of two-dimensional details and building sections which are actually quite abstract. However, with two-dimensional documentation such exploded views must be created from scratch as complete separate drawings and are consequently used only for special construction problems.

In the field of CAD/CAM, solid-modeling systems create projected views of machined parts that are both accurate and easy to understand. As a result, an entire step in the development of a new part is eliminated—namely building a full-size physical model. The cycle of time from design to manufacturing is thus shortened, thereby compensating for the time required to create a computer-based model of the part in the first place. Similarly, justifications for three-dimensional modeling in architecture should include savings in construction costs which are derived from documentation which is more useful than current two-dimensional drawings alone.

Glossary

application A series of interrelated software routines and subroutines designed to perform a specific function

architectural program The analysis and definition of the characteristics of a planned building which meet the requirements of the building users

ASCII Acronym form of American Standard Code for Information Interchange—an industry-standard representation of alphanumerics and punctuation as binary numbers

attribute Often alphanumeric data and typically operator designated, a characteristic which defines the significance of a graphic object or group

audit trail The trail or path left by a transaction; a record from which a transaction can be recreated and its processing continued, should that transaction be disrupted

benchmark A predefined set of operations used in testing either software or hardware products or systems from which an objective measurement or performance can be made

boolean operations Operations in solids modeling, such as union, difference, and intersection, which combine two or more primitives or assemblies of primitives, thus producing a new object

boundary The geometric perimeter of an area, usually a closed series of contiguous, nonintersecting lines

boundary representation, Brep, B-rep Within a three-dimensional model a method of representing a solid object by its spatial boundary; a boundary representation lists all the faces and edges of an object, or the object can be represented by listing its vertices

cell See *voxel*

computer program A set of machine instructions and/or executable procedures combined to perform a task

construction document Legal description of a building project, including architectural and consulting drawings, specifications, and contracts

construction (or working) drawing A drawing showing a plan, elevation, section, detail, schedule, or notes which documents identities, dimensions, shapes, and locations of building elements for the purpose of construction

constructive solid geometry (CSG) A method of modeling in three dimensions whereby objects are represented as ordered "additions" and "subtractions" of simpler solid objects

data base "A collection of interrelated data stored together, without harmful or unnecessary redundancy to serve multiple applications; the data are stored so that they are independent of programs which use the data" [MART77]

data dictionary A centralized set of definitions of all data types, or data fields, within a data base giving their names, structures, intent, and relation to other data

data independence The capability to change the content or the logical or physical structure of the data in a data base system without changing the application software view of the data

direct file A file or data set of nongraphic information that is part of or dependent on the drawing file

drawing file or graphic display file The file of data that describes a drawing with sufficient information to redisplay all or part of the drawing; typically the drawing file consists of a header record to identify the drawing, blocks of data for recording geometric characteristics or grouping structure of each object, and blocks for recording appearance characteristics of each graphic object

extent The space or degree to which a graphic object extends; length, area, volume, or scope; the maximum and minimum *X* and *Y* cartesian coordinates of a rectangle surrounding the object

extractions Copies from a set of graphic objects or their attributes of all those items which meet a specified criterion

field A set of one or more characters which is named and treated as a whole and is the smallest unit of data that has meaning in describing information

file Physical storage or organization of information consisting of records, items or arrays, and data elements

flag Any of various types of indicators used for identification frequently used to tell some later part of a program that some condition occurred earlier

flat file A method of laying out a file as a two-dimensional array of fields; a table

format A specific arrangement of data required to define fields, records, and files

geometry record A record that describes the geometry of a graphic object

global Pertaining to an entire drawing, file, model, or library; a characteristic or function that has an effect reflected in all copies of an object within the graphic system

graphic object Any element within the drawing, such as a point, line, arc, string of letters or numbers, which can be defined with geometry

group Two or more graphic objects which can be operated on as one object

hidden line A line segment that is obscured from view in a projection of a solid three-dimensional object

hidden-edge and hidden-surface removal The process of removing edges or surfaces obscured by visible surfaces when projecting the image of a surface or solid model

index A table used to determine the location of a record within a file

indirect addressing Any method of specifying a storage location whereby the key does not represent a storage location address, such as using the value of an attribute field to select all records from another file whose attribute value matched the initial value

indirect file A file created, stored, and managed independently of the drawing or graphic files, yet containing data associated with graphic objects

integrity A quality of a group whose geometry is shared among all unchanged copies of the group

intensity A number that indicates the brightness and/or color of an object as it is displayed

iteration A logical stage, a single input and output cycle of a set of working drawings or other input and report forms processed by a CAD or other automated system

join See *union*

key A group of characters, usually forming a field, used to identify or locate an item or record within a file

key field Any field that contains a key—a record can have multiple key fields

key word A word used as a key

kind A flag, usually a number, used to mark members of a class or group of objects of the same character or with traits in common

layer A logical concept used to subdivide groups of data within a given drawing for purposes of display and operation

level See *layer*

library A file containing graphic objects or symbols which may be accessed from any drawing at any workstation

logical record A record that includes fields from one or more records or files

macro A series of commands and or alphanumeric input which is recorded and named by the operator and can later be replayed automatically

memory That component of a computer which holds data and instructions; size of memory refers to the capacity of a computer to store information subject to immediate recall within its primary storage area

mnemonic An abbreviation or acronym which resembles the original word so that it is easy to remember

model A framework formally describing an object or process such as a design project recorded as a single unified entity in a computer-processable medium

modeling Creating a comprehensive, coherent description of an architectural design

normalization The reduction of complex data structures into simpler flat files without loss of information

octree A method of recording spatial subdivision used for solids modeling in which the design space is partitioned into increasingly fine divisions of cubes

origin A reference point that defines the geometric location or pivot of a graphic object for the purpose of finding, moving, rotating, or mirroring the object by the system

overlay drafting Also called "registration drafting" and "pin-registration drafting," a method of reusing that information which is common to two or more drawings by drawing it on a base sheet instead of redrawing it

packing The process of consolidating the records of a drawing file so that all records are contiguous and unused records are no longer embedded in storage

pan To display an image while moving along the vertical or horizontal axis, thus viewing a larger image than would fit on a screen all at once

physical record A collection of fields as they are physically recorded in the system's storage medium which are read or written by one machine input/output access

pixel Short for picture element, the finest grain of locations on a screen; rows of pixels form rasters, and the entire screen image forms a matrix of pixels

pointer The exact position or address of a record or other data grouping stored in a file

polytree A hybrid spatial-subdivision methodology for solids modeling whereby aspects of boundary representation and octree encoding are combined

primitive A simple geometric entity visible on the screen, such as a line, arc, text, or point, usually created with a single command

record A set of one or more consecutive fields of data on a related subject treated as a unit

reference symbol A graphic key, not literally shaped or dimensioned, which refers to different parts of the documents

resolution The smallest spacing between points on a graphic device at which the points can be detected as distinct

scale Use of a factor to multiply the values in the internal geometric representation of a graphic object such that the results will be within a range that can be expressed or displayed by the system

search The process of finding the records that meet a given criterion by a systematic examination of the information in specific fields in each record

serial number A unique number, usually assigned in succession, which identifies a design element on the drawings in relation to similar design elements within a project

solid model "While wire frame and surface models define a part's edges or section of its surface, a solid model completely defines its enclosure. A solid model guarantees a physically realizable shape and may be unambiguously interpreted by CAD/CAM applications programs." [JOHN84]

sort The process of arranging the records in a file in sequence by the contents of a specified key field

spatial subdivision A solids-modeling methodology that looks at space as a whole and subdivides it until sufficient detail is realized; each of the primitives in the modeling system are identical, cubes, for example

sweep object A solids primitive created by using a closed two-dimensional and extruding it along an axis

symbol A named group, filed separately from any one drawing, which can be retrieved for use on any drawing

system An interdependent and functioning assembly of procedures, processes, methods, personnel, software, and computerized equipment to perform data processing operations

text That part of a message, made up of both character and numeric data, often in prose form, that contains the information to be conveyed

text file A file, commonly managed with a word processing system, in which all the data is in character format as opposed to internal numeric representations

three-dimensional primitive A set of points, lines or edges, curves, or surfaces that define a single complete and unambiguous volume

transaction An input record used to update an existing file

transaction file A file of transaction records to be processed against a master file

transformation matrix A matrix of coefficients for *X*, *Y*, and *Z* location, scale, and rotation which are applied by multiplication to the coordinates of a point, thus locating the point in coordinate system other than the one in which it was created: typically used to translate a point from three-dimensional coordinates to a two-dimensional coordinate system for visualization

tree structure A hierarchy of groups of data or objects such that the highest level in the hierarchy includes only one group and all others relate to only one group on a higher level than themselves

trigger field A field that when selected or queried activates a software process which captures information from the drawing, such as location, length, or size of an object

union, or join An operation which combines fields from different relations or records, in every instance where the key fields of the records match

vertex In two dimensions, the intersection of two lines; in three dimensions, a point common to three or more surfaces or sides of an object

voxel Cubes or rectangular parallelepipeds, used as a unit of volume

window An area on the display screen selected by the operator or the application program, usually a subset of the whole display

wire frame Objects described in terms of three-dimensional points and lines

zoom To enlarge or decrease proportionately the size of entities displayed on a screen by rescaling the image

References

The quotes in this book are reprinted with permission from the following:

[CARL85] Carlbom, Ingrid, Indranil Chakravarty, and David Vanderschel, "A Hierarchial Data Structure for Representing the Spatial Decomposition of 3-D Objects," *Computer Graphics & Applications,* April 1985.

[DESC82] Descargues, Pierre, *Perspective History, Evolution, Techniques,* 1982, Van Nostrand Reinhold, New York.

[FOLE82] Foley, J. D. and A. Van Dam, *Fundamentals of Interactive Computer Graphics,* 1982, Addison-Wesley, Reading, MA.

[FRIE85] Frieder, Gideon, Dan Gordon, and R. Anthony Reynolds, "Back-to-Front Display of Voxel-Based Objects," *Computer Graphics & Applications,* Jan. 1985.

[HEAT70] Heath, Thomas F., "The Algorithmic Nature of the Design Process," in [MOOR70], p. 57.

[JOHN84] Johnson, Robert H., "Solid Modeling: A State-of-the-Art Report," *CAD/CIM Alert Newsletter,* Chestnut Hill, MA, 1984 and revised 1985.

[LOGC70] Logcher, Robert D., "ICES STRUDL," in [MOOR70], p. 79.

[MART77] Martin, James, *Computer Data-Base Organization,* 1977, Prentice-Hall, Englewood Cliffs, NJ.

[MOOR70] Moore, Gary T., *Emerging Methods in Environmental Design and Planning,* 1970, MIT Press, Cambridge, MA.

[NEGR70] Negroponte, Nicholas, *The Architecture Machine,* 1970, MIT Press, Cambridge, MA.

[PORT70] Porter, William, K. Lloyd, and A. Fleisher, "DISCOURSE: A Language and System for Computer-Assisted City Design," in [MOOR70], p. 92.

[SIPP80] Sippl, Charles, and Roger Sippl, *Computer Dictionary and Handbook,* 1980, Howard W. Sams, Indianapolis, IL.

[STIT84] Stitt, Fred A., *Systems Graphics,* 1984, McGraw-Hill, New York, NY.

Other references cited are:

[CHEN85] Chen, Lih-Shyang, Gabor Herman, R. A. Reynolds, and J. K. Udupa, "Surface Shading in the Cuberille Environment," *Computer Graphics & Applications,* Dec. 1985.

[FARR85] Farrell, Edward J., Wen Yang, and Rosario A. Zappulla, "Animated 3D CT Imaging," *Computer Graphics & Applications,* Dec. 1985.

[FOUR85] Fournier, Alain, and Thomas Milligan, "Frame Buffer Algorithms for Stochastic Models," *Computer Graphics & Applications,* Oct. 1985.

[GILO78] Giloi, Wolfgang, *Interactive Computer Graphics,* 1978, Prentice-Hall, Englewood Cliffs, NJ.

[GREE83] Hall, Roy, and Donald Greenberg, "A Testbed for Realistic Image Synthesis," *Computer Graphics & Applications,* Nov. 1983.

[JORD69] Jordain, Philip, and Michael Breslau, *Condensed Computer Encyclopedia,* 1969, McGraw-Hill, New York.

[PLUN85] Plunkett, David J., and Michael J. Bailey, "Vectorization of a Ray-Tracing Algorithm for Improved Execution Speed," *Computer Graphics & Applications* Aug. 1985.

[POP80] Committee on Production Office Procedures, *Recommended Standards on Production Procedures,* Northern California Chapter, the American Institute of Architects, July 1980.

[REQU82] Requicha, A. A. G., and H. B. Voelcher, "Solid Modeling: A Historical Summary & Contemporary Assessment," *Computer Graphics & Applications,* March 1982.

[SABE83] Sabella, Paolo, and Michael Wozny, "Toward Fast Color-Shaded Images of CAD/CAM Geometry," *Computer Graphics & Applications,* Nov. 1983.

Index

ABOUT THE AUTHORS

TERRENCE G. SCHILLING, AIA, received both his undergraduate training and his M.B.A. degree from the University of California at Berkeley. Formerly a principal in the architectural firm of Schilling & Arnold in Oakland, California, he now manages a CAD system within a 35-person architectural firm and also consults and conducts workshops on the successful application of CAD. Mr. Schilling is a frequent lecturer at CAD conferences around the country.

PATRICIA M. SCHILLING is currently employed as Manager of Business Systems at American Diversified Capital Corp., where she is in charge of developing computer software for specialized applications. Previously, she served as a Principal Software Engineer at CalComp in Anaheim, California, working on CAD graphics software and on a three-dimensional modeling application. In 1980, she founded Design Logic, Inc., a pioneering CAD and data processing service bureau for architectural, planning, and engineering firms. Ms. Schilling holds a degree in architecture from the University of California at Berkeley.